$\mathcal{R}eading$
WOMEN
$\mathcal{W}riting$

a series edited by
Shari Benstock and Celeste Schenck

Reading Women Writing is dedicated to furthering international feminist debate. The series publishes books on all aspects of feminist theory and textual practice. *Reading Women Writing* especially welcomes books that address cultures, histories, and experiences beyond first-world academic boundaries. A full list of titles in the series appears at the end of this book.

Bruce Conner. *Fear of Liberty*. 1990. Paper collage with Yes glue. 8³⁄₁₆ in. ×
5¹⁰⁄₁₆ in. Courtesy of Bruce Conner and Smith Andersen Gallery. Photograph
by Joseph Quever.

Conceived by Liberty

MATERNAL FIGURES AND NINETEENTH-CENTURY AMERICAN LITERATURE

Stephanie A. Smith

Cornell University Press

ITHACA AND LONDON

First published 1994 by Cornell University Press.

Printed in the United States of America

⊛ The paper in this book meets the minimum requirements of the American National Standard for Information Sciences—Permanence of Paper for Printed Library Materials, ANSI Z39.48-1984.

Library of Congress Cataloging-in-Publication Data

Smith, Stephanie A. (Stephanie Ann), 1959-
    Conceived by liberty : maternal figures and nineteeth-century
    American literature / Stephanie A. Smith.
        p.   cm.   (Reading women writing)
    Includes bibliographical references (p.) and index.
    ISBN 0–8014-2924-2 (cloth : alk. paper). —ISBN 0-8014-8150-3
(paper : alk. paper)
        1. American literature—19th century—History and criticism.
2. Mothers in literature.   3. Women and literature—United States—
History—19th century.   4. Feminity (Psychology) in literature.
5. Love, Maternal, in literature.   6. Motherhood in literature.
I. Title. II. Series
PS217.M65S65   1994
810.9'3520431—dc20

94-21658

In memory of my grandmother
Ethel Theresa Lichenstein Smith
(June 28, 1900–August 19, 1992),
who gave me everything.

For my great-grandmothers
Anna Crinnigan Lichenstein
and Alice Avery Smith.

And to my mother,
Carol Marie Wagner Smith,
her mother, Muriel Knerr Wagner,
my sister, Jennifer Carol Smith,
and my aunt, Marjorie Smith,
for always being there,
no matter what the trouble.

Contents

List of Figures   ix

Acknowledgments   xi

Introduction   1

Part I. Governing Sentiment

1. The Mother's State: The Policies and Politics of
   Reproduction in Lydia Maria Child   31

2. Engendering a Body of Truth: Fuller, Emerson, and an
   Embryonic American Literature   69

Part II. Maternal Race

3. Brooding over the Ties That Bind: Harriet Beecher
   Stowe's Monumental Maternal Icon   89

4. Frederick Douglass's Strategic Sentimentality   111

5. The Tender of Memory: Restructuring Value in Harriet
   Jacobs's *Incidents in the Life of a Slave Girl*   134

Part III. Paternal Return

6. Melville, Monstrosity, and Euthanasia: Pierre's Mother
   and Baby Budd   163

7. The Delicate Organisms and Theoretic Tricks of Henry
   James   189

Afterword: Shadows of the National Banner   211

Selected Bibliography   225

Index   239

Figures

Fear of Liberty (Bruce Conner)   Frontispiece

1. The Custom House Eagle   10
2. "A New England Boy's Song"   33
3. Eliza and Harry (George Thomas)   102
4. Eliza and Harry on the ice (George Thomas)   103
5. Eliza and Harry on the ice (James Daugherty)   104
6. A slumbering Harry (George Thomas)   179
7. Harry imitating Uncle Cudjoe (George Thomas)   180
8. Eva and Topsy (George Thomas)   182
9. Eva and Topsy (James Daugherty)   183

Acknowledgments

My first and most urgent thanks go to John Murchek—whose care, curiosity, and incisive intellectual engagement inspired me daily—and to Sandra Gunning, without whose conversation, intelligence, and loving friendship in a difficult time I could not have done this work. My debt to both of them, as colleagues and as friends, is manifold.

I count myself fortunate as well to have had the inspiration and continuing support of Carolyn Porter and Elizabeth Abel.

Gratitude is due also to my colleagues at the University of Florida for sharing their time and their considerable resources. Particular thanks to Elizabeth Langland, who has been a mainstay; to Caryl Flinn, for her invaluable advice; to Daniel Cottom, who read more than his fair share of the manuscript and offered, among other things, free admonishments, bad coffee, and meticulously painful forms of heartburn. Without David Leverenz and his fine-tuned reading of the manuscript I would have committed unpardonable scholarly errors. Ira Clark, Marsha Bryant, and Malini Schueller made Turlington Hall bearable.

Thanks also to the University of Florida's Research and Development Grants program for summer grants in 1991 and 1992 that allowed me the time to complete the project. I am grateful to Rita Smith, of the Baldwin Library, for her help with material on Lydia Maria Child. The graduate students in my feminist theory seminar at the University of Florida (spring 1992), particularly Amy Murphy, Marlene Tromp, and Gary MacDonald, kept me on my toes, as did many of my undergraduates, particularly Ann Rose, Mejgan Zia, and Bill

Hunt. Thanks also to Angela Kelsey for her skillful and knowledgeable help in preparing the final manuscript.

Cornell University Press has been a pleasure to work with, and I offer my appreciation above all to Bernhard Kendler. Readers Philip Gura, Nancy Walker, Shari Benstock, and Glenn Altschuler offered sharp commentary and challenging criticism.

Indeed, many people have given generously of themselves over the years. I owe thanks to Guilia Fabi, Kristen Luker, Eva Cherniavsky, David Elderbrock, Kate McCullough, Susan Schweik, Judith Rosen, Cathy Gallagher, Peter Logan, Richard Hardach, Eric Chandler, and many other people who contributed to this work during my years in Oregon and California. To all, most particularly to the Cortes and Harlow families who gave me respite and shelter, thank you.

My ever-suffering loyal friends Molly and Ed Gloss, Judith McBride, Katrin Snow, Mary and Paul Troychak-Wallulis, Vonda McIntyre, Ursula and Charles Le Guin, Al Wesolowsky, Michael Weston, Peter Korn, and Kris Peterson gave me the courage and the humor to persevere. There is no way I can repay them.

Finally (although hardly last) I thank my family for always being there. Special appreciation to my grandfather, Edmund Dewey Smith, Sr., whose belief in me never wavered. I will miss his love and his constancy.

Portions of this book have been or will be published elsewhere in some form. "Frederick Douglass's Strategic Sentimentality" (Chapter 4) appeared as "Heart Attacks: Frederick Douglass's Strategic Sentimentality" in *Criticism* 34 (Spring 1992) and in *Reading with a Difference: Gender, Race, and Cultural Identity*, ed. Arthur F. Marotti, Renata R. Mautner Wasserman, Jo Dulan, and Suchitra Mathur (Detroit: Wayne State University Press, 1994); "The Delicate Organisms and Theoretic Tricks of Henry James" (Chapter 7) appeared in *American Literature* 62 (December 1990) and in *Major Literary Characters: Isabel Archer*, ed. Harold Bloom (New York: Chelsea House, 1992); "The Tender of Memory: Restructuring Value in Harriet Jacobs's *Incidents in the Life of a Slave Girl*" (Chapter 5) will appear in *Harriet Jacobs and "Incidents in the Life of a Slave Girl": New Critical Essays*, ed. Deborah Garfield and Rafia Zafar (Cambridge University Press, forthcoming.)

S. A. S.

Gainesville, Florida

Conceived by Liberty

Everything begins with reproduction.

—Jacques Derrida

Everything, in the 'last analysis' is political.

—Fredric Jameson

All of western culture rests upon the murder of the mother.

—Luce Irigaray

Introduction

Mid-nineteenth-century "American culture," wrote Ann Douglas, "seemed bent on establishing a perpetual Mother's Day."[1] As *The Public Ledger* declared in 1850, "a mother is, next to God, all powerful."[2] Yet despite how predominantly mothering figured as a trope for, among other things, morality—and despite the cultural currency of what G. J. Barker-Benfield dubbed the "maternal icon"[3]—quintessential American literature of the period has been defined, for the most part, as that which lacks or flees mother.[4] What impact would a sustained reconsideration of so pervasive a sign have on how to read American literature?

This was the foremost question that provoked *Conceived by Liberty*. To say that representations of a sanctified motherhood formed the primary cornerstone for commercially successful writing in the United States of the nineteenth century is a commonplace. But critical articulations of maternal iconography remain scarce. This lack is especially evident in considerations of work not designated commercial or sen-

---

1. Ann Douglas, *The Feminization of American Culture* (New York: Avon, 1977), 5.

2. Quoted in Gerda Lerner, *The Grimké Sisters from South Carolina* (New York: Schocken, 1971), 3.

3. G. J. Barker-Benfield, *The Horrors of the Half-Known Life: Attitudes toward Women and Sex in Nineteenth-Century America* (Boston: Harper and Row, 1976), 10–15.

4. Perhaps Leslie A. Fiedler's *Love and Death in the American Novel*, rev. ed. (New York: Dell, 1966) is the most widely known study proposing such a "flight." Other critics to whom I refer in this study have demonstrated how profoundly American literary history in the United States academy has been shaped by arguments structuring both American literature and the "American Renaissance" in opposition to sentimental motherhood as a trope.

timental. It is well, as Jane Tompkins writes in *Sensational Designs*, to talk about novelist Susan Warner's sentimental mothers, but Hester Prynne is quite another matter.[5] This point was brought home to me recently when a senior colleague said, "You know, I can't think of a single mother in American literature." "Hester Prynne?" I asked. "Oh, right," I was told, "but that's not what's really important about her, is it?"

Why is Hester Prynne's maternity so unimportant? Not all critics have thought so. In 1982 Daniel Cottom saw maternity as a central concern in *The Scarlet Letter*. Reading the novel as if it were a legal brief—Hawthorne v. Hester—on sexual/textual difference,[6] Cottom claimed that the text installed romance as an economy in which the maternal (reproductive) body signified the opposite of artistic production. However, if one should take Hawthorne's case as an incontrovertible proof, if maternal reproduction is the opposite of artistic production, then paying critical attention to how reproduction and the maternal body are themselves literary representations might damage the novel's artistic value. Best to skirt the issue (as it were), even though Hawthorne himself described Hester Prynne as "the image of Divine Maternity, which so many illustrious painters have vied with one another to represent."[7]

Reproducing my colleague's unintentionally punning question here—"Is there not a single mother in American literature?"—is meant less as an anecdotal indictment than as an index to the several aims of this book. The question, however simply, indicates that motherhood has consistently been regarded as less important than other features to an American literary heritage. After all, there is no maternity in Herman Melville's *Moby Dick*. But then again, how, without referring to representations of maternity, does one read Queequeg's "obstetrics" (in chapter 78)? Rescuing Tashtego from a decapitated whale's head, Queequeg "averred, that upon first thrusting in for him, a leg was presented; but well knowing that that was not as it ought to be, and might occasion great trouble;—he had thrust back the leg,

5. Jane Tompkins, *Sensational Designs: The Cultural Work of American Fiction, 1790–1860* (New York: Oxford University Press, 1985).

6. Daniel Cottom, "Hawthorne versus Hester: The Ghostly Dialectic of Romance in *The Scarlet Letter*," *Texas Studies in Literature and Language* 24 (Spring 1982): 62, with reference to Toril Moi, *Sexual/Textual Politics: Feminist Literary Theory* (New York: Methuen, 1985).

7. Nathaniel Hawthorne, *The Scarlet Letter* (New York: Norton, 1988), 41. "The Custom House" in this edition is cited hereafter as *CH* and *The Scarlet Letter* as *SL*.

and by a dexterous heave and toss, had wrought a somerset upon the Indian; so that with the next trial, he came forth in the good old way— head foremost."[8] Is maternity, or at the very least mid-wifery, not at issue in this description?

The Political Religion of the Nation

Most critics of Anglo-American nineteenth-century culture and literature speak to the enormous, if paradoxical, pressure put on maternal iconography as emblematic for a stable, unfractured morality. It would be hard indeed for any sustained consideration of nineteenth-century cultural practices in the United States not to comment on the degree to which maternal iconography signaled utopian perfection, making "mother" a sacred, natural symbol of perfect, reciprocal relations. This symbol served as a self-regulating model for social and familial community and a source of creative generation. Woman performed what Leslie Fiedler characterized as the role of "sexless savior and . . . eternal Mama."[9] Thus by extension was the family, emphasizing maternity as the stabilizing icon of continuity in a (Christian) republic, woven into nineteenth-century discourses both public and private.

Logically, though, the use of the mother as both public and private figure undermined the supposed distance between political and domestic concerns.[10] Abraham Lincoln's 1837 speech to the Springfield Young Men's Lyceum, "The Perpetuation of our Political Institutions," indicates as much: "Let every man remember that to violate the law is to trample on the blood of his father, and to tear the charter of his own and his children's liberty. Let reverence for the laws be breathed by every American mother to the lisping babe that prattles on her lap, . . . in short, let it become the political religion of the nation."[11] Thus the (private) family, educated by a reverent, revered American motherhood, was construed as the moral linchpin in the structure of (pub-

8. Herman Melville, *Moby Dick* (London: Penguin, 1972), 451 (hereafter cited as *MD*). Earlier, Queequeg's famous matrimonial embrace has reminded Ishmael sharply and significantly of his stepmother and her disciplinary actions.

9. Fiedler, *Love and Death*, 90.

10. See also Mary Kelley, *Private Woman, Public Stage: Literary Domesticity in Nineteenth-Century America* (New York: Oxford University Press, 1984).

11. From *Abraham Lincoln's Speeches*, ed. L. E. Chittenden (New York: Dodd, Mead 1895), 21.

lic) liberty. And if Lincoln's speech is a public document, Henry David Thoreau's more private journal offers another example of the maternal icon would serve as pervasive cultural currency for ethical purity: "I lose my respect for the man who can make the mystery of sex the subject of a coarse jest, yet, when you speak earnestly and seriously on the subject, is silent. I feel this to be truly irreligious. Whatever may befall me, I trust that I may never lose my respect for purity in others. . . . I would preserve purity in act and thought, as I would cherish the memory of my mother."[12]

Elevated purity became discursively axiomatic for motherhood. Whether in speech or journal, behavior manual or instruction book, novel or autobiography, a cherished iconic memory of mother lifted the mind toward a better state and away from the sordid. This elevation would effect a clarity of purpose as well as social propriety. Keeping mother in mind meant keeping away from private unruliness that could lead, as Lincoln warned, to the destruction of public political liberty. Ignoring mother could be tantamount to both sociopolitical and personal suicide. Certainly Hester Prynne's demon child, Pearl, and Arthur Dimmesdale's and Roger Chillingsworth's tortured fates attest to the dangerous desires of a passionate, unruled, free body.

Yet if "mother" could intrude upon *Moby Dick* and *The Scarlet Letter* "she" raises the aesthetic spectre that perhaps sentimentality may not be confined to the pages of popular, domestic novels. Deemed aesthetically degrading because sentimental, mother has been left out of most critical assessments and lost or killed off in the narrative, and maternal iconography read, if at all, as banal. Pathetic and linked to, if not the very source of, an ever increasing consumer economy, maternal sentimentality supposedly came to demonstrate the "vitiation" of American culture, the shameful worst of nineteenth-century Victoriana—or so declared Ann Douglas. Since its publication in 1977 her *Feminization of American Culture* has provoked much disagreement, if not outright attack. And yet maternal sentimentality remains a byword for banality. If, as Jane Tompkins labored to prove in *Sensational Designs*, domestic sentimentality was a politically expedient vehicle (primarily although not exclusively for white, middle-class women), invoking the sentimental functioned and can still function as a transparent sign of aesthetic paucity.

12. Henry David Thoreau, *Journal*, in *The Harper American Literature*, ed. Donald McQuade (New York: Harper & Row, 1987), 2:1500.

A few brief examples. In James Fenimore Cooper's sentimental novel *The Deerslayer* (1841), it is of profound and central importance that the mother of the Hutter girls is dead and deeply mourned. She is, in fact, doubly buried, both under the Hutter home and, because that home floats in the middle of Glimmerglass Lake, under the water. The sunken, lost Mrs. Hutter had also been sunk in her own estimation (and *her* mother's) because of her intimacy with a man "who came from Europe, and who could hardly be supposed to wish to form an honorable connection in America." The result of her "great error"? Two illegitimate daughters and a subsequent marriage to another man so far below this woman's social station and respectability in general that even her shameful grave had to be rendered invisible.[13] Still, despite that shame and invisibility, her memory animates the novel's action, and her fate determines that of Cooper's redoubtable Deerslayer.

The other mother in this novel is (chronologically) not yet a mother: Hist-oh!-Hist (Wah-ta-Wah), Chingachgook's beloved and the mother-to-be of Uncas, gives birth and dies in the narrative interstice between *The Deerslayer* and *The Last of the Mohicans*. But without her there would have been no "last" Mohican at all. In this second (chronologically) of the Leatherstocking Tales, published in 1826, both Munro girls have lost their mothers. Cora Munro's dead mother was "a lady whose misfortune it was . . . to be descended, remotely, from that unfortunate class who are so basely enslaved to administer to the wants of a luxurious people"; and consequently, even her doting father calls his daughter "degraded." Represented as inherently unable to have a proper (white) marriage—or, heaven forbid, children—Cora leaps off the famous cliff with the Mohican, Uncas, and so, according to Cooper's text, dies (out) with him and his tribe.[14]

By 1851 the situation of mothers and of those characters who, like Cora Munro, have become known as "tragic mulattas" had changed. They did not always have to die but were presented instead as living

13. James Fenimore Cooper, *The Deerslayer* (New York: New American Library, 1963), 154, 165, 173.

14. James Fenimore Cooper, *The Last of the Mohicans* (New York: New American Library, 1963), 186–87. For discussions of Cooper's textual form of Native American genocide, see also Carolyn L. Karcher's introduction to Lydia Maria Child, *Hobomok and Other Writings on Indians*, ed. Carolyn L. Karcher (New Brunswick, N.J.: Rutgers University Press, 1986), esp. xxxvi–xxxvii; and Lora Romero's "Vanishing Americans: Gender, Empire, and New Historicism," *American Literature* 63, reprinted in *The Culture of Sentiment*, ed. Shirley Samuels (New York: Oxford University Press, 1992), 115–27.

monuments of maternal virtue: Eliza Harris in *Uncle Tom's Cabin* and the later Rosabella Royal of Lydia Maria Child's *Romance of the Republic*, come to mind.[15] Yet even if Eliza and her lover, George Harris, do not die precipitously at each other's feet, they, with their children, do disappear from America to become the extratextual, utopic Adam and Eve of Liberia.

More significant for my argument, though, is the fact that none of these authors—Cooper, Stowe, and Child—have enjoyed reputations as "good" American writers. Both Nina Baym and Judith Fetterley have observed that "in the study of American literature there exists an equation between 'masculinity' and 'Americanness' parallel to the fusion . . . between 'male' and 'American writer.' "[16] Sentimentality has been part of that which is neither masculine nor artistic, and since maternity as a narrative focus is most apparent in the so-called women's sentimental texts, it is not surprising that it has been doubly ignored. Given how pervasively, since the 1940s, texts written by women have been excised from traditional notions of what constitutes America's literary heritage, the chance that maternal iconography might be viewed as a matrix of criticism has been slim.[17] Yet on what evaluative grounds are these sentimental texts being judged? Is sentimentality itself not also an issue for critical debate?

A partial answer as to how one can address the evaluative category "sentimental" is to question the relatively unproblematic vision of

15. It is interesting to note that in Lydia Maria Child's 1842 short story "The Quadroons" (*The Liberty Bell*, an annual giftbook that Maria Chapman edited for the Boston Female Anti-Slavery Society, 1842), which is widely credited with introducing the tragic mulatta as a literary archetype, both mother and daughter die as a result of their "condition"—whereas Child's later *A Romance of the Republic* insisted upon the survival of this figure. See also Karcher's critical introduction to Child, *Hobomok*. Karcher argues persuasively that Cooper's vision of racial antagonism became dominant not because it was any less sentimental than either Child's or Catharine Maria Sedgwick's in *Hope Leslie* but because its vision served the interests of a white, male ruling class. (For extended treatment of Child and Harriet Beecher Stowe, see Chapters 1 and 3 below.)

16. Judith Fetterley, *Provisions: A Reader from 19th-Century American Women* (Bloomington: Indiana University Press, 1985), 18. See also Nina Baym, "Melodramas of Beset Manhood: How Theories of American Fiction Exclude Women Authors," in *The New Feminist Criticism: Essays on Women, Literature, and Theory*, ed. Elaine Showalter (New York: Pantheon Books, 1985). Like Jane Tompkins, Baym delineates theories defining an American literary aesthetic which "in pursuit of the uniquely American . . . have arrived at a place where Americanness has vanished into the depths of what is alleged to be the universal male psyche" (79).

17. See Vincent B. Leitch, *American Literary Criticism* (New York: Columbia University Press, 1988).

what might be said to constitute maternity. As both Judith Fetterley and Eve Kosofsky Sedgwick have noted, "sentimentality" has been an underdefined term, critical shorthand for the mundane of the everyday, the trivial.[18] Furthermore, the Emersonian metaphysical equation of perception with conception has, still, great definitive power; the maternal in the Western philosophical tradition has been overdetermined, to borrow from Julia Kristeva, as a space of material abjection,[19] while its supposed opposite, abstract conception, has been seen as the locus of unquestioned creativity. This represented disjunction between cerebral and corporeal conception affected the American writer particularly, insofar as an emerging nineteenth-century articulation of the uniquely "American" artist rested upon the core idea that to be able to conceptualize the future was to have a unique vision. This special perception would be to the advantage of America's national, cultural destiny. Transcendentalist in origin, clearly dependent on Cartesian metaphysics, this creative ideal was popularized through Ralph Waldo Emerson's works. As Oliver Wendell Holmes was to say, Emerson's essay *Nature* cut the cord that bound America culturally to Great Britain.[20]

Such idealist conceptualization is often claimed as the essence of a pragmatic American creativity, repeatedly identified with utopic "Americanness." As Emerson wrote, the American artist was "a conductor of the whole river of electricity. Nothing walks, or creeps, or grows or exists which must not in turn arise and walk before him as an exponent of meaning. . . . All the creatures, by pairs and by tribes, pour into his mind as into Noah's ark, to come forth again to people a new world."[21] Assimilating the world and peopling it properly with the spawn of a (Christian, American) mind, Emerson's artist gestates

18. See Fetterley, *Provisions*, 20; and Eve Kosofsky Sedgwick, *Epistemology of the Closet* (Berkeley: University of California Press, 1990), 144. I am indebted to Sedgwick, whose 1987 seminar at the University of California, Berkeley, prompted my examination of how the sentimental is still being constructed, and how those constructions might frame an understanding of nineteenth-century narratives. See also Susan K. Harris, " 'But Is It Any *Good?*': Evaluating Nineteenth-Century American Women's Fiction," *American Literature* 63 (March 1991): 43–61, which comments on Jane Tompkins's question as to whether sentimentality can ever be judged as aesthetically "good" writing.

19. See Julia Kristeva, *Powers of Horror: An Essay on Abjection* (New York: Columbia University Press, 1982).

20. Oliver Wendell Holmes, in *Critical Essays on Ralph Waldo Emerson*, ed. Robert E. Burkholder and Joel Myerson (Boston: G. K. Hall, 1983).

21. Ralph Waldo Emerson, "The Poet," in *The Harper American Literature*, ed. Donald McQuade (New York: Harper & Row, 1987), 1:1081.

with electricity. He is a clean conductor, not bound to the temporal or to the mundane uncertainties of flesh. Those uncertainties are assigned rather to a discarded umbilical cord, or to the tribes and creatures that swarm and creep. At the heart of this national identity was the credo that to conceive an idea and give it shape in language was to birth a better world.

But the very term "conception" implies gender, and reproductive metaphors suggesting the maternal were invoked to represent it, even as the maternal itself was assigned to the monstrously multifarious, the uncertain, or the abject. "Conception" became a contested site of cultural value. When antebellum sentimental ideology focused on the maternal, it did so through rhetorical strategies of utopian beatification so that an iconographic economy celebrating the mother as an unconflicted image of utopian stability became dominant.

It was an unstable predominance, however. The sanctified icon of divine maternity kept invoking the scarlet adulteress, even as the icon served as a blind to underlying fears. Anxious questions arose. Who is the divine (demonic) mother's child—precious pearl or evil elf? Would the possibilities of democratic diversity merely precipitate fatal dismemberments—social, moral, and political? By examining ruptures in the dominant maternal iconographic economy, I will show how such fears of disunion shaped—and continue to shape—figurations of "the" maternal.

Moreover, the dominant rhetoric of nineteenth-century sentimental ideology which associated the maternal with "appropriate/d" excess[22]—whether that of beatific serenity or horrific rage—recurred in critical definitions of an American literary aesthetic. As a result, certain elements of the iconography—such as "nurturance"—were naturalized as instinctual rather than recognized as historically conditioned. Reified, sentimental maternal iconography has been situated in opposition to a more restrained "literary" practice and is still seen as such.[23] *Conceived by Liberty*, then, contends that maternal iconog-

22. I have borrowed Trinh T. Minh-ha's term "inappropriate/d" as a pertinent denotation for a site of appropriation that is resistant to the process. See Minh-ha, ed., "She, the Inappropriate/d Other" (special issue), *Discourse* 8 (Fall–Winter 1986–87). See also *Woman, Native, Other: Writing Postcoloniality and Feminism* (Bloomington: Indiana University Press, 1989).

23. See Leitch, *American Literary Criticism*. Although Tompkins's *Sensational Designs* restored to the previously belittled and often invisible maternal sentimentality the didactic power it possessed for nineteenth-century ideology, her revalorization has also served, ironically, to reinforce traditional and standard critical divisions between the

raphy is central both to how a nineteenth-century text such as *The Scarlet Letter* has been interpreted and to how such a text, as an artifact, works in relation to critical conflicts over aesthetic value and canonicity in the United States.

Could It Be Possible That She Has No Maternal Instincts?

My choice of *The Scarlet Letter* as an opening emblem is unavoidable, not only because Hester Prynne is a mother but also because of the myriad critical meanings assigned to her playfully generative or promiscuously infamous signifier, the protean "A." Whether as Angel, Avenger, Adulteress, American, Animal, Anger, or Astonishment, this blazing "A" has been an avatar for the definition and study of an American literary aesthetic since 1879, when Henry James, in his Men of Letters biography *Hawthorne*, called *The Scarlet Letter* its author's "most substantial title to fame, . . . in the United States a literary event of the first importance. The book was the finest piece of imaginative writing yet put forth in the country, . . . America having produced a novel that belonged to literature, and to the forefront of it."[24]

But rather than writing yet another gloss on Mistress Prynne's ambiguous signifier, let me take a slightly circuitous route via two more recognizable icons of popular, national significance: the American bald eagle and the (younger) Statue of Liberty. In 1850, Salem's Custom House bore (as it still bears today, see Fig. 1) "an enormous spec-

---

sentimental and the serious, the popular and the literary. Calling for a critical reinvestment to validate didacticism within its historical context, rather than calling into question the categories of the "sentimental," "popular," and "didactic," *Sensational Designs* links political expediency to sentimental culture and demonstrates that the sentimental "is seen as a derogatory code name for female bodies and the female domestic and 'reproductive' preoccupations of birth, socialization, illness and death." But that linkage has not gotten very far beyond an aesthetic bind that Tompkins herself articulated. In asking in her final chapter "But is it any *good*?" Tompkins reasserts a traditional evaluative dichotomy prevalent in much American literary criticism, which insists on placing aesthetic literary value and political didactic intent in opposition. In addition, according to Susan K. Harris, "There appears to be an unspoken agreement not to submit nineteenth-century American women's novels to extended analytical evaluation . . . because the evaluative modes most of us were taught devalue this literature *a priori*" ("But Is It Any *Good*?" 44).

24. Henry James, *Hawthorne* (Ithaca: Cornell University Press, 1956), 86–87.

Figure 1. The "vixenly," golden-winged republican eagle on Salem's Custom House, carved in 1826 by Jonathan True. Courtesy of Salem Maritime National Historical Site.

imen of the American eagle, with outspread wings, a shield before *her breast* and . . . a bunch of intermingled thunderbolts and barbed arrows in each claw" (*CH*, 6; emphasis added). Gendered as female in *The Scarlet Letter*'s prologue, this truculent spectacle is "vixenly." The narrator of "The Custom House" goes on to relate that the well-armed eagle's foolish progeny often mistake her viciousness for the protective instincts of a domestic hen. Our narrator knows better. Any who think "her bosom has all the softness and snugness of an eiderdown pillow" will find that this untender mother is "apt to fling off her nestlings with a scratch of her claw, a dab of her beak, or a rankling wound from her barbed arrows" (*CH*, 6).

Such an image of a maternalized demon is not surprising. Female monsters are as familiar a trope of nineteenth-century literature in the United States as the Victorian Woman's calling to play Coventry Pat-

more's Angel-in-the-House.[25] Definitive polarities, these cultural twins
the Demon/Angel and the Dark Lady/Light Lady, are densely impacted personifications of a variety of supposedly stable cultural bor-
derlines dividing black from white, evil from good, upper from lower,
normal from perverse. Thus the fate of the Dark Lady/Light Lady
pair displays the catastrophes likely to result from a confusion or
worse a fusion of such definitive oppositions. From Zenobia and Pris-
cilla of *The Blithedale Romance* to Miriam and Hilda in *The Marble Faun*,
Hawthorne's "women" enact this paradigm.[26]

Of course, Hawthorne was not alone in his use of a female Angel/
Demon. Likewise, his casting of the eagle/nation-state as both female
and maternal was (and is) a broadly familiar device. Reconciliatory
political narratives in the postcolonial, post-revolutionary nineteenth-
century United States often figured Britain as Columbia's mother, or
described Columbia herself as maternally protective of Liberty's children.[27] Indeed, a habit of personifying the nation-state as a mother,

---

25. See Coventry Patmore, *The Angel in the House*, 2 vols. (London: Macmillan, 1863).
See also Jean Fagan Yellin, "Nathaniel Hawthorne's *The Scarlet Letter*," in *Women and
Sisters: The Antislavery Feminists in American Culture* (New Haven: Yale University Press,
1989), esp. note 43.

26. Many critics have noted the prevalence of Dark Lady/Light Lady pairs in Hawthorne's works, particularly with regard to "Rappaccini's Daughter." See, e.g., Nina
Baym, "Hawthorne's Women: The Tyranny of Social Myths," *Centennial Review* 15
(1971): 250–72; Judith Fryer, *The Faces of Eve: Women in the Nineteenth-Century American
Novel* (New York: Oxford University Press, 1976); Gloria C. Erlich, *Family Themes and
Hawthorne's Fiction: The Tenacious Web* (New Brunswick, N.J.: Rutgers University Press,
1984); Kristin Herzog, *Women, Ethnics, and Exotics: Images of Power in Mid-Nineteenth-
Century American Fiction* (Knoxville: University of Tennessee Press, 1983); David Leverenz, "Devious Men: Hawthorne," in his *Manhood and the American Renaissance* (Ithaca:
Cornell University Press, 1989), 227–58; and Yellin, "Hawthorne's *The Scarlet Letter*,"
125–52. Indeed, it is still common, particularly in films made in the United States, to
find a "dark" woman of dubious sexuality—say, a "Black Widow"—cast as the dangerous opposite of her "light" and stereotypically innocent sister. Recent and self-
conscious uses of Dark Lady/Light Lady pairs can be found in the film version of
Bernard Malamud's novel *The Natural* (1984, Barry Levinson, dir., Tri-Star/Delphill),
and in Michelle Pfeiffer's campy, schizophrenic Catwoman in *Batman Returns* (1992,
Tim Burton, dir., Warner).

27. There are numerous and frequent references to Mother Britain, Columbia as a
maternal figure, and of course the "motherhood" of the Statue of Liberty. See Martha
Banta, *Imaging American Women: Idea and Ideals in Cultural History* (New York: Columbia
University Press, 1987); and Annette Kolodny, *The Lay of the Land: Metaphor as Experience
and History in American Life and Letters* (Chapel Hill: University of North Carolina Press,
1975). For an analysis of how such perceptions work in national iconography, see Lauren Berlant, *The Anatomy of National Fantasy: Hawthorne, Utopia, and Everyday Life* (Chicago: University of Chicago Press, 1991). For a highly suggestive feminist meditation

however transformed and reshaped by shifting historical contexts, has not vanished. Nor have this figure of speech and the associations it breeds lost their iconographic density or political efficacy. A recent resurgence of American patriotism has linked national pride to appropriate maternal and familial values, if the politically explosive image of American mother/soldiers in the Gulf War was any indication. Women like Captain Yolanda Huet-Vaughn, a family physician who left her son to serve in the Gulf, received both kudos for patriotism and censure for abandoning a child.[28]

Hawthorne's depiction of "The Custom House" eagle as a dangerous, wounding mother points to how its supposed opposite, a fantasy of homogeneous maternal love, was used as a prescriptive model. The ideal maternal icon would contain, and thus mask, any threat of disunion she might also represent. That is, to a republican democratic culture wherein the illusion of achieving univocal political consensus was deemed necessary, emblems of proliferation such as reproduction suggested the potential for squabbling diversity and so were scripted as dangerous—monstrous, perhaps, like Nathaniel Hawthorne's 1851 Medusa, from his collection *A Wonder-Book*.[29] Female, golden-winged, and brazen-clawed, Hawthorne's Gorgon inherited descriptive attributes from the republican "unhappy fowl" perched atop the Custom House. And both demons had "no great tenderness" for mortals (*WB* 41).

The American eagle a fatal Gorgon? Perhaps a more benign and

---

on democratic theory, see Anne Phillips, *Engendering Democracy* (University Park: Pennsylvania State University Press, 1991).

28. The number of women in the American armed forces who served in this war was high; those who left small children behind were displayed in photographs and discussed endlessly, it seemed. Huet-Vaughn caused even further debate when she deserted from Operation Desert Storm after deciding that the U.S. action was "immoral, inhumane, and unconstitutional." As a result, she was court-martialed, and although she was granted clemency, her medical license was revoked, despite the fact that her practice as a doctor had never been in question. See "Deserter Regrets War Protest Failed," *Gainesville Sun*, April 12, 1992. See also Valerie Hartouni, "Containing Women: Reproductive Discourse in the 1980s," in *Technoculture*, ed. Constance Penley and Andrew Ross (Minneapolis: University of Minnesota Press, 1991), 27–56.

29. Nathaniel Hawthorne, *A Wonder-Book*, p. 1 (New York: Houghton Mifflin, 1898), 21–48 (hereafter cited as as *WB*). Hawthorne describes the Gorgon as bearing "some distant resemblance to women . . . [with] wings, too, and exceedingly splendid ones, I can assure you; for every feather in them was pure, bright, glittering, burnished gold, and they looked very dazzlingly, no doubt, when the Gorgons were flying about in the sunshine" (*WB*, 24). The Custom House eagle, carved in 1826 by Jonathan True, is gilded.

embracing icon for democratic motherhood is the Statue of Liberty. Little more than a century old in the 1990s, Lady Liberty retains her fascination. For example, U.S. media coverage of the Chinese student uprising in Tiannanmen Square focused much of its attention on the students' replication of Lady Liberty; her subsequent dismemberment was presented as a horrific emblem of totalitarian oppression. In *The Anatomy of National Fantasy* Lauren Berlant persuasively argues that the Statue of Liberty inhabits a national fantasy of the timeless, indivisible iconic maternal body; however, says Berlant, when such a body is "employed symbolically to regulate or represent the field of national fantasy," her "positive 'agency' lies solely in her availability to be narrativized—controlled."[30] In August 1991 the logic of a campaign poster for the Children's Defense Fund seemed to exemplify this claim. The poster interrogated a photograph of the statue's head with the rhetorical question: "Could It Be Possible That She Has No Maternal Instincts?"[31] Addressed to Americans en masse, the poster's plea stands as a self-evident narrative. Lady Liberty cares.

But this image bears troubling antinomies. The bold rhetorical question may assume a prescripted (controlled) affirmative response—"Of course she has maternal instincts!"—but the poster's frame decapitates the statue, accentuating in close-up Lady-Mother Liberty's stony, frowning brow and her alarmingly spiked crown. Such a medusan image unsettles, threatening to arouse a response opposite the one the poster was presumably designed to evoke. Liberty with her toothy spikes seems to share in the *Wonder-Book* Gorgon's dream "of tearing some poor mortal all to pieces" (*WB*, 41).

Should my reading signal opposition, it also shares in the assumption that the word "maternal" is a synonym for (moral and instinctual) care, just as Hawthorne's sarcastic invocation of the motherly eiderdown pillow one could *not* find in the republican eagle's ample bosom presupposes that such an item ought to have

30. Berlant, *The Anatomy of National Fantasy*, 26–27.
31. Children's Defense Fund Poster, August 1991. Then Vice-President J. Danforth Quayle's much publicized "attack" on the popular representation of single motherhood in the television series *Murphy Brown* is a brief but dense example of the efficacy, no matter whether one reads the consequences as trivial or no, of appealing to the mother-and-child icon in tensely political and conflictual socioeconomic times. Quayle's insistence that a loss of the moral qualities he finds transparently evident in the term "family values" (what sort of family? which values?) demonstrate that an appeal to utopian maternal iconography still masks social conflict.

been there in the first place. The Statue of Liberty, a hegemonic icon of sacred American motherhood, remains a seemingly unalloyed representation that helps instill, if not ensure, proper (hetero)social behaviors. In a national community that still identifies itself as Lady Liberty's ideal home but where traditional, rigidly enforced social and political boundaries are at least *theoretically* in flux, such maternal iconography can function as a conservative guarantee against a tide of unpredictable change. The mother, as a figure, can be used to reinforce conventional certitudes about racial, social, sexual, and political restrictions. Indeed, as Hazel Carby's *Reconstructing Womanhood: The Emergence of the Afro-American Woman Novelist* demonstrates, the nineteenth-century ideology of True Womanhood idealized Christian maternity and made the middle-class, legally married, heterosexual, domestic lady-mother supreme. This Woman, who passively reproduced without expressing sexual desire, and who exercised benevolent authority in the home, became a (white) icon against which any alternative patterns of mothering—or female behavior—were measured.[32]

And yet in the sheer replication of the icon's prescriptive function, the maternal angel points rather insistently toward her own demon and thus at her own fractured instability—or, as Berlant writes, "the unifying utopian figure, which in theory brings time and space into the realm of (discursive, systemic) perfection, shows, in relief, the impermanence and instability of the historical frames within which persons gain (self)knowledge and experience."[33] Maternal iconography was never as untroubled or as static as it was represented to be, rather, it was and is rife with moral, social, and politically charged tensions, subject to persistent conflict, and thus open to dynamic and strategic revisions.

Therefore, it is not surprising to find that "to mother," as Margaret Homans argues in *Bearing the Word: Language and Female Experience in Nineteenth Century Women's Writing*, was represented as both a prescriptive and an imperiled ideal. On one hand, "women's lives were increasingly defined in relation to a standard of motherhood, regardless of whether or not they were of childbearing age"; women who held jobs or who wrote "did so within a framework of dominant cul-

32. Hazel Carby, *Reconstructing Womanhood: The Emergence of the Afro-American Woman Novelist* (New York: Oxford University Press, 1987), 60.
33. Berlant, *The Anatomy of National Fantasy*, 33.

tural myths in which writing contradicts mothering."[34] On the other hand, it is well documented that lower- and middle-class women (and mothers) during the mid-nineteenth century formed an increasingly large sector of the labor market in the United States, particularly in the textile and publishing industries.[35] The dominant maternal ideology did seek to confine women to (sacred) pregnancy and the physical duties of child rearing; popular wisdom held, as Lydia Maria Child's *The Mother's Book* did, that a girl who "feels interested in nothing but books . . . will in all probability be useless, or nearly so, in all the relations dearest to a good woman's heart"—these relations being maternal. Yet Child was herself a prolific author who insisted that "the power of finding enjoyment in reading is above all price, particularly to a woman."[36]

Reading, of course, is not the same activity as writing—or, indeed, as slave-laboring on a plantation. But Child's portrait of the useless girl does indicate that the iconic memory of mother, as Thoreau had imagined his nostalgic idealism, was especially pressing for those persons defined as women. As late as 1887 Mary Virginia Terhune— author of twenty-five novels and numerous short stories and essays, as well as the handbook *Common Sense in the Household*—could still claim that the "woman who rides her hobby of art, literature, social, religious or political reform rough-shod over the wreck of domestic comfort and happiness" was "diseased in perception and judgment."[37] As historian Mary Ryan says, if "by the mid-nineteenth century maternity had assumed its honored position in the center of popular culture, right alongside a familiar variety of American pastry" so that "motherhood was invested with a new glory [and] . . . proclaimed the essence of femininity, 'woman's one duty and function . . . that alone for which she was created.' "[38] then "Mother," for all intents and purposes, meant "woman."

Furthermore, the figure of mother often reduced woman to another

34. Margaret Homans, *Bearing The Word: Language and Female Experience in Nineteenth-Century Women's Writing* (Chicago: University of Chicago Press, 1986), 22.

35. See Mary P. Ryan, *Womanhood in America* (New York: New Viewpoints, 1975); Carroll Smith-Rosenberg, *Disorderly Conduct: Visions of Gender in Victorian America* (New York: Oxford University Press, 1985).

36. Lydia Maria Child, *The Mother's Book* (Boston: Carter, Hendee & Babcock, 1831; rpt. New York: Arno Press, 1972), 20–21 (hereafter cited as *TMB*).

37. Quoted in Kelley, *Private Woman, Public Stage*, 333.

38. Ryan, *Womanhood*, 98–99. Ryan quotes Dr. William Dewees, *A Treatise on the Physical and Medical Treatment of Children* (Philadelphia,1833), 64–65.

and even more restricted image: womb. Put simply, all women, regardless of circumstances, were expected to reproduce under the proper Christian aegis of marriage, and to mother their offspring carefully, in order to be defined as good, solid American women. Similarly, all men were expected to revere and uphold the purity of this maternal icon in order to be defined as true, patriotic, red-blooded American men. Otherwise? A potentially violent melange, potential dissolution—frequently figured in the "bad" woman/mother/womb such as Hawthorne's Custom House editor faces when he is positioned as a nestling seeking shelter at the mother eagle's breast.

But perhaps Hawthorne's brooding fowl-demon may best serve not as an allegorical reference in Western, neoclassical mythology but rather as an index to the sorts of maternal fantasies effective across a broad range of interconnected discourses in nineteenth-century American culture.[39] At the same time, the manner in which Hawthorne's eagle has been interpreted provides an example of how a variety of conflicting discourses not only were but still are readily accommodated by a trope of maternal reproduction as dire instrument of discord.

Liberty, That "Vixen of Contradictions"?

In *The Office of the Scarlet Letter* Sacvan Bercovitch welds the Custom House eagle to Hawthorne's later description—in his famously noninterventionist essay on the Civil War, "Chiefly about War Matters" (1862)—of the *Mayflower* as "the fated womb which in its first labor brought forth a brood of Pilgrims on Plymouth Rock, and, in a subsequent one, spawned slaves upon the Southern soil,—a monstrous birth, but one with which we have an instinctive sense of kindred,

39. In fact the editor's fate—to become a version of Washington Irving's Headless Horseman—associatively draws mythological monster and republican icon closer together, at least insofar as Hawthorne's famous political execution (which rendered *The Scarlet Letter* a "Posthumous Paper of a Decapitated Surveyor:" *CH*, 33) was a beheading performed at the new administration's (medusan eagle's?) behest. For the political relation, within Enlightenment philosophy and pragmatics, between the Medusa and the threat of disorderly conduct, see also Neil Hertz, "Medusa's Head: Male Hysteria under Political Pressure," and related discussions by Joel Fineman, Catherine Gallagher, and Neil Hertz, "More about 'Medusa's Head,' " *Representations* 4 (Fall 1983): 27–55; and Larry J. Reynolds, "*The Scarlet Letter* and Revolutions Abroad," *American Literature* 77 (1985): 44–67; Yellin ("Hawthorne's *The Scarlet Letter*", in *Women & Sisters*, 133) also comments on Hawthorne's thorny relation to revolution and politics.

and so are stirred by an irresistible impulse to attend their rescue even at the cost of blood and ruin."[40] Bercovitch claims that this contains "all the major imaginative ingredients of the dominant culture," notably "the legend of the Puritan theocracy, womb of American democracy; the ambiguities of good and evil, agency of compromise; and the ironies of regeneration through violence, rationale for civil war." Hawthorne's tale of a fatal womb, he says, is "a parable of social conflict following upon cultural myth [which] reverberates with ambiguities at cross-purposes with each other—for example, the recurrent American nightmare of miscegenation; the long literary procession of mutually destructive dark-white kin (from *Clotel* through *Clarel* and *Pudd'nhead Wilson* to *Absalom, Absalom!*); the biblical types of the elect and the damned through which the South defended its peculiar institution; and the racist use of the image of Christian sacrifice through which the North sanctified first the Union Cause and then the Martyrdom of Lincoln."[41]

Viewing Hawthorne's *Mayflower*-womb as rhetorical kin to the Custom House eagle, Bercovitch declares both to be versions of "a Frankenstein's monster of the culture: history returning in the guise of figures designed to control it—the most familiar of symbols . . . now streams forth disjunctions." Mother-eagle and womb-ship are (as are the Madonna/Whore Hester Prynne and her endlessly generative scarlet A) "uncannily" ambiguous signs, double-sided coins signifying above all a form of dynamic, if coercive, social continuity, or what Bercovitch calls "the American ideology" of "consensus founded upon the potential for dissent."[42]

Bercovitch's rendering of *The Scarlet Letter* as a definitive symbol of liberal ideology is remarkable for the breadth of concerns he identifies as embedded in the "Mayflower-eagle, mother of nationhood and vixen of contradictions."[43] Yet the interpretive telos of this argument, along with the metaphorics of Bercovitch's rhetoric, uncannily echoes the politics of consensual containment he explores. At certain key moments he presupposes an interpretive consensus without examining the terms of conflict. For example, the syntax of "mother of nation-

40. Nathaniel Hawthorne, "Chiefly about War Matters," *Atlantic Monthly* 10 (July 1862): 42.

41. Sacvan Bercovitch, *The Office of the Scarlet Letter* (Baltimore: Johns Hopkins Press, 1991), 158.

42. Ibid., 159.

43. Ibid.

hood and vixen of contradictions" balances "mother" and "vixen" in a parallel construction that unquestioningly assumes the terms to be oppositional. But why has "vixen," a word that designates genus and sex, come to connote a vexatious or unruly quantity that can be opposed so easily to the term "mother"? And for whom, exactly, is miscegenation a "recurrent nightmare"? Is an American literary heritage indeed a "procession of mutually destructive dark-white kin," or might such kinships be described as mutually constitutive? Bercovitch's assertion that *Clotel, Clarel, Pudd'nhead Wilson,* and *Absalom, Absalom!* are tales of dark-white destruction is one way these texts have been read. But do these particular narratives measure the reach of "our" literary heritage? For instance, in her 1824 novel *Hobomok,* Lydia Maria Child offers a narrative in which interracial relations need not be read as altogether nightmarish.[44] Nor are the kinships of dark and light in Frances Watkins Harper's *Iola LeRoy* or Charles Chesnutt's *The Marrow of Tradition* well represented by the phrase "mutually destructive."

Indeed, the identification of miscegenation as a nightmare, though accurate with regard to many postbellum representations and indeed legalities, also neatly replicates Hawthorne's assertion that slaves were of monstrous, if kindred, birth to the Pilgrims, and that a "fated womb" was the fatal source of such twinned spawn of inevitable discord.[45] It leaves undisturbed the tenacious and intermeshed presuppositions that would read multiplicity, encoded in the words "brood" and "spawn," as associatively female and animalistic—a nightmare of improperly restrained, gendered reproduction.

In turn, those presuppositions serve to determine aesthetic categorization, affect how interpretive strategies operate, and ultimately form the basis upon which texts are chosen as representing "American" narratives. For instance, part of the elegance of Bercovitch's argumentive strategy is the rhetorical ease with which the *Mayflower*-eagle can both serve as the image of mother-womb, teeming with a brood of disjunctions, and be in and of itself a "monstrous birth, a Frankenstein's monster."[46] Using such a totemic Anglo-American cul-

---

44. Child's 1824 *Hobomok* features an interracial marriage that does not end violently. See also Yellin, *Women & Sisters;* and Carby, *Reconstructing Womanhood.*

45. Prior to 1864 amalgamation, not miscegenation, was the term used to designate interracial "commerce." I thank David Leverenz for calling this usage to my attention and John Mason for fleshing out the historical background to these terms.

46. Bercovitch, *Office,* 159.

tural artifact as Frankenstein's monster proves a deft move for Bercovitch's argument, but it also enacts an interesting metaphoric collapse: it substitutes a later, widespread Anglo-American cultural fantasy for the particularity of Mary Shelley's text.[47] The appeal to Frankenstein's monster as metaphor begs a number of critical questions that must perforce redefine Bercovitch's interpretation. For is it not precisely a womb that is notoriously absent in Shelley's *Frankenstein*? Shelley made it clear that her monster was not born and did not consider itself monstrous until shown that it was *viewed* as horrific both by the parent who rejected it and by a hypocritical society that preached an ideal of disinterested Christian love. Shelley's novel figures maternity in various ways.[48] But what does the word "maternal" signify, how, and to whom? What sorts of maternities play through the novel? These are only a few of the suggestive questions that Bercovitch's facile cultural reference leaves out.

In fact, the unspoken source of logical connection that binds the *Mayflower* to the eagle is for Bercovitch the figuration of both as dangerously reproductive—fated wombs. If the ship and the bird are among the "most familiar of symbols"[49] in a national consciousness, and if mother is as "American as apple pie"[50] for the nineteenth century, all three slide together along a metonymic axis of maternal reproduction in Bercovitch's reading. Of course, my question as to why the notion of a fatal, Frankensteinian womb is available, without much critical mediation, as a metaphor for monstrosity is not meant to stand here as a definitive counterpoint to Sacvan Bercovitch's provocative reading of *The Scarlet Letter*. Still, it does serve as a telling reminder that reproduction can function as a metaphor of chaos. The womb remains a "feminized" image of an unquestioned, phantasmal horror about disunion.[51]

Moreover, such metaphors help to fuel contemporaneous argu-

---

47. For various considerations of both Shelley's text and the resulting cultural phenomenon of Frankenstein as a figure, see George Levine and U. C. Knoepflmacher, eds., *The Endurance of Frankenstein* (New York: Methuen, 1983).

48. Ellen Moers, "Female Gothic," in Levine and Knoepflmacher, *The Endurance of Frankenstein*, 11–35; makes the connections between the novel and Mary Shelley's own troubled maternity unmistakable. See also Anne K. Mellor, *Mary Shelley: Her Life, Her Fiction, Her Monsters* (New York: Routledge, 1987).

49. Bercovitch, *Office*, 159.

50. Ryan, *Womanhood*, 98–99.

51. For the cultural viability of the association between womb and phantasmal, dismembering horror, see Slavoj Žižek, *The Sublime Object of Ideology* (London: Verso, 1989), 79.

ments over whether cultural and interpretive diversity will mean pluralism or, worse, an "indeterminism"[52] that will dismember aesthetic
judgment. The charge of indeterminism often implies that diversity
means, ipso facto, a lack of intellectual integrity. Such a lack, it has
been argued, will inevitably result in a sort of formless mess. "We"
will lose sight of the value of "our" American culture in the pursuit
of a spurious cultural relativity. "We" might lose the forest for the
trees. The current tendency to cast either critical pluralism or, in more
contemporary parlance, multicultural literacy as divisive Angel of
Doom has appeared before in other guises. In fact, the treatment of
The Scarlet Letter as an artifact bears the historical scars of a system of
aesthetic evaluation activated by a presupposition that multiplicity
must mean many-headed medusan monster.

When *The Scarlet Letter* was published in 1851, it contained "The
Custom House," composed as the head note to a volume originally
intended to include other works besides the novel. But as Henry James's 1879 discussion of it shows, this preface was first seen as integral to *The Scarlet Letter*.[53] Much subsequent critical debate, however,
acting like Perseus, has quietly decapitated Hawthorne's novel by re-
moving "The Custom House" as its head. Indeed "The Custom
House" writes Nina Baym, has been silently ignored by most critics.[54]
Yet even though Baym argues that the thematic continuities between
the essay and the novel bind the pieces together, her article also treats
them as separable entities insofar as she claims that "The Custom
House" should be respected as a work "in its own right."[55]

But why the assumption that this sketch's ability to stand on its
own serves to guarantee critical respect? In fact, a number of arguments designed to demonstrate the importance of "The Custom
House" do so at the cost of the sketch's impact on and relation to *The
Scarlet Letter* (and vice-versa) as if the political, autobiographical milieu as well as the unreliable tone of the jaunty (or jaundiced) narrator
were either the buzzing of bothersome contingencies or just unnec-

52. As Jonathan Arac notes in "The Politics of *The Scarlet Letter*," in *Ideology and
Classic American Literature*, ed. Sacvan Bercovitch and Myra Jehlen (London: Cambridge
University Press, 1987), 222–47, cries of horror concerning the problem of interpretive
indeterminism have erupted all over the academy.
53. See James, *Hawthorne*, chap. 5. On the shape of later debates over how "The
Custom House" should be treated, see *SL*, 249–78.
54. Nina Baym, "The Romantic *Malgré Lui*: Hawthorne in 'The Custom House,' " in
SL, 265.
55. Ibid., 266.

essary detail. Indeed, one recent study declares that both novel and sketch are simply "twice their optimal length."[56] This supposed excess of "The Custom House," or what Baym called its "mundane materiality,"[57] has often been deemed incompatible with, or only obliquely related to, the balanced and artistically sound body of Hawthorne's most well-shaped tale.[58] For instance, in 1986 Jonathan Arac declared that "The Custom-House" occupies a space that "in its absence would not be recognized as vacant"; it adds "something gratuitous that was not required and thus destabilizes what it claims to support." So although it is a part of *The Scarlet Letter*, "The Custom House" also remains apart, is indeed declared a detriment to what Arac described as an unquestioned "self-sufficiency" of the tale that follows it.[59] Despite arguments demonstrating that the narrative perspective of *The Scarlet Letter* is shaped by the narrator of "The Custom House"[60] and despite evidence that the sketch was composed in the midst of (as well as published with) *The Scarlet Letter*,[61] it still evidently poses aesthetic problems with regard to the question of appropriate form. Though considerable effort has been exerted to make the sketch an "organic part" of *The Scarlet Letter*,[62] it would appear that the organism still bears suspicious sutures.

It is undoubtedly true that issues other than form have long been at stake in critical assessments of *The Scarlet Letter*, and that "The Custom House" is usually taught as preface to, if not as a part of, the romance. What I am more concerned with is how a rhetoric of aes-

56. Camille Paglia, *Sexual Personae* (New Haven: Yale University Press, 1990), 581. Paglia does not specify which parts should have been deleted or exactly why a perfect version would be a shorter one. Like Emperor Joseph of Austria speaking of Mozart (in the film *Amadeus*), Paglia has decided that Nathaniel Hawthorne used "too many notes."

57. Baym, "Romantic *Malgré Lui*," 272.

58. For James, only *The Scarlet Letter* achieved the absolute "indefinable purity and lightness of conception, a quality which in a work of art affects one in the same way as the absence of grossness does in a human being" (*Hawthorne*, 88). Note his use of the term "conception" with reference to purity and lightness to denote both appropriate art and the appropriate human being, and his insistence that material grossness has no place in either.

59. Arac, "Politics," 252.

60. See Cottom, "Hawthorne versus Hester"; and David Leverenz, "Mrs. Hawthorne's Headache: Reading *The Scarlet Letter*," *Nineteenth-Century Fiction* 37 (March 1983), 552–67.

61. See William Charvat, introduction to *The Scarlet Letter* (Columbus: Ohio State University Press, 1962), xxi–xxiii.

62. Robert L. Berner, "A Key to the 'Custom House' " in *SL*, 278.

thetic cohesion can determine a structure of ideological, metaphorical logic which—under the rubric of reason, rationality, self-sufficiency, or, indeed, ordinary common sense—equates multiplicity with monstrosity. This equation, in turn, devalues discussion that seeks to explore the historical conflicts and contexts of diversity, specifically those concerning race, class, and gender. Such a logic continues to allow for the dismissal of particularity *as* particularity, on the grounds that multivalency eradicates standards of reliable value—without a murmur as to the basis of the supposedly reliable standards being upheld. This brand of common sense can render the everyday obsessions of Surveyor Hawthorne's "Custom House" wholly irrelevant to the scarlet romance of literatus M. de l'Aubépine, forcing a thematic separation between two interdependent texts.[63]

The amputation of mundane particularities from the stuff of sublime romance, I would argue, restricts what material can be viewed as valid or even useful for discussion. In addition, although more recent critical work on *The Scarlet Letter* has been aimed at precisely what earlier assessments would have struck off—that is, the "mundane materiality" of historical context (antebellum abolition, the politics of slavery, the women's rights movement, and the European revolutions of 1848)—such pleas for historical specificity themselves can slyly play Perseus.

Let me return, for a moment, to Jonathan Arac's "Politics of *The Scarlet Letter*." Arac seeks a methodology that is historically and ideologically self-reflexive and that would also ground specific, incisive interpretation. In the course of his quest he takes issue with Frederick Crews and, through him, with larger critical debates about literary indeterminacy. In 1982 Crews had proclaimed that those debates which substituted the "empirically dubious sources of authority" of Marx, Nietzsche or Freud for authorial intent contributed to a wholesale "renunciation of rationally based choice between competing theories." Yet Crews, says Arac, "acted neither empirically nor rationally" in declaring authorial intent foundational. Arac calls Crews's declaration a "decapitation of literary studies by a debased pragma-

---

63. Hawthorne lampoons his own literary aspirations with this parodic French rendition of his already anxiously revised last name: Hathorne to Hawthorne. The irony, of course, is that French can still connote cultural anxieties in an American critical context. I think particularly of how French "theory" (often monolithically imagined) is distrusted as ipso facto elitist, inappropriate to discussions of American texts.

tism" intent upon keeping English departments, in a capitalist economy, up and running.[64]

Here I might stop and ask why Jonathan Arac uses decapitation—a politically charged image of formal execution—as an appropriately horrific image for the possible death of certain literary studies. I am more interested, however, in how Arac, despite his validation of the kinds of sociopolitical engagement represented by, say, the use of a Marxist conceptual framework, also performs a closure of debate not unlike the one with which he charges Crews. Although *The Scarlet Letter* addresses "the anonymous toil of women under the barbarism of patriarchy", he writes, *"we must go farther* to understand its immediate and continuing power long before feminism became an unavoidable presence. Slavery was the issue that agitated American politics more deeply in Hawthorne's time, and abolitionism made the young Henry Adams feel that Boston in 1850 was once again revolutionary (emphasis added).[65] Arac's identification of feminist debate about *The Scarlet Letter* as an obstacle to an understanding of slavery as *the* political issue curiously truncates his claim that refocusing on the "politics of *The Scarlet Letter*" will provide a more opened-out apprehension of Hawthorne's narrative. While distancing himself from a charge of indeterminacy, Arac's injunction to "go farther" places "feminism" in the position of a static ideology.

Indeed, Arac's vision of slavery and the abolitionist movement as somehow unmarked by gender politics tacitly severs antebellum abolition as a political movement from its relation to the women's rights movement and, in so doing, Arac disables a portion of the immediate and continuing power he wishes to locate in *The Scarlet Letter*.[66] Nineteenth-century abolition was hardly gender-neutral. The economics and ideology of slavery helped to shape—and were shaped by—the definitive cultural weight placed upon proper maternity. While domestic ideology strove to keep (free) women's labor restricted to the home just as a new, highly mobile marketplace economy demanded

64. Arac, "Politics" (citing Crews), 250.
65. Ibid., 248.
66. As Arac, Bercovitch, Yellin, Berlant, and T. Walter Herbert, Jr. (in *Dearest Beloved: The Hawthornes and the Making of the Middle-Class Family* [Berkeley: University of California Press, 1993]), among others, have claimed, Hawthorne was involved in the issues that agitated the politics of his time, although it is decidedly difficult to argue that he did anything but fence-sit with regard to abolition and the Civil War; indeed, in Yellin's estimation, Hawthorne's inactivity almost amounted to a pro-slavery position.

an influx of (unskilled, often female) laborers,[67] the slavocracy maintained that (female, slave) maternal reproduction was invisible (a slave
supposedly could not be a true mother) even as it grounded economic
security on that reproduction. Along similar lines, while medical theories concerning the radical instability of female anatomy were tying
women ever more severely to a reproductive destiny—a biologically
determined destiny that militated against the kind of social autonomy
still named the American entrepreneurial spirit—many women were
beginning to take political action with regard to abolition, suffrage
and abortion.[68] Sojourner Truth's famous question "Ain't I a woman?"
pinpoints the paradox of an antebellum (hetero)sexual orthodoxy insisting on the one hand, that to be truly feminine and maternal was
to be anatomical weakness personified and on the other hand, enslaving some female bodies in enforced reproductive factories called

67. Ryan, *Womanhood*, 23–25.
68. In the antebellum courtroom, issues of a "free" mother's right to rear her offspring were being contested within a public discourse where issues of a slave's right
to "own" himself (and later the hypocrisies of increasingly complex Jim Crow laws)
had much to do with the legal status of any mother and her children. For example, in
the slavocracy an African-American woman's child might be said, ironically, to belong
to her alone under the euphemistic law that "a slave must follow the condition of its
mother." But this provision allowed "mixed" children to be considered salable commodities, through organized (white male to black female) rape. Such "mass production"
was predicated on several interlocking beliefs that structured the system of racial slavery: (1) that the woman bearing the salable child was not truly a mother, nor could she
be or become (in the majority of cases) free; (2) that the woman bearing the salable
child would, of course, never be white (suicide, infanticide, or a quick sale being preferable to an acknowledgment of such a birth); (3) that even if legally "free," the woman
bearing the child would have no real or binding legal rights to her children, given the
way property laws were written in both the North and the South. That is, since no
woman had legal citizenship, a single woman's right to parent her children was no
right at all. For instance, a white widow whose husband left no clear will might have
to file suit for custody of her children through a male member of her family. Worse, a
widow sometimes found her deceased husband's male relations legally appointed heirs
and guardians to her children; she could even be turned out of her own home as a
burden on the household, and her children (given the laxity of child-labor laws) sent
out to work for the new guardian. Such a patriarchal economy left a black freedwoman
legally powerless with regard to her children, even if she had managed to "liberate"
them from actual bondage. See Suzanne Arms, *Immaculate Deception: A New Look at
Women and Childbirth in America* (Boston: Houghton Mifflin, 1975); Michael Grossberg,
"Who Gets the Child? Custody, Guardianship, and the Rise of a Judicial Patriarchy in
Nineteenth-Century America," *Feminist Studies* 9 (Summer 1983); Viviana A. Zelizer,
Pricing the Priceless Child: The Changing Social Value of Children (New York: Basic Books,
1985); Sylvia D. Hoffert, *Private Matters: American Attitudes toward Childbearing and Infant
Nurture in the Urban North, 1800–1860* (Chicago: University of Illinois Press, 1989). Sig-
nificantly, none of these works address the particular situation of bi- or multiracial
children in the nineteenth century.

plantations and working others to death in "Devil's Dungeon" paper-mills.[69]

Contrary to Arac's suggestion, feminism did not enter the picture merely as a result of twentieth-century critical practice. Not only was racial slavery marked by gender ideology, but abolition took shape through Arac's so-called "unavoidable presence." This would suggest that the relations between revolution, race, and reproduction need critical attention, an attention that Henry Adams was attuned to when he wrote *Democracy's* story as that of a woman whose nurturance is dependent on the imperialist policies of late-nineteenth-century American politics.[70] At the very least, then, I would argue that Arac's American political history is a foreshortened one. It raises troubling questions as to which histories are lost, or remain untold, when "history" is used thus as a means of validating unquestionable truths. Slavery may have been *the* political issue agitating Hawthorne's time, as Arac insists, but it is shortsighted not to inquire how and to what end that issue was represented.[71]

Reproduction, Race, and Revolution

Conceived by Liberty addresses such foreshortenings in order to articulate the rhetoric of reproduction, race, and revolution that constructed and revised dominant, sentimental maternal iconography. The readings that follow seek first to demonstrate how a dominant antebellum maternal ideology put forward an illusion of a coherent, sanctified maternity, an ideology that marked both popular representations of motherhood and texts designated as literary, as I show in Part I: Governing Sentiment. Chapter 1 examines Lydia Maria Child's use of a maternal iconography to show how the creation of an obe-

69. Herman Melville, "The Paradise of Bachelors and The Tartarus of Maids," in *Selected Tales and Poems* (New York: Holt, Rinehart & Winston, 1963), 206–30.

70. Henry Adams, *Democracy: An American Novel* (London: Macmillan, 1882).

71. Joan Scott's persuasive and continuing argument that history as a narrative needs attention with regard to gender is pertinent, particularly given that Arac, for reasons he does not make clear, appears to assume that "feminism" has no history or is a univocal and ahistorical theoretical approach. See Scott, "Gender as a Useful Category of Historical Analysis," in *Gender and the Politics of History* (New York: Columbia University Press, 1988), 28–52. Two useful works on the relation between nineteenth-century feminism and the politics of abolition are Yellin, *Women & Sisters*, and Smith-Rosenberg, *Disorderly Conduct*.

dient yet enterprising and bold citizenry fell most heavily on motherhood—both as pragmatic institution and as figurative symbol—and
structured metaphorical and metaphysical debate. In the philosophical
discussions that "occurred" between the writings of Sarah Margaret
Fuller and Ralph Waldo Emerson, as I argue in Chapter 2, the infra-
structure of "an" American literature and culture was in the process
of being constructed. Fuller's response to Emersonian metaphysics allowed for an aesthetics that demanded diversity as the basis for fecund creativity, an outlook that came to affect Emerson's later essays.

Antebellum maternal ideology was unstable, however. By examining specific representations that indicate rupture in texts that have
been used critically, in one way or another, as central to argumenta-
tion about the shape of various contested American literatures, my
readings propose that a supposedly seamless icon was not only conflicted but also a site of politicized, aesthetic contention. Indeed, the
beatified maternal as political and cultural icon, on which Emerson
and Fuller relied to ground Transcendental metaphysics, also represented fears that the American democratic experiment might prove,
as Henry James put it, a "many-headed monster of universal suffrage."[72] Should America lack appropriate controls, her unchecked reproductive capacity, deemed monstrous, would shatter the singularity
of *e pluribus unum*, rendering a sublime ideal inchoate.

Such fears of maternalized duplicity can be seen most urgently in
work directly addressing slavery and racial conflict as threats to the
Union. Thus, in Part II: Maternal Race, through a sustained discussion
of sentimentality and slavery, I show how the underlying ideal of a
homogeneous maternal love, because it both relied upon and masked
fears of monstrosity, began to lose its symbolic force as a model of
utopian unification during the Civil War. Sentimental maternity, often
daring in its defiance of the expected, symbolized community for a
dominant nineteenth-century American culture (Chapter 3, on Harriet
Beecher Stowe). Yet because it was unstable, its power (Chapter 4, on
Frederick Douglass) to propose startling alternatives to convention was
also uncertain (Chapter 5, on Harriet Jacobs).

Finally, I argue that in treating sentimental maternal iconography,
critics have reinforced elements of the dominant ideology as natural.
As a result, such criticism is often locked into the very ideology it
seeks to expose. In Part III: Paternal Return, I show how the Civil

72. James, *Hawthorne*, 111.

War's shattering of the maternal ideal as cultural icon allowed for the consolidation of a benevolent paternal ideology, which gained a definitive critical priority by providing a "new" principle of social and aesthetic unification. A univocal American cultural identity emerged as phantasmaly unscarred by conflict, fully coincident with Emerson's early credos of "Self-Reliance." In the project of renationalization, however, from Reconstruction to the turn of the century, the attributes of sentimental maternity were regendered: imaginative creativity, aesthetic purity, and moral idealism, all once associated with the maternal, became primarily paternal attributes.

Nevertheless, the reductive, rejecting denigration of the maternal upon which an emerging twentieth-century definition of quintessentially American identity would come to rest was a forced and painful process that left traces of agony. This agony and the system of paternalized aesthetics that it marks haunt the shape of late nineteenth-century narrative and, indeed, the ensuing shape of an American canon. Both the process of paternal reinstatement and the agony of maternal rejection are evidenced, albeit quite differently, in the work of Herman Melville (Chapter 6) and Henry James (Chapter 7). Therefore, what became a prevailing twentieth-century definition of an American literary aesthetic was dependent upon but apparently unconnected to a previously central maternal icon, now lost. This book seeks to address both the conditions and the consequences of that loss.

Part I

Governing Sentiment

The Mother's State:
The Policies and Politics of
Reproduction in Lydia Maria Child

> The first rule, and the most important of all, in education, is that a mother govern her own feelings, and keep her heart and conscience pure.
>
> —Lydia Maria Child, *The Mother's Book*

From 1844 to 1846 a collection of small gift books, titled *Flowers for Children*, was issued by the well-known *Juvenile Miscellany* editor (1826–34), Lydia Maria Francis Child. The second volume contained "A New-England Boy's Song: About Thanksgiving."[1] This twelve-verse poem, later set to music, became the popular song "Over the River and through the Woods." Taught in elementary schools as a traditional ditty for Thanksgiving, it can still be found in children's books.[2] Indeed, the song has become something of a cultural icon, fostering a picture of domestic security nearly as all-American as the Statue of Liberty or the bald eagle.

Over the river and through the wood
To grandfather's house we go;
The horse knows the way to carry the sleigh through the white and
    drifted snow
Over the river and through the wood
To grandfather's house away! We would not stop for doll or top, for
    'tis Thanksgiving Day.

1. Lydia Maria Child, *Flowers For Children*, vol. 2 (New York: C. S. Francis, 1845; Boston: J. H. Francis, 1845), 26–28; see also William S. Osborne, *Lydia Maria Child* (Boston: Twayne, 1980), 117.
2. When I was a child on Long Island, my grandmother taught me to sing this song on Thanksgiving. At a middle school where I taught creative writing in 1992, I came across it in the children's library; my sister and my mother—a teacher and a librarian—confirm that the song is still being reprinted and taught.

Over the river and through the wood
When grandmother sees us come
She will say, "Oh, dear, the children are here, bring a pie for
  everyone."
Over the river and through the wood
Now grandmother's cap I spy! Hurrah for the fun! Is the
  pudding done? Hurrah for the pumpkin pie!

Or so goes Brinton Turkle's 1974 illustrated edition, which uses the first and last stanzas of Child's poem.[3] Providing a scene of shelter and security set against the backdrop of a New England winter, the song stipulates Grandfather's house as yearned-for destination, over which Grandmother evidently presides with her traditional pumpkin pie and pudding—as in the original 1844 illustration (Fig. 2). Thanksgiving dinner, we are told, is more fun for children than dolls or tops. The toys are shown scattered and deserted at the children's feet, as they follow Grandmother and pudding.

In the 1990s, however, Thanksgiving Day has become a politically troubled site. Indeed, although some might stage regional tussles over whether Grandmother's pecan, apple, or pumpkin should signify as the American pie—apple being favored, as in the saying "American as mom and apple pie"—far greater and more vexed public dispute has broken out over whether the violences of European colonization— forced departures, captivities, betrayals, genocide—have been white-washed by the myth of Thanksgiving as a day of egalitarian co-operation, when Native Americans and European colonists suppos-edly shared a feast.[4]

Native American political activism—though not phrased as such, and situated within a very different set of historical circumstances— would have been familiar to the author of "Over the River," an abo-litionist editor and an advocate of emancipation. Child's most popular fictional works—Hobomok: A Tale of Early Times, Philothea: A Romance, and "The Quadroons"—were profoundly shaped by political ques-tions. Even though in the 1990s many aspects of her work, such as the figuration of the New England scene in "Over the River," have

3. Lydia Maria Child, *Over The River and through the Wood*, illustrated by Brinton Turkle (New York: Coward, McCann & Geoghegan, 1974). My grandmother's version had no grandfather in it, however.
4. See William Bradford, *Of Plymouth Plantation*, ed. Samuel Eliot Morison (New York: Knopf, 1952). The meal frequently identified as the first Thanksgiving is a des-ultory affair that my students seldom recognize as the feast they've been taught it was.

28   THE NEW-ENGLAND BOY'S SONG.

Over the river, and through the wood—
    When grandmother sees us come,
        She will say, Oh dear,
        The children are here,
    Bring a pie for every one.

Over the river, and through the wood—
    Now grandmother's cap I spy!
        Hurra for the fun!
        Is the pudding done?
    Hurra for the pumpkin pie!

Figure 2. The last two stanzas, with original illustration, of "A New England Boy's Song." Courtesy of the Baldwin Library, Gainesville, Florida.

become highly questionable parts of a nationalist tradition, Child was committed to causes deemed radical for a white woman of her class. And though many critics and scholars of nineteenth-century American culture have demonstrated that the mulatto, mulatta, and quadroon, as figures for "the notion of the 'white Negro,'" were part of strategy of representation "tacitly subscribing to the racist ideology of the color line" (to quote Susan Gillman), Child was undeniably committed to the antislavery cause.[5]

Of course, such commitment is itself hard to gauge and difficult to evaluate. In *The Word in Black and White: Reading "Race" in American Literature, 1638–1867*, Dana Nelson argues that "no matter how progressive the impulse of the text—in discussions of 'racial' intermarriage from Byrd's *Histories* to Child's *A Romance of the Republic* . . . or how suggestively the text deconstructs its own racist privilege," the "white"-authored narrative addressed to a "white" audience "always maintains at least some last vestige of 'white' privilege."[6] Other critics, writing about Child's interaction with Harriet Ann Jacobs, have questioned the impact of Child's editorial assistance on Jacobs's *Incidents in the Life of a Slave Girl*: Child insisted upon sentimental conventions as a means to veil slavery's horrors—specifically that of African-American women's sexual exploitation in racial slavery—so that the work might find a genteel, middle-class, white, female Northern audience. The forced collaboration between Child and Jacobs (the publisher, Thayer and Eldridge, accepted Jacobs's manuscript only on the condition that Child provide an introduction) has been read as an illustration of the racial "limits of sisterhood."[7] The resulting text bears

5. Susan Gillman, "The Mulatto, Tragic or Triumphant? The Nineteenth-Century American Race Melodrama" in *The Culture of Sentiment: Race, Gender, and Sentimentality in Nineteenth-Century American Culture*, ed. Shirley Samuels (New York: Oxford University Press, 1992), 221. The figure of the mulatto has been the source of a large number of critical studies, among them Judith R. Berzon, *Neither White Nor Black: The Mulatto Character in American Fiction* (New York: New York University Press, 1978); Hortense Spillers, "Notes on an Alternative Model—Neither/Nor," in *The Difference Within: Feminism and Critical Theory*, ed. Elizabeth Meese and Alice Parker (Philadelphia: John Benjamins, 1989); Carolyn Karcher, "Lydia Maria Child's *Romance of the Republic*: An Abolitionist View of America's Racial Destiny," in *Slavery in the Literary Imagination*, ed. Deborah E. McDowell and Arnold Rampersad (Baltimore: Johns Hopkins University Press, 1989), 81–103; Dana D. Nelson, *The Word in Black and White: Reading "Race" in American Literature, 1638–1867* (New York: Oxford University Press, 1992); Yellin, *Women & Sisters.*

6. Nelson, *Word,* 132.

7. I've used Jeanne Boydston, Mary Kelley, and Anne Margolis's title for their book on conflicts in the Beecher family, *The Limits of Sisterhood: The Beecher Sisters on Women's*

the sentimental inscription of the race, class, and gender "norms" constructed by the Cult of True Womanhood. In fact, in critic Karen Sánchez-Eppler's view, the sentimental strategies that abolitionists used to arouse white, middle-class sympathy obliterated "blackness" because white was consistently washed over black, and so, "by identifying with her enslaved sister, the free woman [came] to betray her."[8]

That Lydia Maria Francis Child occupied the space of a free, white, middle-class, well-connected abolitionist editor in 1860, when she and Harriet Ann Jacobs began corresponding, cannot be denied. But did this relative position of power, as P. Gabrielle Foreman has claimed, "place her in the position of the (benign) Southern patriarch"? Is Child's sentimental language "informed by a patron-child hierarchy which mirrors slave patriarchy"?[9] Sánchez-Eppler seems to agree: the sentimental conventions of abolitionist discourse "obliterate[d] the particularity of black and female experience."[10] Although Sánchez-Eppler goes on to say that she is not "interested in attempting to defend either authors or audiences" from the charge of racism which, in part, determines Foreman's evaluation, she nevertheless constructs Child as a "defensive" writer who "backs away from her argument" and whose "very effort to depict goodness in black involves the obliteration of blackness."[11]

Child did enjoy a middle-class readership and critical esteem in her own day, although much if not most of her fictional work has since been forgotten.[12] Such invisibility is the complicated result of what

---

Rights and Woman's Sphere (Chapel Hill: University of North Carolina Press, 1988) in a rather different context here. See also Lydia Maria Child, *Selected Letters, 1817–1880*, ed. Milton Meltzer and Patricia G. Holland, 94; Yellin's introduction to Harriet Jacobs, *Incidents in the Life of a Slave Girl*, ed. Jean Fagan Yellin (Cambridge, Mass.: Harvard University Press, 1987); and Chapter 5 below. Although Child wrote, "We certainly have done all we could to secure the deadly hostility of the red man and the black man, everywhere," when it came to writing about the reproductive economy of slavery and those breeders "of slaves for traffic," she could only call it "that most disgusting feature of slavery, which abolitionists have been obliged to leave partially veiled, for decency's sake." See esp. P. Gabrielle Foreman, "The Spoken and the Silenced in *Incidents in the Life of a Slave Girl* and *Our Nig*," *Callaloo* 13 (Spring 1990), 313–24; and Bruce Mills, "Lydia Maria Child and the Endings to Harriet Jacobs's *Incidents in the Life of a Slave Girl*," *American Literature* 64 (June 1992).

8. Karen Sánchez-Eppler, "Bodily Bonds: The Intersecting Rhetorics of Feminism and Abolition," in Samuels, *The Culture of Sentiment*, 104.

9. Foreman, "The Spoken and the Silenced," 316.

10. Sánchez-Eppler, "Bodily Bonds," 95.

11. Ibid., 102.

12. For example, before Child's publication of her anti-slavery treatise, *Appeal in*

Carolyn Karcher terms "censorship, American style" and the "limits of genre."[13] Child was never legally censored or officially silenced; rather, when her *Appeal in Favor of That Class of Americans Called Africans* effectively curtailed her career in 1833, she experienced "social ostracism, economic boycott, . . . mob violence, . . . [and] the censoriousness of her fellow abolitionists"; finally, says Karcher, she engaged in self-censorship by acceding to the limitations of sentimental representation.[14] In order to get difficult or controversial material published, Child eschewed her earlier, more direct political tracts, such as the *Appeal* in favor of writings designed to arouse pity and compassion. Self-censored, unremarked, untaught, unread, and for the most part now unavailable, Child's fiction has been overlooked, as Dana Nelson has shown, even by the very work that sought to reclaim a nineteenth-century women's tradition for the twentieth century.[15]

In other words, although I agree that the sentimental conventions of abolitionist discourse Child used did both mirror and give rise to antebellum social hierarchization, I wonder at Foreman's desire to see Child in the place of a southern patriarch, or Sánchez-Eppler's insistence that "blackness" was utterly obliterated in Child's work, since it would seem that such critical narratives reproduce the power of the patriarchy and the obliteration of which they complain. Instead of discussing how "blackness" might signify, they help to render "blackness" blank. So while I am persuaded to discover in Child what Nelson calls the "inevitable conservatism" resulting from the complacency of texts by "white" authors addressing "white" readers,[16] I am puzzled by readings that regard Child as a writer who (for being

Favor of That Class of Americans Called Africans (Boston: Allen and Tichnor, 1833), which insisted upon immediate emancipation thirty-odd years before the Civil War, the *North American Review* wrote: "We are not sure that any woman in our country would outrank Mrs. Child" (quoted by Karcher in her introduction to Child, *Hobomok*, xi. *Hobomok* is hereafter cited as *H*).

13. See Carolyn L. Karcher, "Rape, Murder, and Revenge in 'Slavery's Pleasant Homes': Lydia Maria Child's Antislavery Fiction and the Limits of Genre," in *Women's Studies International Forum* (1986): 331; rpt. in Samuels, *The Culture of Sentiment*, 58–72; and "Censorship, American Style."

14. Karcher, "Censorship American Style," 285. Karcher goes on to describe such tacit censorship policies as a "tendency to discourage the publication and distribution of works that go beyond the bounds of acceptable opinion; but the opinion in question will be attributed to the public, rather than the government, and the rationale for rejecting the offending works will be economic rather than political."

15. See Nelson, *Word*, 160, n. 22.

16. Ibid., 132.

politically incorrect, racist, or heterosexist) deserves a critical beating. Why such rhetorical interest in tongue-lashing an already largely invisible object?

Sentimental Verities

Of course, I am not arguing that whipping Child was anyone's primary intent. Without Dana Nelson's careful consideration of Child's *A Romance of the Republic*, for example, I could not have written this chapter. Yet Nelson, too, sees Child's rhetorical strategy of sympathy as forestalling "a fuller questioning of the biases in Anglo-American culture that permitted slavery and patriarchy and continued to foster 'racial' prejudice."[17] In thus capitulating to the dictates of "white" sentimentalism, says Sánchez-Eppler, Child unfortunately bowed to the "power of social sanctions," since she clearly sought "a different answer" to racial prejudice from one dependent "upon the black being washed white."[18] For Nelson and, to a greater extent, for Sánchez-Eppler, whitewashing would seem to be the inevitable result and the inherent flaw of sentimental rhetoric. Indeed, as both Nelson and Karcher point out, Child's fourth and last novel, *A Romance of the Republic* (1867), has been generally viewed as flawed precisely because it uses sentimental conventions and so could not exceed the representational limits of racially inflected cultural prejudice. Commentary on this novel in the early 1980s sees its author as wedded to antebellum concerns—"The novel did not speak to readers in postwar America," writes William Osborne—and misguided in her use of the romance as postbellum political vehicle.[19] And although Nelson calls such judgment dated in the wake of more recent critical reassessments of the sentimental romance, she, too, finds that Child's novel "fails to imagine cross-*cultural* relationships that would complement the cross-*racial*

17. Ibid., 88.
18. Sánchez-Eppler, "Bodily Bonds," 102.
19. Osborne, *Lydia Maria Child*, 157. Osborne writes in his preface: "Devoted as she was to political and civil freedom for all men and women, she was unable to subordinate propaganda to the subtler demands of fiction. Worse, she employed an outdated novel tradition—the domestic romance so popular in America in the 1850s" (preface). Yet much evidence indicates, as Nelson (*Word*) shows, that sentimentality and sentimental romance conventions were both more complicated than such commentary might allow and in any case still quite popular well beyond the 1850s. Nelson concludes that such critiques are outdated.

ones." *A Romance* does not "seek out the voices and experiences of the victim/object of American racial hisory and representations" but rather "unquestioningly endorses 'white' bourgeois class structure and culture" by situating racial Otherness as victimized or trapped Object; thus Child "preserved a class structure which ensured the continued cultural (and economic) domination of the Anglo-American majority."[20]

Later in this chapter, I reconsider these assessments of *A Romance*. More broadly, however, I want to examine Child's career as an emblematic case of the "sentimentality" that is still regarded as a sign not only of aesthetic paucity in the mid-nineteenth-century American domestic romance[21] but also of the racist and (hetero)sexist political limitations of middle-class cultural production. In fact, critiques of Child's fiction in general have condemned her reliance on a hobbling strategy of sentimentality that was racebound, genderbound, and classbound.

Indeed, Child's status as a white, abolitionist author of domestic romance and "literary ephemera"[22] —such as *The Mother's Book* and *Flowers for Children*—seems to have marked her out ipso facto as a source of that which is often said to be both in bad taste and in bad faith. For even though, as Dana Nelson writes, "scholars need no longer apologize or rationalize their interest in sentimental novels," thanks to "a reassessment of the role their constructions of sympathy played in the cultural dialogue of the 1800s"[23] (an ongoing critical endeavor to which *Conceived by Liberty* is addressed) such scholars more often than not come to the conclusion, as Franny Nudelman does in "Harriet Jacobs and the Sentimental Politics of Female Suffering," that domestic sentimentality merely effects a reproduction of victimization and subjection.[24] For Nudelman, the vacillations of sentimental discourse (what she has called the play between excessive "fanfare" and coy "reluctances")[25] can produce a narrator who might indeed alter—or, to use her term, "contaminate"—a (supposedly) nor-

20. Nelson, *Word*, 145.

21. See Douglas, *Feminization*, 3.

22. Although Child's work generally is characterized as sentimental and domestic, Osborne, *Lydia Maria Child*, identifies *The Mother's Book* particularly as "literary ephemera."

23. Nelson, *Word*, 67.

24. Franny Nudelman, "Harriet Jacobs and the Sentimental Politics of Female Suffering," *ELH* 59 (1992): 939–64.

25. Ibid., 960.

mative sentimental narrative voice.[26] Yet this contaminating voice, despite being that of an agent, is still also and inevitably the voice of a victim and sufferer.

Why does Nudelman assume that as late as 1861 (years after Frederick Douglass and Harriet Wilson, to name only two authors, began writing), sentimental discourse still represented an unfractured, normative, or typical white, middle-class voice? And why hear Jacobs's voice as a *contamination*? Furthermore, when Nudelman claims that "sentimentality relies on generic rather than eccentric reactions—fear, indignation, sorrow," which allow for a utopically universal, reciprocal "sentimental exchange,"[27] I am left with a number of troubling questions. How, for example, did fear, indignation, and sorrow become generic rather than eccentric? Concurrently, what is an eccentric reaction? Once an emotion such as fear is involved in a process of representation, when is it not shaped, even negatively, by generic convention? How is exchange imagined here, if the situation is from the start unequal or assymetrical? Nudelman appears to concur with Sánchez-Eppler that "sentimental antislavery stories are constructed on the foundation of a presumed alliance between abolitionist goals and domestic values, an alliance . . . fraught with asymmetries and contraditions."[28]

Both critics see these asymmetries denied by sentimental harmonies. But if sentimentality depends on the denial of contradictions and the eradication of difference, if sentimentality produces only the attenuation of pain or the obliteration of the very persons taken as "objects" of solicitation, then one must conclude that sentimentality itself is deeply suspect, a tool only and forever of the status quo. It may become contaminated, as Nudelman claims, but certainly not altered in such a way as to shift or fracture the norm. Logically, then, all texts that use sentimentality—say, Frederick Douglass's *My Bondage and My Freedom*—have also engendered denial and contributed to the obliteration of "blackness." What interests me is how such sentimental texts, once devalued as aesthetically void abolitionist propaganda, are now being devalued under the surprising rubric of the politically naïve—a devaluation that is in the end reductive to the complicated

---

26. Ibid., 962.

27. Ibid., 945. Private conversations with Sandra Gunning helped me to think through the implications of Nudelman's language.

28. Sánchez-Eppler, "Bodily Bonds," 109.

situation of—and ambivalent racial, sexual, and cultural politics in-scribed in—sentimental iconography.

A caveat: I am not claiming that sentimentality cannot be, at the very least, a two-edged sword.[29] Child's domestic Thanksgiving Day scene in "Over the River" has helped to screen official U.S. policies of what, in the 1990s, might bear the euphemism "ethnic cleansing." At the same time, this Thanksgiving scene can, in and of itself, pro-duce much less blinding or idealized associations than those it has been said to represent. For example, one might note that the original twelve-verse poem, as opposed to the shortened song, presents a very conflicted attitude toward the verities of domestic ideology. The poem conjures up the idea of domestic warmth, but images of home are absent; it remains a longed-for but unrepresented shelter against the cold, dangerous environment the totemic boy of the title (and the chil-dren in the sleigh) endure. "Oh how the wind does blow. / It stings the toes / And bites the nose / As over the ground we go"[30] does not sound altogether like the fun we are told it is. And although the house is owned by Grandfather, he is neither heard from nor identifiably present at the holiday scene. And Grandmother, making her appear-ance only in the last stanzas, has been reduced to a few worried words, a cap in the window, and food on the table. Indeed, although the destination of the horse-drawn sleigh is the grandparents' house, the primary scenes in the poem are of white and drifted snow, of endless, empty, threatening tracts of river and woods, windswept and freezing, which only the horse knows how to navigate. Nipped and frozen, careening across silent woodlands at the mercy of a horse's knowhow, the boy of this song fantasizes that the sleigh may tip over, sending the children onto the ice. Even the original illustration is cu-rious (see Fig. 2). The large, platter-bearing grandmother seems to have scattered not just the toys (were they dropped in eagerness or out of fear?) but the children, too. And, at the risk of sounding mel-odramatic, I might also ask what, exactly, is on that steaming platter Grandmother bears—plum pudding or swaddling clothes?

By her own account, the more lighthearted aspects of Child's works

29. A word on phallogocentrism seems necessary here. Although "two-edged sword" is a cliché and one that might be said to employ phallic imagery, it may be useful to remember the labrys—also a two-edged weapon, but the double-headed axe doesn't carry quite the same phallic connotations. A labrys, then, suggests how one might reread figures and revise figures of speech.

30. Child, Flowers, 25.

were nostalgic fabrications, the construction of a childhood past that she did not remember experiencing. "Cold, shaded and uncongenial was my childhood and youth," she wrote to a friend. "Whenever reminiscences of them rise up before me, I turn my back on them as quickly as possible."[31] Knowing this, we begin to see "Over the River" as a fantasy substitution for difficult memories, a screening picture that nevertheless bears traumatic traces. So, too, I argue, do sentimental representations screen, reveal, substitute for, and bear problematic inscriptions. Consequently, I question whether or not sentimentality always reproduces exactly the "same" class structure and "white" culture from which it emerges and which it helped to define. In other words, if a child (a word that of itself begs questions as to its content: which child? from what background? how constituted as a child?[32]) is still taught to sing "Over the River" in public elementary schools, must we not also ask how he or she is educated and what she and he—or we—are taught to hear, when told *to* hear a sentimental sound? How might sentimental middle-class cultural productions be read against the so-called dominant grain so as to produce a reading where "black" might not always be obliterated, or "woman" might not always signify the margin?[33]

Domestic Loving

In 1831, two years before the *Appeal* would send her career into a precipitous fall, Lydia Maria Francis Child published *The Mother's Book*, a guide to child rearing suitable for "popular use" among the "middling class in America" (*TMB*, 1). Child's dedication, "To American Mothers, on Whose Intelligence and Discretion the Safety and Prosperity of the Republic so Much Depend, This Volume is Respectfully Inscribed," posts three central tenants: (1) that "Woman" was intelligent, (2) that Woman's intelligence was a national concern, and (3) that American mothers would be responsible for producing the prosperity of the Republican body politic. Like *Flowers for Children* and

31. Child, *Selected Letters*, 1.

32. It is impossible not to observe that Child's own last name circulates oddly through a chapter focused on mother and child.

33. In thinking through the framing questions of this chapter, I was influenced most by the work of Judith Butler, Hazel Carby, Sandra Gunning, Donna Haraway, Barbara Johnson, Eve Kosofsky Sedgwick, Kaja Silverman, Hortense Spillers.

The Juvenile Miscellany, this text was designed for a *"middling*-class" family, because, as Child often wrote, too many books were addressed to childish frivolity or the folly of wealth, rather than to the real, day-to-day concerns of middle-class life, particularly those of the woman whom she called "The Frugal Housewife."

The Mother's Book became an indispensable middle-class household item, part of a burgeoning educational literature aimed at inculcating the appropriate virtues—such as cleanliness, piety, restraint, and compassion—in children.[34] This education, as Mary P. Ryan's *Womanhood in America* shows, both arose from and installed antebellum constructions of narrowly particular, separate, and gendered spheres. Such an inscription of appropriate virtues and definitive gender roles in turn shaped representations of a middle-class domesticity. The orderly, religious, serene Home, presided over by the Mother, was a private, compassionate retreat from the hurly-burly, greed, and destitution of public life.[35] By the 1840s, writes Ryan, "the positions in the female labor force had proven ill-paid and arduous and grew ever more dehumanizing with the advance of industrial technology. The doctrine of women's influence promised women that rarest of delights, having one's cake and eating it too. They could remain at home and still achieve . . . a real but indirect power in society."[36]

The Mother's Book, however, sits at the cusp of a shift between eighteenth-century parenting conventions and antebellum domesticity. Following an already long-standing cultural tradition in the United States of what Linda Kerber has usefully named "republican motherhood,"[37]

34. As Child herself says, libraries—private and public—were becoming an adjunct to every well-run, middle-class household; she "can hardly suppose that any person can really want a book, in this country, without being able to obtain it" (*TMB*, 88). *The Mother's Book* enjoyed an extensive popularity; on the sixth (revised) edition the *New York Herald Tribune* (December 24, 1845) commented: "This work is widely known and highly appreciated by multitudes. . . . we know of no work of its class worthy to be compared with it and we could wish that a copy were placed in the hand of every mother in our land."

35. The separate-sphere inscription of gender roles, the Cult of True Womanhood, would soon make "feminine" signify delicacy and a static retirement—unlike eighteenth-century conventions. Woman became an influential but not a performative force. See Carby, *Reconstructing Womanhood*; Nancy Cott, *The Bonds of Womanhood: "Woman's Sphere" in New England* (New Haven: Yale University Press, 1977); Linda Kerber, *Women of the Republic: Intellect and Ideology in Revolutionary America* (Chapel Hill: University of North Carolina Press, 1980); Kerber, *Women's America: Refocusing the Past* (New York: Oxford University Press, 1982); and Ryan, *Womanhood*.

36. Ryan, *Womanhood*, 91.

37. See Kerber, *Women of the Republic*.

Child envisioned an active, civic function for the mother. Domestic ideologies that required a woman to be brought up in "petted indolence, or shut from the sun and air, for fear of injury to her beauty, or her gracefulness" (*TMB*, 57) were pernicious: "It is a universal remark that American women are less vigorous and rosy, than women of other climates; and that they are peculiarly subject to disorders of the chest and the spine. I believe the sole reason of this is, that our employments and amusements lead us so little into the open air" (*TMB*, 58). Child represented domestic confinement as cognate with another domestic American institution. Slavery, according to abolitionists like Child, was a patriarchal institution that produced a luxuriant, "oriental" despotism, the opposite of true, neoclassical republicanism.[38] Slavery was family gone wrong. Good mothers did not sell babies, as Child once scathingly remarked.[39] Good (middling class) mothers were gentle and strong, sweet and active. A "spirit in tranquillity and purity" (*TMB*, 4), the true mother knew how to govern her home without becoming an "oriental" despot.

Still, *The Mother's Book* depends on domestic arrangements that do sequester mother and child in the home. From the 1830s through the late 1840s popular northern educators such as Horace Mann, Catharine Beecher, and Lydia Sigourney, despite their work for "public" education, espoused the conventional logic of a domestic maternity that made the child's early education a mother's entire purpose.[40] Indeed, a sequestered maternity was represented as vital. Child's book, as indicated by her dedication, demonstrates how seriously the private yet evidently political task of the mother was taken to be.[41] Mothers who betrayed this educative, moral ideal could wreak untold and widespread disaster on both present and future members of a democratic republic. So Child would write: "It is beyond all doubt that the state of the mother affects her child . . . and who can tell how much

38. See Child's neoclassical novel, *Philothea, a Romance* (Boston: Otis Broaders, 1836); and Child, *Selected Letters*.
39. See Yellin, *Women & Sisters*, 64: in responding to southerner Margaretta Mason's taunts about her womanhood, Child "suggests that the claim that slaveholding women sympathize with their slaves is hypocritical. She charges that if sympathy and benevolence constitute true womanhood, as Mason asserts, southern women are not true women because as slaveholders they profit from the sexual exploitation of their female slaves: 'I have never known an instance where the "pangs of maternity" [wrote Child] did not meet with requisite assistance; and here at the North, after we have helped the mothers, *we do not sell the babies.*' "
40. See Ryan, *Womanhood*, 92–111.
41. See also Kelley, *Private Woman, Public Stage*.

moral evil may be traced to that state of mind indulged by a mother" (*TMB*, 6). Since "what the child is, the man will probably be" (*TMB*, 37), what was at stake in the mother's proper management of the sequestered home, and in the management of the her own state of body and soul, was the production of an appropriate future citizenry, a strong body politic.

But what sort of body would this future citizenry take? What kind of state would be attained? Out of which domestic arrangement, patriarchal slavery or a free middle class, would the best citizen be born? In 1854 George Fitzhugh envisioned "free society" as "a monstrous abortion"; slavery, he said, was "the healthy, beautiful and natural state of being."[42] Fitzhugh here reversed the abolitionist rhetoric that figured slavery as a she-devil who ought to be "stripped of her veil . . . exposed in all her monstrous deformity"[43] or as "a cage of obscene birds," or as "one grand menagerie."[44] Thus did tropes of monstrosity and animalistic obscenity serve *both* North and South to damn deformities (for abolitionists, slavery) or excessive states (for pro-slavery advocates, free society).

Thoreau's journal affords an example of how a rhetoric of obscenity marked off the excessive. Zealous abolitionists like Henry C. Wright, says Thoreau, in seeking one's sympathy, could "not keep their distance, but cuddle up and lie spoonfashion with you, no matter how hot the weather or how narrow the bed. . . . They lick you as a cow

42. George Fitzhugh, *Sociology for the South; or the Failure of Free Society* (Richmond, Va.: A. Morris, 1854), 41. See also Fitzhugh, *Cannibals All! or Slaves without Masters* (Richmond, Va.: A. Morris, 1857), esp. the preface; and Lydia Maria Child, *The Patriarchal Institution, as Described by Members of Its Own Family* (New York: American Anti-Slavery Society, 1860).

43. Salmon Chase, quoted in Peter F. Walker, *Moral Choices: Memory, Desire, and Imagination in Nineteenth-Century American Abolition* (Baton Rouge: Louisiana State University, 1978), 309.

44. Characterizations of the South as an oriental bordello, a pen, a den of iniquity were very common. Jacobs, in *Incidents in the Life of a Slave Girl*, 52, calls the domestic situation in the South a cage of obscene birds; Child, *Patriarchal Institution*, 19, quotes Thomas Jefferson Randolph's speech before the Virginia legislature in 1832, characterizing the Ancient Dominion as one grand menagerie (Chapters 3, 4, 5, below, deal with these images in more depth). See also Francis Smith Foster, *Witnessing Slavery: The Development of the Ante-Bellum Slave Narrative* (Westport, Conn.: Greenwood Press, 1979); Karcher, "Lydia Maria Child's *Romance of the Republic*: An Abolitionist View of America's Racial Destiny," in *Slavery in the Literary Imagination*, ed. Deborah E. McDowell and Arnold Rampersad (Baltimore: Johns Hopkins University Press, 1989), 81–103; Nelson, *Word*; Yellin, *Women & Sisters*; Walker, *Moral Choices*; Ronald G. Walters, "The Erotic South: Civilization and Sexuality in American Abolition," *American Quarterly* 25 (May 1973): 179–80.

her calf. They would fain wrap you about with their bowels. . . . I do not like the men who come so near me with their bowels. . . . Men's bowels are far more slimy than their brains."[45] Linking sympathy to sweat and intimacy to slime, however, and invoking a gendered maternity through an image of animal husbandry, Thoreau forces matter and mind, bowels and brains, into proximity even as he strains, through disavowal, to separate them. Such images—like those of advocates who called slavery a "parental relation" but strenuously denied actual parentage, particularly when slave-owners chose to sell, whip, or rape their own children; or like those of abolitionists who fought the auction block but nevertheless envisioned themselves stripping a female Slavery as if "she" were standing there—trade in the very scene they are meant either to attack or to ward off. Thus while condemning "men who come so near," Thoreau envisions a curiously intimate range of possible domestic immediacies—narrow beds, tight cuddlings, nurturing licks.

By the 1830s, however, enclosed privacy that signified "home" for both North and South[46] was, in fact, changing; various countercurrents were disrupting the proper flow of instruction between sequestered mother and child. Commodities such as games, toys, magazines, children's books—and, indeed, *The Mother's Book* and *The Juvenile Miscellany*—began to appear, as if to offer guidance through the cultural shifts that these items themselves signified. Mary Ryan describes some examples: "Games for girls were carefully differentiated from boys' amusement. . . . On a boys' game board the player moved in an upward spiral, past temptations . . . until the winner reached a pinnacle of propriety and prestige. A girls' playful enactment of her course in life moved via a circular, ever- inward path to the 'mansion of happiness,' a pastel tableau of mother and child."[47] Such items evidently served to reinforce ideological conventions, but their introduction into the home also showed the need for a repeated "implantation" of correct values.[48] The games trace out a repetitive trajectory, as if the course of life might otherwise go awry.

45. Journal entry for June 17, 1853 in *The Writings of Henry David Thoreau*, ed. Bradford Torrey, (Boston: Houghton Mifflin, 1906), 11:263–65.

46. I do not mean to suggest that North and South were completely analogous in this regard, only that both imagined the home as a private sphere.

47. Ryan, *Womanhood*, 92.

48. I am following here the logic of Michel Foucault, *The History of Sexuality: An Introduction*, trans. Robert Hurley (New York: Vintage, 1980).

Moreover, although the home was where a child's education began, "both sexes left home in the nineteenth century to enter the growing public school system."[49] The child might be "obliged to serve an apprenticeship to the five senses" as Child described the state of infancy, in order to learn "his trade" of adulthood (*TMB*, 6), but as the century drew on, a systematic, educational apparatus became imperative. The mother might still serve as first master—if sometimes unreliable and in need of guidance herself—but the United States was becoming more urban and mobile. A larger and more organized system was needed for the appropriate training of clearly distinct managerial (master/owner/capitalist) and labor (slave/worker/proletariat) forces.

That pedagogical institutionalization had moral, political, and economic valence for antebellum culture was made evident in the *Richmond Examiner* (1856): "Free farms, free labor, free society, free will, free thinking, free children, free schools, all belong to the same brood of damnable isms. But the worst of all these abominations is the modern system of free schools. The New England system of free schools has been the cause and prolific source of the infidelities and treasons that have turned her cities into Sodoms and Gomorrahs, and her land into the common nestling places of howling bedlamites. We abominate the system, because the schools are free."[50] At pressing issue, then, as early as the 1830s but with mounting urgency by the late 1850s, was the definition of the word "free" and its relation to "labor," "society," and "education." What was a free government? What did free republicanism or free capitalism mean? Did such "isms" need to be herded into a pen with all other damnable "isms" belonging to the same, potentially profligate, illegitimate brood? This nightmare scene of sexualized and reproductive horror figures "free schools" as especially worrisome, a treasonous traffic in the abominable.[51]

Indeed, after William Lloyd Garrison began to publish *The Liberator* in January 1831, such freedoms would come under increasingly severe pressure as abolitionist liberatory rhetoric insisted upon calling into

49. Ryan, *Womanhood*, 92–93.

50. Quoted in Child, *Patriarchical Institution*, 7.

51. Of course, teaching slaves to read was illegal in most southern states. Frederick Douglass's is perhaps the most famous narrative account of the importance of "education," but slave narratives in general frequently include scenes of illegal schooling (see Part II below). Free public schools were among the first institutions that provisional Reconstruction governments set up; see *The Journals of Charlotte Forten Grimké*, ed. Brenda Stevenson (New York: Oxford University Press, 1988), 589.

question the nature and shape of a free (democratic) republic, an insistence to which anti-abolitionists responded with their own definitions. In 1835 Governor George McDuffie of South Carolina offered that "slavery is the corner-stone of our Republican ediface. . . . Domestic slavery is the only institution I know of which can secure the spirit of equality among freemen, so necessary to the true and genuine feeling of republicanism, without compelling the body politic into the dangerous vices of agrarianism, and legislative intermeddling between the laborer and the capitalist."[52] McDuffie's concern that an appropriate, virtuous, and unregulated relation between capital and labor be sponsored was a shared one; similar rhetoric can be found in, for example, a report from the Southern Commercial Convention at Vicksburg, Mississippi, in 1859: "The eminent advantage of slavery over free institutions is that the continuance of the association is systematic. . . . the slave works not as *he* pleases but as his *master* pleases. Indeed, slavery is nothing more than labor obeying unchecked, unregulated and irresponsible capital."[53]

Irresponsible? Such slaveholding logic was ridiculed as incoherent by abolitionists, as Child's sarcastic redeployment of the Convention's language indicates: "In all [slavocratic] communities, capital is irresponsible by law. . . . This circumstance renders the regulation of labor exceedingly convenient; it being placed entirely in the hands of 'unchecked, unregulated, and irresponsible captial.' "[54] How could legalized irresponsibility provide anything like an appropriate system of either economics or government? Abolitionists were clear about their answer: it could not. "Free labor," Salmon Chase claimed, was "locked in a mortal struggle with slavery."[55]

In addition to producing economic irregularities, slavery was obviously licentious, said abolitionists. The South was imagined as a libidinal pit or, as Wendell Phillips famously remarked, a "great brothel," where "wrongful profit as well as unbridled sexuality," writes Peter Walker in *Moral Choices*, fused "sex and economics."[56] With sexual government and economic propriety so linked, Walker argues, abolitionists like attorney David Child, who supported agricultural systems designed to undermine slave labor, and Lydia Maria

---

52. Quoted in Child, *Patriarchical Institution*, 5.
53. Quoted in Ibid., 4–5.
54. Ibid., 49.
55. Quoted in Walker, *Moral Choices*, 309.
56. Ibid., 288–89.

Child, who boycotted slave-produced goods, heard the term "free labor" not only as an idea "expressive of the aspirations of the small independent entrepreneur" but also as "a powerful ideological device that provided much of the moral sanction for the social behavior of the emerging middle class."[57] The debates carried out between North and South about nature and morality, social and familial behavior, economic and governmental regulations were often couched in fantasmatic, eroticized scenarios featuring dangerous vices, prolific broods, indecent illegitamicies, or sweaty abominations.

Thus, through ideally opposed but often congruent images did abolitionist and anti-abolitionist debate the questions: who embodied the true spirit of a democratic republic? What systems would reproduce those moral values appropriate to an American body politic? McDuffie's image of dangerous vices being foisted upon the body politic in the name of freedom (or the *Richmond Examiner*'s worry that free schools made Sodom[ized] northern cities the nestling Gomorrahs of howling bedlamites) presents freedom as a potentially ungovernable, wild theory, a morally outrageous threat to natural morality.[58]

Indeed, images of sexualized and gendered profligacy shaped both pro- and anti-slavery representations of the possible consequence of complete emancipation. For example, Child was one of the first abolitionists to demand both legal emancipation and an end to anti-amalgamation laws. But in December 1835, when Child's brother, Convers Francis, charged "democracy with being the mother of evil," Child's reply was cautious: "I do not wonder at it," she says about her brother's fear, "for these are times when its best friends have need of faith. But I believe the difficulty ever is in a lack of republicanism."[59] For Child, an aristocracy had survived within a so-called democratic republic—an aristocracy bred by the wealth of northern industrial capitalism and by the privilege of southern slavocratic *noblesse oblige*. It was the accumulation of capital that continued to poison the purity of democratic libations.

But her caution here, and her frequently stated concern that profligacy resulted when modest discipline was not enforced, suggests the vexatious nature of emancipatory rhetorics. Her own logic often

57. Ibid., 308.
58. Child, *The Patriarchical Institution*, 4–5.
59. Child, *Selected Letters*, 41–42.

scripted excessive freedom as vice. Eager passions, like inordinate ardency or, indeed, volatile spirits,[60] were the particular dangers that an American mother, and America as a nation, faced. "If the inordinate love of wealth and parade be not checked among us, it will be the ruin of our country, as it has been, and will be, the ruin of thousands of individuals. What restlessness, what discontent, what bitterness, what knavery and crime, have been produced by this eager passion for money! Mothers! as you love your children, and wish for their happiness, be careful how you cherish this unquiet spirit" (TMB, 12). The movement of the word "love"across this passage indicates how troubling a definition could become. Love was necessary for domestic happiness, but where and when did love turn inordinate? Where and how did passion become ruinous? Child's distrust of wealth is the subject of this passage, yet the images and language of a seduction novel—love, passion, restlessness, knavery—make desire the motivating and potentially ruinous force of the economy.[61]

Evidently, for Child, only the steady love that the domestic sphere generated was reliable and not inordinate. And only a mother's familial love could stand as a coordinate to happiness. A mother's goal was "to have the various members of a family feel a common interest, as if they were all portions of the same body." This "beautiful sight" of a well-proportioned body that the mother has produced was the picture of a harmonious social order (TMB, 155).

The logic of familial harmony and healthy bodily proportions also subtends the report of the May 1859 Southern Commercial Convention, however. True freedom, said the report, could be assured only by the kind of systemic and regulated affectional association that a traditional patriarchal family would provide. There were advantages to a system of patriarchal domesticity claimed southern papers, which the North, with its "greasy mechanics, filthy operatives, small-fisted

60. Child spoke out against alcoholism both privately and publicly. See Helene G. Baer, The Heart Is Like Heaven: The Life of Lydia Maria Child (Philadelphia: University of Pennsylvania Press, 1964); Child, Selected Letters; and Milton Meltzer, Tongue of Flame: The Life of Lydia Maria Child (New York: Dell, 1965).

61. Child disapproved of seduction novels such as Susannah Rowson's Charlotte Temple, which "has a nice good moral at the end, and I dare say was written with the best intentions, yet I believe few works do so much harm to girls of fourteen or fifteen" (TMB, 91)—yet her language in these passages could have come from that novel. On the language of the seduction novel, see Cathy N. Davidson, Revolution and the Word: The Rise of the Novel in America (New York: Oxford University Press, 1986), esp. 101–10.

farmers and moon-struck theorists," had failed to consider. "The great evil of Northern Society is that it is burdened with a servile class of mechanics and laborers, unfit for self-government, and yet clothed with the attributes and powers of citizens. Master and slave is a relation in society as necessary as that of parent and child."[62]

It would seem, then, that abolitionists and pro-slavery advocates alike feared that excess—whether of vices, passions, or inordinate freedoms—would disfigure or infect the sexual and reproductive health of the body politic, without the judicious restraint and guidance of appropriate domestic relations. But each claimed that the other's system corrupted those relations.

That the definition of appropriate parental guidance hinged most emphatically upon the mother's role in the domestic realm—a scene within which a host of other concerns might be euphemistically inscribed, such as how property was to be distributed with regard to gender and class, and how such relations were regulated with regard to (slave/free) labor in a consumer market—is evident throughout *The Mother's Book*. In a passage where Child seeks to address "the greatest evil now existing in education. I mean the want of confidence between mothers and daughters on delicate subjects" (*TMB*, 151), the mother becomes both the fount of all knowledge and the source of that fount's pollution. Children, writes Child, have a natural, innocent curiosity, and information and knowledge pertaining to these unnamed "delicate subjects" are best provided by rational explanation. It is because a rational explanation is so frequently wanting that such subjects become the source of restlessness and excitement.

Child did not, I wish to stress here, posit knowledge or the subjects themselves as the cause of such excitation but rather their treatment by the mother. The mother's want of confidence breeds impropriety: "Information being refused them at the only proper source," warns Child, "they immediately have recourse to domestics or immodest school-companions; and very often their young minds are polluted with filthy anecdotes of vice and vulgarity. This ought not to be. Mothers are the only proper persons to convey such knowledge to a child's mind. . . . A girl who receives her first ideas on these subjects from the shameless stories and indecent jokes of vulgar associates has infact prostituted her mind by familiarity with vice" (*TMB*, 151–52).

62. Quoted in Child's *Patriarchical Institution*, 6–7.

Thus, a mother's refusal to handle knowledge rationally can lose her daughter to prostitution.

Child's curiously worded conclusion to this cautionary tale is also intriguing. "Many a young lady," she says, "has fallen a victim to consumption from a mother's bashfulness in imparting necessary precautions; and many, oh, many more, have had their minds corrupted beyond all cure" (*TMB*, 152). Disease becomes a metaphor for necessary knowledge improperly handled. Just as a mother's silence might allow her daughter's body to become infected by a virus, so it might also allow the girl's mind to be infected by the loose conversation of "vulgar associates." But the disease here is vague—despite the terminology of consumption, Child does not appear to be addressing tuberculosis—and yet also,because of the earlier passages, linked to both social intercourse (with servants in the home and associates at school) and the consuming pleasure of conversation (as in stories and jokes).

If the knowledge of sex is the unnamable delicate subject here, it is not, in and of itself, deadly, excessive, errant, or vulgar; unnatural filth is a result only of a mother's lapse with regard to how this knowledge is circulated in the domestic sphere. Indeed, Child wishes to warn mothers about the corruptions breeding in their own homes when she advises that "it is a bad plan for young girls to sleep with nursery maids. . . . From a large proportion of domestics this danger is so great, that I apprehend a prudent mother will very rarely . . . place her daughter in the same sleeping apartment with a domestic" (*TMB*, 153). Thus, although the home is imagined as sacred and sequestered, it is also the terrain of wandering and possibly profane domestics. Coded as a "private" domain, it is evidently involved in a "public," possibly consumer, economy.

In addition, I find it intriguing that these passages speak of "children," yet it is only the fate of a daughter whose mother lacks prudence that is made clear. What the fate of a son might be whose interests are not fully satisfied in conversation with his mother is left open to conjecture. Child seems a little worried, too, that her advice might produce the opposite of prudence: "I would not by any means be understood to approve of frequent conversations of this kind between parent and child" (*TMB*, 152). If mother and the *domus* for which she serves as primary icon are the source of strong, prudent love, both are equally liable to blame for the production of dangerous, prurient liaisons.

Home Productions

Contestations over the definition of freedom, republican democracy, and the body politic, then, were often played out in images of a sexualized political economy particularly concerned with the domestic management of a productive reproduction, imagined as the specific provenance of the female and the maternal. Exhorted to procreate the citizenry, told to be fruitful and multiply, "woman" was at the same time associated with images indicating that those visceral subjects to which the definition of "woman" was bound—subjects such as pregnancy and variously represented carnal knowledges—could generate a social, economic, or political mess. As Mr. Conant, the Puritan patriarch in Child's first novel, remarks, women "are the source of every evil that ever came into the world. I don't refer in special manner to that great tree of sin planted by Eve; but I say they are the individual cause of every branch and bud from that day downwards" (*H*, 25). Even though Child portrays Mr. Conant as a hypocrite and shows that his identification of woman as the profligate origin of a branching and budding sin is not only historically dated but indeed outmoded in its own time, the text nevertheless situates "woman" at the site of disorder. Even if Mr. Conant groundlessly fears that new (world) liberalities would make of New England "a cage for every unclean bird. A free stable-room and litter for all kinds of conscience" (*H*, 46), Child's text activates and substantiates such a fear, because it links uncleanliness and disorder either to inappropriate maternal inheritances (Governor Endicott sees in King James's management of the British crown "a taint of hereditary evil from his Moabitish mother" [*H*, 71])[63] or to out-of-control daughters. For example, Mary Conant's too devoted love for Charles Brown (a "hypocritcal son of a strange mother," thunders Mr. Conant [*H*, 77]) inspires her to wish for her mortally ill mother's death, a destructive sin that she cannot forgive herself.

"Love," as the unnamed narrator playfully remarks, "usually finds means to effect his purpose, and it seems he laughed as loudly at

---

63. It is useful to note in this context Jonathan Goldberg, "Bradford's 'Ancient Members' and a 'Case of Buggery amongst Them'" (on William Bradford's *Of Plymouth Plantation*) in *Nationalisms and Sexualities*, ed. Andrew Parker, Mary Russo, Doris Sommer, and Patricia Yaeger (New York: Routledge, 1992), esp. his analysis of the role the "mother" is made to play—and how "she" vanishes—in structuring a homosocial relation between the ancient "members" of the Puritan Church.

locksmiths in 1629, as he does in these degenerate days" (*H*, 81). Despite the teasing tone, degeneracy hovers near: love is seen as inherently errant. And when Mary—brokenhearted not only over the long-awaited (guilt-laden) death of her mother but also over the rumored death of Charles Brown—marries Hobomok, the reader is told that "her own nation looked upon her as lost and degraded; and, what was far worse, her own heart echoed back the charge" (*H*, 135). A woman's love breeds disorder, wickedness, and national degradation. Or as Mary herself remarks about her first attachment to Charles Brown, "it makes me shudder to think of the wickedness of such devoted love" (*H*, 82).

In fact, although the text would have it that Mary's mother-love for her child by Hobomok is a beneficent force more "than she thought she should ever again experience" (*H* ,136), this maternal love, too, is associated with disgrace and economic debt. When Charles Brown returns (word of his death having been mistaken), Hobomok instantly understands that his wife of three years must be relinquished because "Mary loves him better than she does me" (*H*, 139). And so (without asking Mary, I should point out) Hobomok disappears. "And this I doe, that Mary may be happie" says the writ of divorce he "nobly" leaves behind (*H*, 146). Whereupon Charles asks Mary, "Will you . . . say that you will be my wife, either here or in England?" "I cannot go to England," she replies. "My boy would disgrace me, and I never will leave him; for love to him is the only way that I can now pay my debt of gratitude" (*H*, 148). To love her disgracing child is akin to paying off a debt of gratitude to lost love. It would seem, as the text says, that all love is the "source of woman's greatest misery" (*H*, 111).

For Child, then, passion—here literalized in Mary Conant's errant loves resulting from her own badly tended need for affection, since her father too often "stifled the voice of nature, and hid all his better feelings beneath the cold mask of austerity" (*H*, 119)—can produce adults who are ill equipped to regulate their own morality. Without care, a woman (daughter, wife,) like Mary might become a part of the sordid and indolent "multitudes of people who do wrong from mere emptiness of mind, and want of occupation" (*TMB*, 20)—as Mary indeed does when she dabbles in witchcraft. Such ill-educated bodies could in turn (re)produce "disgrace," the term Mary applies to her own son.

Thus Child repeatedly calls for the strict but healthy management of love as a means to combat the potentially ruinous results of desire.

"When a strong *wish* to excel in any particular thing is once excited," she claims, "there is no danger but it will find means to satisfy itself; and this is one reason why we should be more careful what we teach children to *love*, than what we teach them to *remember*" (*TMB*, 161). Most particularly, she is worried about a mother's regulation of her daughter, for "the greatest and most prevailing error in education consists in making lovers a subject of such engrossing and disproportionate interest in the minds of young girls" (*TMB*, 163). Indeed, a mother who does not learn how to rouse her daughter to properly managed love is truly reprehensible; such a mother would "be willing to sell her [daughter] to the Grand Sultan, to grace his seraglio" (*TMB*, 164).

Like many abolitionists, Child uses the image of the seraglio here to question what sort of governmental polity will come from an improper attention to domestic bliss. Calling erring mothers slaves—to fashion, wealth, and frivolity—she then asks "what *republicanism* there is in such rules of conduct?" (*TMB*, 128). When inordinate excess is encouraged rather than curbed, republicanism goes out the window. Or as Henry Wright proclaimed in various ways in his popular mid-century works (*The Unwanted Child: The Empire of the Mother over the Character and Destiny of the Race*, 1863; *Marriage and Parentage; or, The Reproductive Element in Man, as a Means to His Elevation and Happiness*, 1855, the nation was getting deeper and deeper into a political, economic, and moral "state of wild delirium" that had to be checked not only by the "thorough regeneration" of women—in order to "make them what God designed they should be, healthy mothers of healthy children"—but also through the strict domestic management of the "Reproductive Element."[64] "Destiny is determined by organization—organization is determined by maternal conditions. So far as human agency is concerned the mother makes the man" claimed Wright.[65] Such a statement echoes Child nearly word for word.

But the appropriate (maternal) management of what Wright called the Reproductive Element is, as I have demonstrated, devilishly hard to define. It is one of those delicate subjects too often avoided by mothers when they try to prepare their children for marriage (*TMB*, 152). In her private letters, Child was more explicit. Indiscreet, immodest habits, poor family organization, poor diet, but, above all, bad

---

64. See Walker, *Moral Choices*, 300–305.
65. Quoted in ibid., 300.

marriage customs made for "fitty ricketty children," she wrote. "It is wrong to have children unless people love each other."[66] Yet how was one to know truly and to understand and then manage love? What system was best? Certainly not marriage itself. In commenting to her friend Louisa Loring on the separation of Louisa's cousin John King and his wife, Jane, Child admonishes her not to grieve for the separation of married people who found themselves incompatible: "Look around you and see . . . what miserable organizations, mind and body, are the consequences of wide-spread, legalized prostitution!" As the editors of her letters remark "the description of marriage as 'legalized prostitution' is noteworthy in an era immersed in the ideology of the 'woman's sphere' and the sanctity of marriage."[67]

Thus, while Lydia Maria Child exalted both the mother's role and married, domestic life, she was also extremely wary, even confused, about how exactly to manage maternal, matrimonial, and domestic intimacies. For example, she was a lifelong supporter of legalizing interracial marriage, but because she also saw the institution of marriage as potentially indecent (legalized prostitution), her advice on the matter was often incoherent. Legalizing interracial marriage would end illegitimacies that slavery had legitimated, but profligacy still haunted the scene. Emancipation was necessary, but what freedoms were good ones? After all, if Mary Conant's devoted love of her son, the child of an interracial union, is presented as admirable, it is also scripted as the source of social and cultural disgrace. "Restless" and "roguish" (H, 149) little Charles Hobomok Conant must be made over into Charles Brown. The traces of both his maternal and his Native American heritage are lost as he becomes a version of his "white" father. As an entitled Cambridge graduate, Hobomok Conant vanishes into Charles Brown: his biological father "was seldom spoken of; and by degrees his Indian appellation was silently ommitted" (H, 150).

Carolyn Karcher claims that "Child's response to the call for an authentic national literature does not succeed in resolving the central contradictions of American history itself, . . . that white Americans win their political freedom . . . and cultural independence by expropriating the cultures of the peoples they have systematically debased, devalorized and deprived" (H, xxxvii). I would add that Child's concept of such expropriation was shaped by and resulted from her vision of

66. Child, *Selected Letters*, 235.
67. Meltzer and Holland in Child, *Selected Letters*, 234–35.

love as it should be: a well-managed economy of rational freedom, with heterosexual reproduction serving to generate a properly disciplined body politic. But love, like freedom, unavoidably aroused potentially irrational scenarios. Jean Fagan Yellin reports a telling instance. In a letter written during the anti-slavery riots of 1835, Child says that "the atmosphere in New York . . . had been whipped up by 'a virulent little paper . . . buzzing about here, called the Anti-Abolitionist. Over it is a large wood cut, representing men and women, black and white, hugging and kissing each other; and on the table are decanters marked ATB—which signifies Arthur Tappan's Burgandy.' Her comment," writes Yellin, "is intriguing because, while the masthead of the Castigator and New York Anti-Abolitionist pictures black and white men and women within a domestic setting, they are not 'hugging and kissing each other.' "[68]

Moreover, as noted previously, excessive or frequent intercourse between a mother and child—specifically between a mother and daughter—could produce what Child called "unmingled disgust" (TMB, 153) rather than natural, divine, and orderly love. A mother who indulged in inappropriate levels of intimacy with her child could create unspeakable indecencies. Yellin correctly states that Child's work often resembles "the narratives of fugitive slaves in interpreting as political these private dramas of relationships involving parents, children and siblings and in viewing them as instances of institutionalized tyranny and the struggle against it."[69] But Child's logic often founders on the question of just how the private could be managed so that it would not run amok and grow sin every where one looked, as Mr. Conant feared, or become degrading, as Mary's own choices strike her.

Indeed, a terrified vision of profligacy and an out-of-control generation that became associated with the female/maternal as inherently visceral and deranging—a cancerous disaster of (economic) overproduction always about to happen—was one source of the categorical antebellum terms for supposedly precise "racial" denominations. Half-breed, quarter-breed, mulatto and mulatta, quadroon, octoroon all identified persons through a commodity accounting of so-called "blood" heritage which kept the purity of white America intact lest a reproductive version of liberty and republicanism cross unspeakable

68. Yellin, *Women & Sisters*, 62–63.
69. Ibid., 71.

boundaries.[70] Abraham Lincoln's oration denouncing the 1857 Supreme Court Dred Scott decision subsumes excessive, immoral "over-production" and reproduction in an economic rhetoric. In order to prove that amalgamation was a threat only in the slavocracy, Lincoln argued that there was a natural disgust in both "black" and "white" that would keep them from "free" converse. "In 1850 there were in the free states, 56,649 mulattoes; but for the most part they were not born there—they came from the slave States, ready made up. In the same year the slave States had 348,874 mulattoes—all of home production."[71]

Child wrote a mother's guidebook on how to manage "secluded, domestic education," only to claim in it that she "would have no scheming, no managing, no hinting. [She] would never talk to girls about the beaux, or suffer them to associate with those who did. [She] would leave everything to nature and Divine Providence" (*TMB*, 167). Like Child's, Lincoln's logic is, at the very least, odd. By calling a northern "free" economy naturally separatist, Lincoln supposed he had prevented naming what went on in (restrained) northern homes as anything like what happened in (excessive) southern boudoirs and slave quarters. In appealing to a natural racial economy of "free" commerce that would assert itself once the unnatural economy of "unfree" enslavement was abolished, he produced a political solution to private amalgamations: once naturally "free" racial economy of reproductive practices could be legally guaranteed, the confusing, dreaded multitudes of "home production" would come to an end.[72] But the fact is that only an underlying logic of consumer capitalism which allows all children to be equated with "ready made up" marketplace commodities can either imagine or rationalize such a vision.[73] Lincoln's precise numbering of beings, produced like baby dolls in a madly mismanaged factory, reveals a pervasive cultural perception that reproduction—the Reproductive Element—was a potentially dangerous process in need of a continual (but fractured and anxious, if Child's

70. For one of the most provocative readings of the terms "mulatto" and "mulatta," see Spillers, "Notes on an Alternative Model," 165–87.

71. *Abraham Lincoln's Speeches*, 70.

72. Lincoln shared a widely held nineteenth-century belief that "mulatto" signified a "race" unto itself, a dangerously licentious but (it was hoped) sterile group that was growing by leaps and bounds only because of that laxity of masculine self-government in the tyranny known as the slavocracy. Thus mulattoes would die out, once the North restored natural law.

73. See Zelizer, *Pricing the Priceless Child*.

work is any indication) management. Otherwise, the population of the United States might become so confused as to be ungovernable. Perhaps as mixed and wild as a pack of dogs? Middle-to-late-nineteenth-century writers, from Confederate apologists Thomas Dixon and Thomas Nelson Page to African-American novelist Pauline Hopkins, used the term "mongrel" (albeit for very different purposes) to identify Americans of mixed heritages.[74]

This threat of a too ardently mixed population produced by contaminated, uncontrolled practices of "home production," haunted mid-nineteenth-century American sociopolitical culture. If the naturally licentious children of Egypt attained their liberation, or worse, if the mothers of a war-torn America took the *Gettysburg Address* far more literally than Lincoln meant and "brought forth a new nation," who knew what sort of horrific "Congress" might result? Jean Fagan Yellin reports President John Tyler's not atypical view: "Woman is to be made the instrument of destroying our political paradise, the Union of these states; she is to be made the presiding genius over the councils of insurrection and discord, she is to be converted into a fiend, to rejoice over the conflagration of our dwellings and the murder of our people.[75] Tyler was referring to women who had become public speakers for abolition, but as the crisis of the Civil War became more urgent, dire scenarios of unnamed perversities and peculiar amalgamations added to such a view of fiendish conflagration.

Romancing the Republic

High-pitched rhetoric, then, raised the specter of reproduction and sexualities gone wild and seemed to knell the ruination of true freedom and the loss of the sexual, racial, and economic integrity of the Republic's body politic. Aroused by images of Sodom and Gomorrah or descriptions of "spoonfashion" intimacies; made palpable through

74. This brand of racially inflected commodity logic has a long half-life. The white, mid-nineteenth-century "nightmare" of miscegenation, to which Lincoln's 1857 speech refers, has resurfaced (if indeed it was ever submerged) in twentieth-century white supremacist movements and chants: "We don't want a mongrel America." Sandra Gunning points out the longevity of this term in "Facing 'A Red Record': Racial Violence, Class, and Gender in Turn of the Century American Literature" (Ph.D. diss., University of California, Berkeley, 1991).

75. Quoted in Yellin, *Women & Sisters*, 3. Tyler, it might be noted, had two wives, each of whom bore him eight children.

spurious population figures such as those Lincoln quoted in 1857; or crudely incited by tales of sassy Negresses who tempted innocent white boys to their doom, fear about the national "integrity" circulated in recurrent images of racial and sexual disarray.[76] From the 1830s to the 1860s both overt and covert accusations of "improper" interracial or aberrant sexualities were hurled back and forth between pro- and anti-slavery activists in their debates over commerce, labor, and education; conflicting ideological constructions of race, class, and gender also divided abolitionists against themselves. Vituperative innuendo and condemnation were flung by both South and North at "white" women (Angelina and Sarah Grimké) and "black" women (Sojourner Truth and Maria Stewart) who became public speakers.[77] In addition, both pro-slavery activists and abolitionists accused such men as Frederick Douglass and Henry C. Wright of excessive or salacious interests.[78] Indeed, more than forty years after Garrisonian abolition got rolling, and two decades after the Civil War, these sorts of accusations remained culturally viable. When Frederick Douglass married his long-time secretary Helen Pitts in January 1884, Pitts was disinherited in disgust by her abolitionist father and uncle. Douglass's children by his first wife also disapproved. And one African-American newspaper commented that for many of its readers Douglass's second marriage was a racial and sexual betrayal; his once-revered image was to be taken down from the walls of proper (middle-class) parlors and hung out "in the stables"[79] where, presumably, it now belonged.

Although sexualized vituperations took on a variety of configurations that shaped and were shaped by the specific concerns of Reconstruction politics, worry over the degradation of the body politic was activated most visibly through racially coded, gendered evocations of generative riot. These were most often figured as spectacles of carnal impropriety: monstrous abortions, animal appetites, mongrel populations, sweaty seductions—all sorts of "peculiar" images deemed ru-

76. See Gunning, "Facing 'A Red Record.'"
77. "Why are all the old hens abolitionists? Because not being able to obtain husbands they think they may stand some chance for a negro, if they can only make amalgamation fashionable." Quoted in Lerner, *The Grimké Sisters from South Carolina*, 147. See also Yellin, *Women & Sisters*, esp. chapter 2.
78. See Thoreau's earlier quoted comment about Wright. As various biographers of Frederick Douglass note, Garrison accused him of being sexually involved with British abolitionist Julia Griffiths, who helped finance Douglass's anti-slavery newspaper. See also William McFeely, *Frederick Douglass* (New York: Norton, 1991).
79. Quoted in McFeely, *Frederick Douglass* (New York: Norton, 1991), 320–21.

inous to domestic order and economic prosperity. And among these images, "Woman" remained one of the most frequently cited origins for whatever freedom or civil right might be considered inherently destructive to the perceived status quo of democratic civilization. That view is reflected in Augusta Evans Wilson's denunciation of suffrage in the late 1860s: "The day which invests [women] with the elective franchise would be the blackest in the annals of humanity, would ring the death-knell of modern civilization, of national prosperity, social morality, and domestic happiness! and would consign the race to a night of degradation and horror infinitely more appalling than a return to primeval barbarism."[80]

Yet even as such views were taking shape in the antebellum period, sentimental "acts" and maternal "attachments" were being widely extolled as Christian solutions to all ills. Evidently "woman," the "maternal," and the "domestic" were fractured, contested, and contentious sites. Profane unions and damaging domesticities that encourged those "attachments" later labeled miscegenations, barbarities, or sodomies—for which "mother" was designated as probable source—were depicted as a spreading stain of delirium ruining the antebellum social fabric.[81] Would shoring up the strength of domestic union override the impending strife, soon to become the Civil War? Or would such a forced union simply produce civil fragmentation? And what sort of union would be born? The answers to these questions were by no means certain, even within those texts that were determined to produce a dominant and stable definition.

In many ways, the "mother" of *The Mother's Book* embodies this national and domestic paradox. Identified as the rock of the republic, called upon to bear and instruct an obedient, enterprising citizenry, Child's "mother" is also unpredictable, perhaps ungovernable. "Every look, every movement, every expression, does something toward forming the character," says Child to the mothers of America. "You must drive evil passions out of your own heart" (*TMB*, 9), because "the thoughtless, indolent parent . . . has in fact the most trouble; for the evils she would not check at first . . . afterward grow too strong for her management" (*TMB*, 16). So mother must severely govern

---

80. Quoted in Kelley, *Private Woman, Public Stage*, 333.
81. The U.S. cotton industry's 1992–93 ad campaign—"the touch, the feel of cotton, the fabric of our lives"—comes to mind, particularly given the slave-labor history of cotton production in the United States.

her own wayward sentiments, lest she produce ungovernable ones in others.

This is a system of regulation whose logic—and the logic of the images it relied upon to convey meaning—is rife with contradiction. Among other conundrums, it requires a mother to identify erring sentiments that she is not supposed to know well or exhibit at all. *The Mother's Book* repeatedly locates excess as a female trait while calling on females to be the guardians of restraint. Vulgar, material desires—love of equipage and ease, frippery and finery, indulgences and indolences, passions and pleasures—define "Woman" even as Child offers to save her from them. The text imagines Woman as especially prone to disseminating fatal passions and ruinous impulses: "Children have died in convulsions, in consequence of nursing a mother ... under the influence of violent passion or emotion" (*TMB*, 4); untutored, Woman is wont to choose bordello decor for the nursery, "glaring red curtains and brilliantly striped Venetian carpeting" (*TMB*, 6); she is ruled by impulse not principle (*TMB*, 5).

Child warns her readers that a woman must develop a keen-eyed, never flagging vigilance over herself. "You will find that a smart, notable housewife is always an '*observing* woman.' What constitutes the difference between a neat, faithful domestic and a heedless, sluttish one? One pays *attention* to what she is about, the other does not. The slut's hands may be very dirty, but she does not *observe* it; every time she takes hold of the door, she may leave it covered with black prints, but she does not *observe* it" (*TMB*, 18). But, Child admits, "years of self-education have hardly yet enabled [her] to cure the evil" of careless, hasty habits (*TMB*, 42). She herself was prone to make inkblots on pages or to leave other such "black prints." Indeed, this image, within which guilt, uncleanliness, and disorder are impacted, haunts the narrative voice.[82] Does Child see herself as the source of "blackness" or as a domestic "slut"? Hardly. But her rhetoric excites the "jesting, or double meanings" (*TMB*, 152–53) she seeks to condemn in others.

In other words, disgust and desire appear to shape and determine each other.[83] Images such as that of black fingerprints often lovingly,

---

82. Child's image of fingerprints sets up an interesting resonance with Mark Twain's use of fingerprinting as an indelible mark of (black) identity in his postbellum antislavery novel *Pudd'nhead Wilson*. I am also indebted here to both Sandra Gunning and Anne Goldman.

83. See Peter Stallybrass and Allon White, *The Politics and Poetics of Transgression* (Ithaca: Cornell University Press, 1986), esp. chap. 4. Thanks to John Murchek.

even lavishly, produce the supposed horror they seek to hide, censure, castigate, and deny. Interestingly, the evident logical paradoxes that pertain to sentimental anti-slavery discourse, noted at the outset of this chapter, are not confined to the nineteenth century. That is, sentimentality is frequently treated *sentimentally* in critical responses both to the texts of domestic ideologues such as Lydia Maria Child, and to domestic sentimentality itself as an economy of representation. That is, critical discourse on the sentimental frequently employs, if it does not exploit, the highly charged images it seeks to censure as sentimental practice. As a result, the fractures and contestations within nineteenth-century sentimentality tend to vanish. Such critical readings "suture" over conflict and indeed bury the traces and remains of conflict, thereby reproducing the phenomenon they examine.[84] A brief example: if "blackness" is, as Sánchez-Eppler would have it, utterly "obliterated" in sentimental anti-slavery texts, what should one do with Child's telltale black prints? "Blackness" as a figure is not missing but constitutive. Of course, objections to this can be raised immediately. For one, *The Mother's Book* is not an anti-slavery text. Yet it was written by an abolitionist clearly conversant with sentimental conventions. Second, "black" as used in this context is not intended as a sign for race. Yet certainly the semiotic resonance of the term had racial significance in the United States of 1831 (as indeed still in 1994). Third, Child has not given "black" the "positive" meaning critics such as Sánchez-Eppler seek. Yet the image here does provide the black prints with a fairly positive physicality and presence, if one uses "positive" in the sense of actual, incontrovertible being or existence. Black print on a (presumably) lighter surface is, in and of itself, an interesting image, particularly given Child's frequent reference to the necessity of reading (but not too much, since "the circulating libraries have been overrun with profligate and strongly exciting works, many of them horribly exciting," *TMB*, 93) and writing with a fair hand (although, she says, "I have made mistakes both in conversation and writing, concerning things which I knew perfectly well, merely from an early habit of heedlessness" [*TMB*, 42]).

All in all, what I want to stress here is that despite Child's evident attempt to get rid of or foist off "blackness"—and hence blame, disorder, disarray—she cannot. Her text makes *her*, as its origin, the

84. Following Kaja Silverman's use of the term "suture" in *The Subject of Semiotics* (New York: Oxford University Press, 1983).

source of "blackness" as a figure for heedlessness, sluttishness or disorder. And it is this circular effect of the sentimental representation, one that points to a conflicted and by no means certain logic, that most critical responses to Child void. Child's last novel, *A Romance of the Republic*, has been read as a simple failure (a) because it employed outdated sentimental conventions, and more recently, (b) because it supposedly ensured the cultural and economic domination of an Anglo-American majority. And indeed, this postbellum (1867) novel ends with a sentimental staging of an iconographic *tableau vivant* that appears to support a reading of the book as a failure to imagine "adequate alternatives to the social order she had so brilliantly anatomized," as Carolyn Karcher explains: "Within literary conventions that veiled the realities of race, class, and gender relations and that necessitated euphemism and obliquity, Child found it impossible to envision a truly egalitarian, multicultural society."[85] But I want to reexamine this tableau as a means to illustrate how twentieth-century critical responses to nineteenth-century sentimentality produce their own sentimental veils, which hide the traces of alterity or suture over the conflicts embedded in nineteenth-century representations.

The iconographic tableau occurs at the same locale where I began this chapter—so, off to (Grand)father's New England house we go: that is, to the proper Bostononian home of one Mr. Alfred Royal King, whose journey from heir/financier to wounded Union soldier the novel chronicles. His wife, Rosabella Royal King, and her sister Floracita are the daughters of New Orleans businessman Alfred Royal, who is so close a friend of the King family that he calls young Alfred King not only his namesake but also his cousin.[86] Rosa and Flora's deceased mother, Eulalia Gonsalez, was the daughter of a Spaniard from St. Augustine and a French West Indian slave (*RR*, 19). Separated for many pages by the circumstances of her cultural and racial status as an octoroon, Rosa and Alfred marry; Flora, after many adventures, marries a German immigrant, Florimond Blumenthal. Both sisters have been aided in the escape from slavery by their slave-then-freedwoman, Tulee; both have had several children, including Rosa's daughter Eulalia and Flora's daughter Rosa.

At the elder Alfred's birthday party, these two cousins and their

---

85. Karcher, "Child's *Romance*," 99–100.
86. Lydia Maria Child, *A Romance of the Republic* (Boston: Ticknor & Fields, 1867), 2–6 (hereafter cited as *RR*).

former slave playmate, Benny, romance the republic by staging the following *tableau vivant*:

> Under festoons of the American flag, surmounted by the eagle, stood Eulalia, in ribbons of red, white, and blue, with a circle of stars round her head. One hand upheld the shield of the Union, and in the other the scales of Justice were evenly poised. By her side stood Rosen Blumen, holding in one hand a gilded pole surmounted by a liberty-cap, while her other hand rested protectingly on the head of Tulee's Benny, who was kneeling and looking upward in thanksgiving. [Then] all the family, of all ages and colors, joined in singing "The Star-Spangled Banner" (*RR* 441)

As Carolyn Karcher remarks, this *tableau* sums up "the strengths and weaknesses of the vision *A Romance of the Republic* offers of America's destiny." Although the Republic "has risen out of the ashes of slavery" so that "here the emancipators are themselves children of emancipated slaves, yet the class relations between the two groups persist."[87] Jean Fagan Yellin points out that this postbellum image is quite similar to a widely used, almost standardized antebellum icon of emancipator and kneeling ex-captive, a vignette of which appears as the cover design on both Yellin's *Women & Sisters* and Lydia Maria Child's 1838 *Authentic Anecdotes of American Slavery*. Of the *Romance* tableau, Yellin writes: "As in pre-Emancipation versions of the double emblem, this assignment of the role of liberator to the light-skinned girl and the role of grateful, kneeling ex-slave to the dark child suggests an endorsement of white superiority that contradicts egalitarian claims . . . proposing miscegenation as the solution to the American race problem, *A Romance of the Republic* colors the multiracial American family not from white to black, but only from white to beige.[88]

Both Karcher and Yellin's readings are persuasive, yet they leave me with two questions. First, how did Child manage the domestic situation that gave rise to this moment? Second, and more urgently, if this iconographic display enacts a sentimentally violent effacement of prior conflicts, does it not also expose and complicate them? I would not overlook Child's evident equivocations—many of which she was herself aware—and I would agree with Karcher's and Nelson's ob-

87. Karcher, "Child's *Romance*," 98–99.
88. Yellin, *Women & Sisters*, 75.

servations that the class status of Child's heroines in this novel hardly approximates the situation of most postbellum freedman. And yet, in describing *both* Alfred King's Boston heritage and Rosabella's colonial one, Child uses the terms "affection", "attachment," "alliance" interchangeably to signify the devotion of *any and all* domestic relations. Curiously, too, the sisters have so obsessively named children after each other and fathers and grandparents that the families read as incestuous replications that cancel each other's duplications out, as if to create one stable, domestic family portrait. Rosa's little Alfred has died, but Flora's Alfred is on his way to college; Rosa's little Flora has died, but Flora's little Rosa—also called Rosen Blumen—has become a replica of her aunt. Flora's fair-haired Lila is a younger version of Rosa's surviving daughter, the "Circassian" beauty Eulalia (*RR*, 306). Meanwhile, Rosa's "almost-white" illegitimate son, Gerald Fitzgerald, whom she had lost when she switched him for his legitimate "white" half-brother, George Falkner, dies in the Civil War. George marries a mulatta, Henriet, and repudiates his "whiteness."

Still, these domestic duplications and dreadful deaths do continue to suggest that the multiracial family is colored within a narrow spectrum that serves both to construct and to validate what would seem to be a middle-class, white, bourgeois ideal. Indeed, we are told, George Falkner is easily "made" into a gentleman while his "good-natured and unassuming" wife, Henriet, is educated "in a degree somewhat suitable to her husband's prospects" (*RR*, 413–15). Thus, as Dana Nelson has argued, "although *Romance* makes a provocative suggestion—along with focusing on 'blacks' who look 'white,' the text proposes that 'whites' can in fact look 'black.' "[89] The preferred look and the suitable education remain faithful to prevailing standards.

But are these supposedly dominant white, middle-class standards not subtly altered and rearranged by such an icon as the *tableau vivant*? I find it very curious that none of the critical readings of *A Romance* trace out the implications of the odd Rosa/Rosen figure, the *middling* figure of the icon. Rosa/Rosen Blumenthal "bears a striking resemblance" (*RR*, 289) to her aunt, that tragic-mulatta Rosa, a mother who in fact replicates in name and description both Child's much earlier Rosalie from "The Quadroons" and a slave whose "actual" history fascinated Child.[90] Neither as fair nor as ethereally graceful as her

89. Nelson, *Word*, 83.
90. See Lydia Maria Child, "The Quadroons," in *The Other Woman*, ed. Susan Kop-

angel-cousin Eulalia, nor as dark and as strong as the ex-slave child Benny, Rosa/Rosen mediates black and white in the tableau; why not read this figure as a link between a nation-state embodied as a light-skinned girl and the emancipated, laboring population embodied as dark (man)child? Yellin's reading of the icon usefully identifies what might be called the dominant hierarchy—although from a nineteenth-century perspective, postbellum Eulalia is not "white," and Benny, however equivocally, is still a member of the family—but in so doing, her reading reinscribes "black/male" and "white/female" as separate categories denoting "low" and "high." The middle is not even visible in her description; Rosa/Rosen is left out.

Therefore, though I might agree with Nelson that *A Romance of the Republic* does appear to uphold "'white' bourgeois class structure and culture," because the "racial Other . . . remains trapped, forever an Object,"[91] I would also ask, what precisely is a text if not an Object? In an act of representation, who or what is not subject to objectification? In other words, Nelson's objection to this Objectification of "the" racial Other suggests that somehow, in some way, "whiteness" is not also an Object in a text, subject to generic convention and rhetorical modes of objectification. Why not try to read the Object itself as a site of historical conflict? After all, wasn't an emerging economic and legal middle class still under construction in 1867, subject to fluctuating cultural descriptions and distinctions, under legal and political pressure to shift and change its composition?

More specifically, if the Royal King family can be read as a "white" aristocracy, signified by angelic Eulalia's blondness; and if an emancipated but laboring class can be read as "black" through the subjected position of Benny, how does Rosa/Rosen signify exactly? Child distrusted an aristocracy that would not, as she put it, soil its hands with the abolitionist cause.[92] Obviously, she also feared the vulgar, dirty hands of sluttish, low-class domestics. But if white "queen" Eulalia mimics the white wealth of the nation-state, while poor black Benny kneels as her subject, it is dark, prosaic Rosa/Rosen who must embody the dynamic and potentially mixed middle (class). Neither black nor white, neither fabulously rich nor working poor, this twelve-year-old's gender and ethnic assignment are also in flux. Indeed, when

pelman (Old Westbury, N.Y.: Feminist Press, 1984), 1–12; and Child, *Selected Letters*, 87–88, 92.

91. Nelson, *Word*, 132.

92. Quoted in Karcher, "Rape, Murder, and Revenge," 331.

her name vacillates across the text between Rosa and Rosen, what resonances can be heard? Is this child a (quadroon) girl, Rosa (following her mother's ancestry), or perhaps an (Austrian Jewish) boy, Rosen (following her/his father's ancestry)? The descriptions of the child compound such resonances. She wears both a "crimson merino" and a "Greek cap" from which "the dark mass of her wavy hair . . . [and] dark curls strayed . . . like the tendrils of a delicate vine; and nestling close to each ear was was a little downy crescent, which her papa called her *whisker*" (*RR*, 288; emphasis added). Whiskers on a girl do not immediately suggest to me a normative nineteenth-century standard of feminine beauty.

Moreover, the emblematic gestures assigned to Rosa/Rosen present a rather odd picture, particularly if one should ascribe gender confusion to the figure, since she/he is pictured "holding in one hand a gilded pole surmounted by a liberty-cap, while her other hand rested protectingly on the head of Tulee's Benny." What (phallic) object is Rosa/Rosen holding onto here? More seriously, as Neil Hertz writes in "Medusa's Head: Male Hysteria under Political Pressure," the liberty-cap itself—the *bonnet rouge de la Liberté*—is a confusing icon: "The cap was taken [during the French Revolution] to stand for liberty because it had stood for liberty in Rome: under the Empire it had been awarded to slaves on the occasion of their manumission." But, continues Hertz, "the question of what the Roman cap of liberty actually looked like gets interestingly tangled." The round-peaked cap that droops forward, adopted by the French as a Roman sign of liberty, has been associated by historians not with the Roman *pilleus* but with the ancient Phrygian "*tiara* . . . well known to the Greeks; they used it to designate not only Persians but Orientals in general: Scythians, Amazons, Trojans." These "exotic" associations function in a manner similar to Rosa/Rosen's tropical heritage. And if the iconographic cap elicits "uncertainties about the stability of sexual difference, uncertainties that could resonate with those developing out of the blurring of differences in social status—between, for instance, citizens, freedmen and slaves" so, too, does Rosa/Rosen.[93] Thus while the domestic and sentimental iconography of "American" liberty seeks to mask divisions by scripting frozen harmonies, it also complicates them, to charge diversity with potentiality.

And what of Eulalia? To read the tableau as a reconstitution of a

93. Hertz, "Medusa's Head," 41, 43, 45–46.

middle-class, white American family is to read Eulalia as representing that family. Indeed, to Karcher, Child's "concession to the bigotry she had explicitly criticized, . . . far from promoting the valorization of African beauty, has the effect of endorsing an ethnocentric preference for approximations of white beauty."[94] And yet through Eulalia's great-grandmother, grandmother, and mother, she inherits—like her cousin Rosa/Rosen—a "mixed" African-American, French West Indian heritage.[95] If one chooses to see the child Eulalia as a "white" beauty rather than as a confused figuration for "whiteness," then her *maternal* and *multiple* heritage vanishes.[96] For does not Lady Liberty's iconic standard-bearer, Eulalia, also bear the name of her French, West-Indian grandmother? If one reads African-American Eulalia Royal as simply "white," then the maternal, as a multiple site of contestation, has once again been forced to signify absence and to disappear.

94. Karcher, "Child's *Romance*," 88.

95. Eulalia Gonsalez is first described as a beautiful quadroon, half? French and half? Spanish, "who danced like Taglioni and sang like Malibran" (*RR*, 13); later, however, we are told that her daughter Flora "on the paternal side . . . descends from the French gentry and the Spanish nobility; but her mother was a quadroon slave" (*RR*, 277). So what happened to her French and Spanish heritage? Flora refers to her *great*-grandmother as the dark-complexion source of African heritage, as if somehow this Eulalia were not also African and Spanish and French (*RR*, 281).

96. At the American Studies Association's annual conference (November 2, 1991), Mark Patterson skillfully pointed out in his talk "Redefining Motherhood: Surrogacy and Race in American Reconstruction" that when the antebellum familial logic of slavery—the child must follow the condition of the mother—legally collapsed, the maternal as a legal, cultural category became more visibly incoherent: "What 'condition' does the mother have after Emancipation?" Patterson argued that Child's *Romance* foreshadowed present-day debates about surrogacy (see the Afterword below). But what most intrigued me about Patterson's talk was that he saw Rosabella's family as an artificial family, especially because she and Alfred King choose to suppress Eulalia's heritage—yet I can find no textual evidence that Eulalia's African, Spanish, French West-Indian heritage will be kept from her once she has become an adult.

2

Engendering a Body of Truth:
Fuller, Emerson, and an
Embryonic American Literature

We two that planets erst had been
Are now a double star.
                    —Henry David Thoreau, "Love"

In *Nature*, Ralph Waldo Emerson writes that Truth in Art has been
named by "man in all ages and countries ... FATHER."[1] Logically,
then, Mother cannot be abstract Truth. Rather she must be concrete
form or, as Emerson defined it, the Not-Me of phenomenological Nature, she who "stretches out her arms to embrace man ... [and]
bend[s] her lines of grandeur and grace to the decoration of her darling child" (*Nature*, 987). A primary embodiment of the Not-Me, upon
whose "steady and prodigal provision" a "kingdom of man over nature" will be built, maternal Nature is vital but ultimately "ancillary
to man" (*Nature*, 983, 1008, 987), just as Mother Britain will become
but an ancillary antecedent to her "free" offspring, Columbia.

As fully inculcated in this Cartesian philosophic tradition as Emerson, Sarah Margaret Fuller nevertheless conceptualized Truth differently: "Truth," she claimed, "is the nursing mother of genius." Like
Emerson, she called for "the spirit of truth [to be] purely worshipped."[2] Yet, for Fuller, Truth was best figured by the body of a
nursing woman. Despite being lodged in the position of the Not-Me
by reason of her sex, and held there by a Western metaphysical tradition that trails back to Plato, Fuller repeatedly expressed a desire to

1. Ralph Waldo Emerson, *Nature*, in *The Harper American Literature*, ed. Donald
McQuade (New York: Harper & Row, 1987), 1:989. Emerson's *The American Scholar, An
Address, Self-Reliance, Circles, Fate, and Illusions* also appear in vol. 1 of this edition and
are hereafter cited by title and page number.
2. Margaret Fuller, "American Literature: Its Position in the Present Time, and Prospects for the Future" (1846), in *The Harper American Literature*, 1:1214 (hereafter cited by
page number in the text).

salvage the material and represent Mother Nature not simply as a frame for man, nor as blind form waiting to be seen, but as a creative force with a vision of her own. In pursuing this goal, Fuller represented maternal power as the foundation for a uniquely American cultural heritage.

A Bounteous Lap?

Adopting an oracular, plural identity in her 1846 essay "American Literature: Its Position in the Present Time, and Prospects for the Future," Fuller evidently identified with her own posited nursing mother Truth as a caretaker of American cultural achievement: "We are joyous, too, when we think that though our name may not be writ on the pillar of our country's fame, we can really do far more towards rearing it than those who come at a later period and to a seemingly fairer task" (1214). Demurring from the pillar of American fame, Fuller instead lends a hand to its erection, an activity she then represents as far more primary, if less "fair," than inscription. And, as if to underscore the primacy of such unscripted *jouissance*,[3] Fuller warns that without Mother Truth "all attempts to construct a national literature must end in abortions, like the monster of Frankenstein, things with forms and the instincts of forms, but soulless and therefore revolting" (1213).

Margaret Fuller has been often portrayed as a decidedly unsettling personality within that circle of New England Transcendentalists whom Edgar Allan Poe lampooned as the Frog-Pondians.[4] Certainly, to personify Truth as both maternal and inescapably necessary to the "rearing" of art must have struck some of her contemporaneous readers as itself revolting, illogical. Concord's elite philosophical circle was far more likely to agree with Emerson that the inspiriting Truth of Art was best represented as the Creator/Father, while Mother was more accurately cast as an embodiment of Nature. Fuller, by suggesting that the former representation of Truth was, at best, philosophically deriv-

---

3. The way Fuller uses "absence" or lack to signify as a space of joy demands general alignment with the Lacanian concept of *jouissance*.

4. Fuller's construction as a figure both marginal and yet unsettling to the Transcendentalist aggregate is demonstrated in her contemporaries' representations of her—most notably if one reads Hawthorne's Zenobia in *The Blithedale Romance* as a portrait of Fuller.

ative, challenged the prevailing epistemology, discursively placing the essence of an "American" poetics in hands other than those of the Father.[5]

This is not to say that Fuller's work escapes the metaphysical binary of the (masculinized) Me and (femininized) Not-Me. Her book *Woman in the Nineteenth Century* and her *New York Tribune* essays (reprinted in 1846 as *Papers on Literature and Art*) are all replete with gendered polarities. Her work is shaped by the very traditional metaphysical categories with which she (and Emerson) struggled: soul/flesh, idea/form, art/nature—which enact a split between (masculinized) conceptions of abstracted spirit and (feminized) conceptions of material form.

Thus I seek not to polarize Fuller and Emerson as antagonists but rather to reconstruct Fuller's deliberate and deliberated philosophical discussion with Emersonian metaphysics over what would be, theoretically, the unique shape of American (literary) culture. Fuller's argument with Emersonian metaphysics allowed for an aesthetics that demanded diversity as the basis for fecund creativity, an outlook that came to affect Emerson's own vision. Indeed, if Margaret Fuller's version of what constituted an ability to "conceive" dovetails with Emerson's in significant ways, her reconceptualization of metaphysical Truth nevertheless also served to redefine early Emersonian versions of such an ability. And yet Emerson's early vision and definition of Truth came to dominate and still serves to construct definitions of Transcendentalist ideology, as well as the way an evolutionary history of nineteenth-century American cultural history is imagined.

For both essayists, creativity as a category relied heavily on maternal metaphors. But for each the maternal was an unreliable power, undeniably associated with those material verities that formed the concrete needs of corporeal existence, and thus associated with the mortal. For instance, Fuller often imagined, in images quite similar to those of her one-time friend and later bitter enemy Nathaniel Hawthorne, a Mother Nature who produced for humanity's benefit. Fuller would have agreed with Hawthorne that "the lap of bounteous Nature [was] . . . filled with breadstuff" for the delectation of men.[6] Em-

5. Fuller's ambivalence about the "originality" of Emerson's symbolism and philosophy, particularly as expressed in his poetry, can be seen in a number of her commentaries about him; see esp. "American Literature," 1215–17.

6. Nathaniel Hawthorne, *The American Notebooks* (New Haven: Yale University Press, 1932), 102–5; this edition is based on original manuscripts in the Pierpont Morgan Library.

erson tried to flee from the corporeal in search of a self-generation
that would bypass the limitation of the material. Although this imaginative flight was decidedly checked in his later essays, American cultural history has discarded *Fate* in favor of *Self-Reliance*, which weds
the American artist and American art to individual, disembodied,
masculinized autonomy. Fuller addresses the consequences that such
a paradigm involves for those who would not and could not flee their
corporeal particularity, primarily with regard to femininity. Staking
out a claim for art that did not require autonomy, Fuller's work questioned the metaphysical grounds on which the twentieth-century par-
allelism between masculinity and the American writer would grow.
She offers an alternative field from which another, less homogeneous
body of American culture can be generated.

The Virgin Dynamo

Like many writers in the nineteenth century, from Emerson to
Henry James, Fuller declared that an American literary genius would
not arise until "the physical resources of the country [are] explored,
all its regions studded with towns, broken by the plow, netted together by railway and telegraph lines." Only after Mother Nature had
been overcome would "talent . . . be left at leisure to turn its energies
upon the higher department of man's existence" ("American Literature," 1213).

Yet despite her evident belief in Emerson's prospective rule of man
over nature, Fuller's vision had some radical quirks. For example, her
description of the tamed natural world lacks the romantic nostalgia
for simpler times that marks Hawthorne's popular sketches and Thoreau's journals; Fuller even suggests that the electric telegraph will
"raise" the character of the newspaper by enabling communication to
flow more freely. This faith in technology as a medium for democracy
was one that many of her fellow Transcendentalists did not share. She
also suggests that in the future America a healthy creativity will depend upon a "fusion of races among us." Although the way she modifies this claim reveals her dependence on the same philosophical
drive toward Unity that structures much of Emerson, her use of such
a suggestion still startles. Fuller confidently names the forces that will
"animate an American literature" as those arising from "a mixed race
continually enriched with new blood from other stocks the most un-

like that of our first descent" (1213). Like Emerson, she undermines this heterogeneity by declaring the goal of American literature to be "a homogeneous or fully organized state of being" (1219, 1213); still, her call for a conversation among races may have jolted, if only subconsciously, people who were clearly aware of and in some cases embroiled in abolitionist polemics.[7]

Many of Fuller's literary reviews contain similarly jolting moments. In her December 4, 1845, review of *America and the American People*, by the German history professor Frederick Von Raumer, who had become a popular pro-slavery lecturer, Fuller employs what one might call unruly imagery to deauthorize Von Raumer's pedantry. The first two columns of her essay are soberly written, balancing guarded praise for the author's intentions against accusations of inaccuracy. Then suddenly she remarks, "In conclusion, we confess that we cordially hate this book as we do all judicious, dull, gentlemanly well-informed, kind, cool persons and all that emanate from them." To support her devastating estimation, Fuller offers an America designed to counteract Von Raumer's prejudice: America "has, as the foreigner thinks, the unmannerly tricks and disagreeable obtrusion of an overgrown child. Like children of a rich and energetic nature, prematurely brought forward, she is peculiarly likely to offend the decorum and even the good feelings of uncles and aunts. She makes dirt pies, kills flies and oversets the teapot. Still she is learning all the while.[8]

America is an unmannerly girlchild? Worse still, this picture would seem to validate James Russell Lowell's complaint that Fuller's work was always a tale of herself, "dotted as thick as a peacock's with I's."[9] This national girlchild does resemble Fuller, who was, as she wrote

7. See Leo Marx, *The Machine in the Garden: Technology and the Pastoral Ideal in America* (New York: Oxford University Press, 1964), 3–34, on technology, the pastoral, and Transcendentalist philosophy. Many New Englanders attempted to figure America as the "so long gathering congress of the world" (Henry David Thoreau, *Collected Poems*, ed. Carl Bode [Baltimore: Johns Hopkins University Press, 1970], 135), where an idealized, often agrarian community that would allow for a profitable mixture of races would bring about a true New World. That vision, however, was well threaded with fears of "miscegenation" and "amalgamation." See also George M. Frederickson, *The Inner Civil War: Northern Intellectuals and the Crisis of the Union* (New York: Harper Torchbooks, 1965); and *The Journals of Charlotte Forten Grimké*, ed. Stevenson.

8. Margaret Fuller in the *New York Tribune*, 1 December 1845, 1.

9. James Russell Lowell, *A Fable for Critics* (Boston: Houghton Mifflin, 1890), 73. See also "Fuller and Lowell's *A Fable for Critics*," in *Critical Essays on Ralph Waldo Emerson*, ed. Robert E. Burkholder and Joel Myerson (Boston: G. K. Hall, 1983), 255–56. Of course, Lowell leveled a similar accusation of self-interest at Emerson as well.

elsewhere, "prematurely brought forward" by her father, Timothy Fuller, a disciplinarian who literally frightened his five-year-old daughter into learning Greek.[10] The American girlchild also foreshadows the antics of a better-known figure of national literary pride: namely, Pearl of *The Scarlet Letter*. Yet Fuller's sprightly fly killer does not appear to need either the fatherly approval of a Timothy Fuller or the identifying seal of a paternal kiss to make her frantic obtrusions cohere into worthwhile creative endeavors.

Fuller admits that the child is "vain." But her vanity is of no consequence, because the girl "show[s] great promise. . . . Her pothooks and trammels are of giant size." If in her vanity "she insists that they are also of as refined beauty as Raphael's drawings," and if "the more she does so, the more she is laughed at," she nevertheless shows "vast prospect." All it takes for her beauty to be seen is a prophet great enough to comprehend "not the child but the horoscope that foreshows its destiny" (Fuller, review of *American People*, 1). Perhaps a spoiled brat, America is still a heroine, struggling toward a hyperbolic grandeur of her own. She may copy European models but does not rely on them. She does not need the title of nobility, unknown but clearly European, that validates Pearl's future. Fuller's America has a vast, nurturant promise that needs fulfilling in ways that will just have to be reckoned with. American literature will be not only a prodigy but a prodigious female beauty with enormous pothooks and teapots, a domestic of gigantic proportions grown up from a forward child.

It is no wonder that James Russell Lowell was not alone in his distaste for Margaret Fuller. Such a female-oriented version of American destiny could have produced only the puzzlement or downright rage reflected in derogatory assessments of her work from many of her contemporaries.[11] And it is also no wonder that Margaret Fuller left her New England Brahmin cloister in favor of Horace Greeley's New York–based *Tribune* where she continued—and, as Hawthorne

10. On Timothy Fuller, see Perry Miller, *Margaret Fuller: An American Romantic* (New York: Doubleday, 1969), x–xxviii, 1–23; David Watson, *Margaret Fuller: An American Romantic* (New York: St. Martin's Press, 1988), 3–12; Bell Gale Chevigny, *The Woman and the Myth: Margaret Fuller's Life and Writings* (Old Westbury, N.Y.: Feminist Press, 1976).

11. On Fuller's relation to her contemporaries, with emphasis on Emerson, see Miller, *Margaret Fuller*, 52–55, 108–32, 277–78, 295–98; Watson, *Margaret Fuller* 13–23, 91–104; Chevigny, *The Woman and the Myth*; *Selections from Ralph Waldo Emerson*, ed. Stephen E. Whicher (Boston: Houghton Mifflin, 1960); John McAleer, *Ralph Waldo Emerson: Days of Encounter* (Boston: Little, Brown, 1984).

might have put it, perversely—recast Truth as an unbounded maternal creativity endowed with an unsettling power and a wild joy.

Fuller's image of dynamic maternity as a primary source of creative
power exists in its most elaborate form in her best-known work,
Woman in the Nineteenth Century.[12] Although at first glance it would
seem that her categorizations unproblematically split conceptions of
the mind from conceptions of the body, she repeatedly searches for a
way to salvage the feminized material world and ennoble the reproductive function of the female body. In order to do so, she attempts
to purge the female of her contact with material Nature. To thus validate maternity while dodging physicality—the "sordor and filths" of
what Emerson termed "disagreeable appearances" (*Nature*, 1007)—
Fuller used electricity as a purified analogue for the unreliability of
flesh. Evacuating the "blood and heat" of Woman to give her a trans-
fusion of magnetic, electrical flux, making her the "conductor of a
mysterious fluid" instead of the source of menstrual flow, Fuller represents the power of female conception in a form that cannot fall into
the trap of blooded sexuality. In her re-creation of the female, "the
especial genius of woman . . . [is] electrical in movement, intuitive in
function, spiritual in tendency," and so "Earth knows no fairer, holier
relation than that of a mother" (*Woman*, 114, 104, 115, 96).

Of course, the divine maternal evokes Emerson's belief that Nature,
if seen clearly through the eyes of true Art, will be revealed as God's
emblem. Sanctified maternity becomes, as well, a central image for the
nineteenth-century white, middle-class Cult of True Womanhood that
made Mother synonymous with Woman. Fuller was raised with the
paradigm that Mother was emblematic of social decorum and divinity,
and in many ways her use of the image merely takes it to its logical
extreme: she assimilates all women to Woman, Woman to mother, and
mother to Madonna. This universalizing iconography maintains the
severance of the soul from the body and leads Fuller to claim as her
ideal the Virgin Mary, who could bear without blood and who was
powerfully "charged" yet lacking in "the heat of wild impulse . . . and
passionate error" (*Woman*, 77).

Yet Fuller did not leave this universalizing iconography as it was.
Anticipating Henry Adams's later observation that the "force of the
Virgin . . .seemed to be as potent as X-rays" and that Woman, at least

---

12. Margaret Fuller, *Woman in the Nineteenth Century* (1845; New York: Norton, 1971),
hereafter cited as *Woman*.

"in France . . . still seemed potent, not merely as a sentiment, but as a force. . . . she was the animated dynamo; she was reproduction—the greatest and most mysterious of all energies."[13] Fuller conflates electricity, the Madonna, and reproductive force. Adams, who wrote "The Dynamo and the Virgin" section of his autobiography in 1900, lamented that American literature was sexless, hell-bent upon covering over the dynamism of sex with fig leaves; he turned to Europe to find female potency. Fuller, writing in the 1840s when the notion of an American literary tradition was still quite embryonic, did not see the Madonna as wholly European. Rather, she attempted to make room in America for female potency and an American Madonna.

I do not mean to suggest that Fuller's electric Madonna is an unproblematic icon for female potency.[14] On the contrary, Fuller traces out the sentimental maternal image that is stamped like a cookie-cutter pattern—although under various names and guises, with varying degrees of complexity—all through antebellum literature, from Hawthorne's Hester Prynne ("an object to remind [us] of the image of Divine Maternity": *SL* 41) to Harriet Beecher Stowe's evocation of St. Clare's mother. "My mother," cries St. Clare, "she was divine! Don't look at me so—you know what I mean! She probably was of mortal birth; but, as far as ever I could observe, there was no trace of any human weakness or error about her; and everybody that lives to remember her, whether bond or free, servant, acquaintance, relation, all say the same."[15] St. Clare's exclamation "you know what I mean," along with his invocation of a universalized memorial that crosses all barriers of sex, race, and class, points up the blanket assumption of the sanctity in motherhood that lies behind Emerson's "devout" Nature-Mother standing "with bended head, and hands folded upon the breast" (*Nature*, 1002).

Fuller's celebration of the beatified mother appears throughout the fabric of *Woman in the Nineteenth Century*. As she says, "no figure that has ever arisen to greet our eyes has been received with more fervent reverence than that of the Madonna," and it is to this standard that all women are held (*Woman*, 56). Still, for Fuller, the icon of the cherished mother functions differently than it does in Emerson—at least

13. Henry Adams, *The Education of Henry Adams*, ed. Ernest Samuels (Boston: Houghton, Mifflin, 1973), 379–80, 384.
14. Certainly not, given the argument of this book as a whole.
15. Harriet Beecher Stowe, *Uncle Tom's Cabin* (New York: Penguin American Library, 1985), 333.

the Emerson of the 1840s, though long after he had lost "his only audience," as he once called Margaret Fuller,[16] her vision of a female conceptual power haunts his later writings.

In his essays before 1844, the year that the original version of *Woman in the Nineteenth Century* appeared in *The Dial*, Emerson metaphorized the material maternal as that which, through the alembic of Spirit, would be abolished. If, as he says in *Nature*, "even the corpse has its own beauty," that beauty can be revealed only through the soul's light because "the material is degraded before the spiritual . . . [and shall be] transferred . . . into the mind and [which will leave] matter like an outcast corpse" (*Nature*, 985, 1000). Later, he asks, "Why drag about this corpse of your memory?" (*Self-Reliance*, 1036). The objective is to consign matter, which he repeatedly associates with the past and the natural and hence with the mother, to a discardable memory that may be overcome through the future-oriented potency of individual mind. As he says in *The American Scholar* (1016), man's fear of the unknown or mysterious—more concretely, the incomprehensibility of origins or the mysterious process of birthing—must be eradicated. "Manlike let him turn and face it. Let him look into its eye and search its nature, inspect its origin—see the whelping of this lion . . . and . . . hence-forth defy it and pass on superior."

Fuller, who often wrote of her wish to give birth, may have been uncomfortable to see birth assigned the name of "whelping." Indeed, Fuller's relation to whelping is less assured of the superiority of transcendence. Despite her endorsement of the sexless Madonna, she does not wish to lose sight of the mother's distinctive ability to become pregnant in the flesh. But given the mother's traditional alignment with Nature, even Fuller keeps falling into the sordid filth of the imperfect phenomenological. She is also less willing than Emerson to let go of memory. To Emerson, the past is apparently of small consequence: "These roses under my window make no reference to former roses or to better ones; they are for what they are; they exist with God today. There is no time to them" (*Self-Reliance*, 1040). For Fuller, who ransacked history, mythology, and fable to supply *Woman in the Nineteenth Century* with a catalogue of former roses, birthing and memory have different values. The mother is neither a ghostly memory nor an

---

16. Ralph Waldo Emerson, *Emerson in His Journals*, ed. Joel Porte (Cambridge, Mass.: Harvard, 1982).

outcast corpse whose beauty can be discovered only through the il-
lumination of spirit.

Fuller's image of electricity to displace muck and mire does more
than simply displace the "disagreeable appearances" of a female reproductive cycle. It also begins to reanimate the corpse that the mother
had become in the tradition reworked and popularized in Emerson.
By the conclusion of *Woman in the Nineteenth Century*, the memory of
mother has become something other than nostalgic. Rather than serving as memory, pointing toward purity, or hanging about the ankles
like a fleshly ball and chain, it electrifies. In fact, if not properly channeled, it may also electrocute.

Electronic Eyes

When Fuller wrote that man "is of woman born and her face bends
over him in infancy with an expression he can never quite forget,"
her description echoes Emerson's and is congruent with the sentimental ideal of maternity. She herself acknowledges that she is writing a
"hackneyed observation," since "most men of genius boast some remarkable development in the mother. The rudest tar brushes off a tear
with his coat-sleeve at the hallowed name" (*Woman*, 49). Here she
makes the same claim as St. Clare: mother-reverence is universal.
Moving from genius to common sailor as if the two were synonymous
in that both are sons, Fuller also erases class difference in an appeal
to gender and maternity:

> The other day, I met a decrepit old man of seventy . . . who challenged
> the stage company to guess where he was going.
>   They guessed aright, "To see your mother." "Yes," said he, "she is
> ninety-two, but has good eyesight still, they say. I have not seen her these
> forty years and I thought could not die in peace without." (*Woman*, 49–
> 50)

The old man's story is juxtaposed to a little boy's school recital of a
poem that is not specifically about Mother but rather about loss, yet
he recites only a part of the poem before the implied memory of his
mother interrupts his speech. The ensuing tears "shamed him from
the stage." Fuller uses this double portraiture to support her claim
that the mother's gaze identifies her as someone "come from heaven,

a commissioned soul, a messenger of truth and love." This maternal gaze, "a Rosicrucian lamp [that] burns unwearied, though condemned to the solitude of tombs" is, as well, a permanent fixture in a man's mind (*Woman*, 50–51).

Fuller's emphasis here is on sight and on the self-evident importance of the mother to infancy. Everyone can *see* why the old man is making a journey, without being told; he boasts that his ancient mother's eyesight is still good; the memory of mother fills a boy's eyes with tears; and the maternal gaze sheds a benign, supernatural light. Sight is key for Fuller—as it is for Emerson when he writes: "To speak truly, few adult persons can see nature. Most persons do not see the sun. At least they have a very superficial seeing. The sun illuminates only the eye of the man, but shines into the eye and heart of the child. The lover of nature is he ... who has retained the spirit of infancy even into the era of manhood" (*Nature*, 982). Yet the rays of light affecting the heart are gendered differently: for Fuller the lamp is the mother's gaze; for Emerson the Sun is God's lamp. So he remarks in *Circles* (1060), "The eye is the first circle; the horizon which it forms is the second; and throughout nature this primary figure is repeated without end. It is the highest emblem in the cipher of the world. St. Augustine described the nature of God as a circle whose centre was everywhere and its circumference nowhere." Unlike God's eye or the famously dismembered, transparent eyeball into which Emerson's being dissolves, making him "part and parcel of God," the white father (*Nature*, 983), Fuller's sanctified eyes have a particular bodily source.

Moreover, these eyes have a peculiar tendency to look back at the one who regards them. However long delayed, Fuller's maternal sanctified gaze is one that returns a look. It is, as well, a gaze that shrinks universal manhood into universal childhood. It might, as Emerson hoped, help the man regain his infancy, but infancy for Fuller is not a reminder that "infancy conforms to nobody" (Emerson, *Self-Reliance*, 1033). Instead, it is a reminder that the man is, forever and always, some woman's child—just as Jesus, the light of the world and Emerson's often cited example of the perfected man, is the son of the Madonna. While Emerson would forget Jesus' humanity, Fuller insists that "the earthly parent of the Savior of souls was a woman" (*Woman*, 57). Fuller's primal circle is not a mirror in which man perceives his perfected nature, and it does not wholly consume or dissolve that which stands before it. To see is not simply self-knowledge; to see is to be *seen*. The child, opening his eyes, views neither just himself nor sublime nothingness but rather the eyes of mother. The sight of this other gaze disrupts, interrupts, or redirects his own. The old man goes home to look upon his mother's eyes; the young boy's gaze, disrupted by the memory of his mother, is veiled with tears.

Whenever Fuller portrays the relation between the male and the female, she insists upon the agency of the woman's gaze.[17] With regard to such portraits, she says that she "could swell the catalogue of instances far beyond the reader's patience" and then proceeds to do so, as if validation of Woman as equal partner and equal soul relied upon the sheer circuitry of repetition (*Woman*, 61). This replication is not reproduction without difference, however. The catalogue runs the gamut from myth to experiential anecdote, enlisting to her cause—without regard for contextual violence—Native American, "Hindoo," German, French, and African images. Yet although her portrait collection assimilates, subordinating difference to universal types, she attempts to enumerate what she believes are the exact particulars of each image.

One mother-son vignette introduces the Flying Pigeon, which Fuller admits is an "imperfect sketch of a North American Indian." The Flying Pigeon "died when her son was only four years old, yet left on his mind a feeling of reverent love worthy the thought of Christian chivalry. Grown to manhood, he shed tears on seeing her portrait." Up to this point, the new portrait is just like the old. Indeed, Fuller adds that the Flying Pigeon's "brow is as ideal and the eyes and lids as devout and modest as the Italian picture of the Madonna" (*Woman*, 88–89). The Madonna overlies the face of the Native American and so colonizes it with the European ideal.

Nevertheless, the portrait of Flying Pigeon has some peculiarities. First, it is disjunctive; the eyes belong to the Italian Madonna, but the rest, Fuller insists, is Indian. Second, it allows Fuller to inscribe a maternal primacy that was not dependent on European models but intrinsic to America. Finally, as the tears of the Christianized Native American son pour down, he is moved to speech. Unlike the boy of her earlier story, this son's utterance is not cut short but evoked at length; Fuller seems compelled to render his words in full. It is an odd speech, for while the words are typologically Christian, this son does not describe his mother as either a memory or a visual object.

17. Fuller often uses a brother-sister pattern of deep, affectional relation that can be read as incestual; for her, however, the theoretical lack of physical intimacy made this bond an ideal relationship (*Woman*, 119–28).

Instead he animates her through the description of particular activities. These actions, though romanticized and Christianized, name Flying Pigeon as "Ratchewaine": that is, as Native American. The son's tearful gaze recreates not his mother's appearance but his mother's behavior. His verb tenses negate her death, and the details he chooses designate her cultural distance from the Italian Madonna: "And she has been known to give away her last blanket—all the honey that was in the lodge, the last bladder of bear's oil, and the last piece of dried meat . . ." (*Woman*, 89).

I want to emphasize: I am not claiming that Fuller's appropriation of the Flying Pigeon does not efface the specificity of the Native American; clearly, it does so. Yet Fuller struggles to retain the particular, because to obliterate all difference in search of Unity (or the Oversoul) would be to negate what she is attempting to voice: the particular power of "Femality" (*Woman*, 114). "Harmony," she claims, "exists in difference, no less than in likeness" (*Woman*, 79). Thus, while Fuller does not escape the Me/Not-Me binary, she does unsettle its implied hierarchy by ascribing agency to both sides of the dichotomy. For her, the European Madonna is and is not an American Madonna. Man is and is not pattern for woman. Consider this passage: "The well-instructed moon flies not from her orbit to seize on the glories of her partner; No; for she knows that one law rules, one heaven contains, one universe replies to them alike. It is with women as with the slave . . . .Tremble not before the free man, but before the slave who has chains to break" (*Woman*, 63). Fuller may restrict the moon, the woman, and the slave to their orbits, yet she also suggests that those orbital chains must be sundered.

Returning later to a Native American milieu, Fuller offers a story that illustrates what such an emancipation meant in the past and could mean again: "A woman dreamt in youth that she was betrothed to the Sun. She built her wigwam apart, filled it with emblems of her alliance and means of an independent life. There she passed her days, sustained by her own exertions, and true to her supposed engagement" (*Woman*, 101). Note that the Sun, one of the ever-widening circles at the center of Emerson's universe, has been reduced to an emblem for the woman. In effect, Fuller takes Emerson's strategy and turns it on him; what he has done to "nature," she does to the "sun." Indeed, at this point every son is gone; Woman needs only symbols of him, no longer needs to become a symbol for him.

It is significant as well that at this point, having removed Woman from her orbit around Man, Fuller resumes the electric imagery with redoubled intensity. Now the electric fluid does more than simply magnetize Woman. Now, it threatens. Those who seem overladen with electricity frighten those around them. " 'When she merely enters the room, I am what the French call *hérissé*,' said a man of petty feeling and worldly character of such a woman." This electric woman has an eye "overfull of expression, dilated and lustrous; it seems to have drawn the whole being into it" (*Woman*, 104). This Womanly gaze does not beam benignly, nor does it simply see all without in order to assimilate all within. Instead, it ambiguously draws being inward even as it overflows outward.

Now that Fuller has reminded man of his sonship and has made the sun into an emblem, a female electricity is unleashed that can "invigorate and embellish, not destroy life." Channel it incorrectly, though, as in the making of a bad marriage, and the electricity will electrocute: "Sickness is the frequent result of this overcharged existence," and women are their own victims, burned up by their overflow (*Woman*, 104). They speak in "a language unknown to themselves"; indeed, to some they seem "the inhabitants of another planet." But Fuller warns that to denigrate the electric Woman will result in sterility. Not only will life be incomplete without the seeming aliens, but in fact real life, the real life Emerson exhorted his American scholars to live, is animated only by such electricity: "These rare powers belonged to no other planet, but were a high development of the growth of this [earth] and might, by wise and reverent treatment, be made to inform and embellish the scenes of every day" (*Woman*, 162).

For Fuller as for Emerson, America is the promised land where such a real life can be rediscovered: "All these motions of time, tides that betoken a waxing moon, overflow upon our land. The world at large is readier to let Woman learn and manifest the capacities of her nature than it ever was before and here is a less encumbered field and freer air than anywhere else" (*Woman*, 107). Waxing as wild as her own unleashed electric Madonna, Fuller closes by positing a future where it is specifically the American woman's gaze that clarifies. Even so, this woman is also aware that any gaze, however exalted, will need improvement: "Every spot is seen, every chasm revealed. Climbing the dusty hill, some fair effigies that once stood for symbols of human destiny have been broken; those I have with me show defects in this broad light" (*Woman*, 178).

In *The American Scholar* (1011), Emerson wrote, "I had better never see a book than to be warped by its attraction out of my own orbit, and made a satellite instead of a system." And in *Circles* (1061), he exulted, "Moons are no more bound to spiritual power than bat-balls." The eccentric trajectory of Fuller's little book may have warped his own orbit a little more than he liked. After all, Fuller reminds the primal Sun that he is only someone's son, and that his planetary influence can be matched by that of another star, "a pure and perfected intelligence embodied in feminine form, and the centre of a world whose members revolve harmoniously around her" (*Woman*, 128).

The mother's electric gaze may universalize, fusing difference into sameness, and yet for Fuller it also particularizes. The desired fusion that both Emerson and Fuller celebrate is always, in Fuller's writings, an incomplete Unity, and the manchild names his mother as frequently as the mother names her child. The two never become entirely one, as they often do in Emerson's writings. There, images of a sacred mother-child dyad generally emphasize the primacy of the "son," as when Emerson painted his portrait of this devotional Mother Nature: "The aspect of Nature is devout. Like the figure of Jesus, she stands with bended head, and hands folded upon the breast" (*Nature*, 1002). Regendering the "she" as "he" in renaming Nature as Jesus, Emerson repeatedly makes the "dead fact" of Nature's materiality into the "quick thought" of her Son's spirit (*The American Scholar*, 1010). Sometimes merely shrinking Mother Nature—"Man . . . seems a young child, and his huge globe a toy" (*An Address*, 1020)—Emerson elsewhere debases the facts of "her" materiality: "All the facts of the animal economy, sex, nutriment, gestation, birth, growth, are symbols of the passage of the world into the soul of man, to suffer there a change, and reappear, a new and higher fact" (*The Poet*, 1074). Emerson obscures and finally absorbs the mother in order to appropriate her gestative economy and then to exalt that creativity as it reappears under the rubric of the (male) child.

Fuller's electrifying planetary woman with the stars in her eyes may well have made Emerson feel a bit *hérissé* toward his contemporary's ability to turn his created, unified world of the mind back into her phenomenological one, thus claiming for herself that affective connection to Nature he both wished to have and yet felt separate from. For the power of the mother, as Fuller imagined it, seems to return from its transcended position in *Nature* and the earlier essays to haunt Emerson in his later years with an ineradicable, stubborn influence. For example, in *Fate* (1102) he remarks, "The book of Nature is the

Book of Fate," and "Men are what their mothers made them. . . . when each comes forth from his mother's womb, the gate of gifts closes behind him." The Mother Nature of endless provision, who had supplied man with his paintbox, is now an intractable limitation; the pitfalls of genetic inheritance and the demands of the flesh cannot be ignored.

By 1860, Emerson's Nature has become a deceitful mother who reminds her child of his defects. Almost as if responding, in some fashion, to Fuller's accusation that men have foolishly discarded perfection by shutting off their wives' electricity, Emerson now blames women and specifically Mother: "Women are the element and kingdom of illusion"; therefore, "we are not very much to blame for our bad marriages. We live amid hallucinations; and this especial trap is laid to trip up our feet with, and all are tripped up first or last. But the mighty Mother who had been so sly with us, as if she felt that she owed us some indemnity, insinuates into the Pandora-box of marriage some deep and serious benefits and some great joys. We find delight in the beauty and happiness of children that makes the heart too big for the body" (*Illusions*, 1119). The world-building power of a limitless mind that, in 1836, could construct a purified reality has given way, by 1860, to a diminished hope expressed by the image of a child who swells the heart to a dangerous size: an image that introjects and then displaces a pregnancy that reminds Emerson only of mortality.

Coda: Literary History and the Recontainment of the Dynamo

Claiming the dynamism of the Virgin as an emblem of female power is in itself an overwhelming task, as Fuller's contradictory text might be said to demonstrate. She herself was aware that the overflow of her examples tried the patience of her readers. The template of the Madonna also hid, or in some cases eradicated, the very differences she claimed to celebrate. And after her death this template was placed, like a plastic map overlay, upon Fuller's major text by its first two editors, her brother Robert and her former employer, Horace Greeley. Greeley celebrates the memory of Margaret Fuller by appealing to the reading public through his invocation of the mother as oppressed provider for abandoned babes—an invocation whose appeal had an especially pathetic ring, considering Fuller's well-publicized fate (she, her Italian husband, and infant son drowned within sight of the Long Island coast). However, Robert Fuller's anxiety-ridden introduction to the posthumous reprinting of *Woman in the Nineteenth Century* has an even more striking motivation. He remarks: "It is often supposed that literary women, and those who are active and earnest in promoting great intellectual, philanthropic or religious movements, must of necessity neglect the domestic corners of life. It may be that this is sometimes so, nor can such neglect be too severely reprehended; yet this is by no means a necessary result. Some of the most devoted mothers the world has ever known ... have been women whose minds were highly cultured" (*Woman*, 6). He then presents his sister, whom he refers to as Margaret Ossoli (to remind his readers that she was literally a wife and mother) as among the devoted in motherhood.

Thus begins the recontainment that was enacted upon Margaret Fuller's memory and upon her image of what American literature, as an embryonic body of work, might have grown up to contain. Even Emerson, whom she trusted to co-parent that literature, mangled her original manuscripts as her editor—mangled them so badly that they became virtually unreadable.[18] By the end of her century this influential, magnetic woman and the body of her work seem to have suffered the sort of death or contamination of the flesh from which she sought to save Mother Nature. As a woman, she was repeatedly accused of having "fallen," despite her family's protestations that she had been properly married. In 1884 the rumor was revivified when Julian Hawthorne republished his father's journals, including the excoriation of Fuller that Sophia Hawthorne strove to repress. Fuller could not, Hawthorne remarked, "recreate or refine ... the very woman" that she was; "a rude old potency" bestirred itself, and she "fell as the very weakest of her sisters."[19]

By 1903, Henry James could observe that "her written utterance being naught," what was left of her was only a "haunting Margaret-ghost, looking out from her quiet little upper chamber at her lamen-

18. On the handling of Fuller's memoirs, see Watson, *Margaret Fuller*, 91–98; Madeleine B. Stern, "A Biographer's View of Margaret Fuller," in Robert E. Burkholder and Joel Myerson, *Critical Essays on Ralph Waldo Emerson* (Boston: G. K. Hall & Co., 1983), 264–67.

19. See Julian Hawthorne, *Nathaniel Hawthorne and His Wife* (Boston: Houghton Mifflin, 1884), 252–62. See also Oscar Cargill, "Nemesis and Nathaniel Hawthorne," in Burkholder and Myerson, *Critical Essays on Ralph Waldo Emerson*, 178–91.

table doom."[20] Yet James could not wholly consign Margaret Fuller (or her work) to the confinement of the madwoman's attic.[21] His description goes on to admit that despite her ghostliness, she "still unmistakably walks the old passages" of an American literary house[22]— as she still does. Yet in tracing out Margaret Fuller's often startling conception of how American cultural aesthetics might have been based on modulations and difference, and in remapping her "place" as central to Transcendentalism's philosophical discourse, it is clear that she more than immaterially haunts the upper regions of the house. Rather, her work offers the metaphysical foundations upon which to rebuild a cultural heritage more consistent with the diversity of the Americas and with diverse cultural experiences in the United States.

20. Henry James, *William Wetmore Story and His Friends* (Boston: Houghton Mifflin, 1903), 127–31.

21. With thanks and apologies to Sandra Gilbert and Susan Gubar; James's image for Margaret Fuller begs comparison with the patterns that emerge from Gilbert and Gubar's groundbreaking study *Madwoman in the Attic* (New Haven: Yale University Press, 1979).

22. James, *Wetmore*, 131.

Part II

Maternal Race

3

Brooding over the Ties That Bind:
Harriet Beecher Stowe's
Monumental Maternal Icon

Get a man and a woman together,—any sort o' woman you're
a mind to, don't care who 'tis—and one way or another she gets
the rule over him, and he jest has to train to her fife.
—Harriet Beecher Stowe, "The Ghost in the
Cap'n Brown House"

To write anything at all about sentimentality, domestic ideology, or
maternity in nineteenth-century America is to invoke Harriet Beecher
Stowe. As biographers and critics alike have reminded their readers,
not only was Stowe a mother to what has been termed a "brood"[1] of
children, but as an author she made motherhood and domesticity the
central motivating "pictures"[2] within the panorama of *Uncle Tom's
Cabin*. Stowe, writes Jane Tompkins, sought to proselytize an increasingly pragmatic and secular America in order to make over what was
viewed as the "private" sector of personal religion and domestic sentiment into a "public," political, didactic force.[3] Morality, for Stowe
and for the abolitionist circle into which she was born, *was* politics.
To those who might condemn her for "introducing politics into the
pulpit," she responds in *A Key to Uncle Tom's Cabin*: "Since people
will have to give an account of their political actions in the day of
judgment, it seems proper that the minister should instruct them . . .
as to their political responsibilities."[4]

1. Harriet Beecher Stowe, *Uncle Tom's Cabin*, ed. Ann Douglas (New York: Penguin
American Library, 1985), back cover. (This edition is cited hereafter as *UTC*.)
2. Not only did Stowe refer to her novel as a series of pictures, but a number of
critics have commented on the emphasis on vignettes and "photographic" set pieces
she employed to carry the story forward. See Douglas, *Feminization*, 293–309; Eric J.
Sundquist, ed., *New Essays on "Uncle Tom's Cabin"* (New York: Cambridge University
Press, 1986), and Yellin, *Women & Sisters*.
3. Tompkins, *Sensational Designs*, 123–39.
4. Harriet Beecher Stowe, *A Key to Uncle Tom's Cabin, Presenting the Original Facts
and Documents upon Which the Story Is founded together with Corroborative Statements Verifying the Truth of the Work* (Cleveland, Ohio: John P. Jewett; London: Low, 1853), 255
(hereafter cited as *KUTC*).

The Garrisonian abolitionist strategy of moral suasion embodied this ideal. Outright rebellion was discouraged; slavery would be ended by a passive Christian shift away from that sin. Gradually, moral suasion would see to the liberation of men, both "black" and "white," from the actual and moral fetters under which they were laboring unfree (a strategy, in one form or another, endorsed by nearly all the Beechers).[5] Stowe's morality, however, carried the caveat that Woman's inherent capacity for maternal love, her "essence," and thus her particular destiny were more than merely linked to moral perfection. As Stowe's cry in *A Key to Uncle Tom's Cabin* suggests—and as she frequently stated with fervent directness in private letters[6]—for her the purest essence of Christianity was the essence of femininity. If Stowe's question "When shall we be Christ-like, and not manlike, in our efforts to reclaim the fallen and wandering?" (*KUTC*, 255) asks a reader to behave like Christ, in *Uncle Tom's Cabin* those persons who either were mothers or acted as if they were mothers exemplified this Christian perfection. Indeed, as Elizabeth Ammons has shown, in much nineteenth-century American narrative the extent to which Woman took on the attributes traditionally assigned to Christ was astonishingly great. To Emerson and to Stowe alike, "Christ and his mother were virtually one."[7]

"Full of Fire and Softness . . ."

In *Uncle Tom's Cabin* this sacred medium of maternal (Christian) love resolves all strife, political and moral. As a result, all God's children will be saved. Stowe said of her Quaker maternal ideal, Rachel

5. On a variety of issues surrounding the Beecher family, see Douglas, *Feminization,* 293–309; Sundquist, *New Essays on "Uncle Tom's Cabin"*; Moira Davison Reynolds, *"Uncle Tom's Cabin" and the Mid-Nineteenth-Century United States* (Jefferson, N.C.: McFarland, 1985); Annie Fields, *Life and Letters of Harriet Beecher Stowe* (Boston: Houghton Mifflin, 1898); Charles Edward Stowe, *The Life of Harriet Beecher Stowe* (Boston: Houghton Mifflin, 1889); Forrest Wilson, *Crusader in Crinoline: The Life of Harriet Beecher Stowe* (Philadelphia: Lippincott, 1941); Jeanne Boydston, Mary Kelley, Anne Margolis, *The Limits of Sisterhood: The Beecher Sisters on Women's Rights and Woman's Sphere* (Chapel Hill: The University of North Carolina Press, 1988).

6. See Fields, *Life and Letters of Harriet Beecher Stowe*; and Boydston, Kelley, and Margolis, *The Limits of Sisterhood.*

7. Elizabeth Ammons, "Stowe's Dream of the Mother-Savior: *Uncle Tom's Cabin* and American Women Writers before the 1920s," in Sundquist, *New Essays on "Uncle Tom's Cabin,"* 167.

Halliday, "headaches and heartaches innumerable had been cured there,—difficulties spiritual and temporal solved there" (*UTC*, 215–16). And Ammons sees as the central message of *Uncle Tom's Cabin*: "Rupture the maternal bond and society [will] stand at risk. Support the work of mothers and a moral society [will] emerge."[8] Thus, as Stowe's reviewers and critics are both wont to point out, whether in praise or blame of her apocalyptic novel, it is a work obsessively focused on questions concerning the Christian morality of social, political, and familial relations within a democratic republic that had been consecrated to independence and ostensibly raised under Lady Liberty's protection. For Stowe, the hypocrisy of American independence, the "vain-glory" of a country that condemned the despotism of Europe while enslaving a whole people, could be righted only under the peaceable influence of a motherly Christianity. Maternal Christians would restore Lady Liberty to her rightful place as a motherly influence of gentleness and justice. All this without bloodshed—in Stowe's words, the Church "must undertake" this mission "because she alone can perform the work peaceably" (*KUTC*, 123, 251).

Challenging her readers to action, Stowe demanded that they put themselves in a mother's shoes: "Would you think it too much honor, could you, like Mary, have followed [Jesus] to the cross, and stood a patient sharer of that despised, unpitied agony?" Since "*that* you cannot do. That hour is over," (*KUTC*, 256), it would be prudent to look to the moral and political sin of slavery haunting the Promised Free Land, that "disastrous spot of dim eclipse, whose gradual widening shadow threatens a total darkness" (*KUTC*, 250-1). America might still become a Christian utopia, but only when, abolitionists claimed, the "immoral subversion of the appropriate relationships between Creator and moral creature"[9] was eradicated.

One of the chief anti-slavery emblems used to encapsulate this immoral subversion was the sundering of familial bonds most often figured as the theft, loss, or death of a child—an emblem to which this book will often return.[10] The horror of such a bereavement was a particularly effective tool in mid-nineteenth-century Anglo-American narrative. Not only did it attempt to stir up a Christian indignation and make personal bereavement replicate the typology of Mary's agony at the foot of the Cross, but it also appealed directly to the wide-

8. Ibid., 160.
9. Yellin, *Women & Sisters*, 7.
10. See Jacobs, *Incidents in the Life of a Slave Girl*; and Yellin, *Women & Sisters*.

spread experience of infant mortality. Further, Sylvia Hoffert and Mary Ryan both suggest, as middle-class familial patterns shifted from extended agrarian family groupings to the smaller, nuclear family units of increasingly industrial urban communities—particularly in the northern states—the cultural ideology of childhood and parenting shifted as well.[11] Childhood became progressively differentiated from adulthood. There was a gradual shift away from the cultural and religious (Calvinist) construction of the child born morally depraved toward a view of the child come from heaven morally pure.

These changes not only emphasized what became a narrative about the unique character of childhood but also heightened the bereavement associated with the loss of a child. When Stowe exhorts her reader to hearken to her novel's message—"And oh! mother that reads this, has there never been in your house a drawer, or a closet, the opening of which has been to you like the opening again of a little grave! Ah! happy mother that you are, if it has not been so" (*UTC*, 154)—she evidently appeals to what she believes is a commonly shared experience apprehended similarly by all mothers. As Hoffert notes: "The cult of motherhood, which demanded that women invest considerable time, effort and affection in their children and measured their contribution to society by their success in fulfilling their maternal obligations, made the death of an infant a particularly tragic occurrence."[12] Because many middle-class women depended upon their motherhood for self-definition, "the death of their babies deprived middle and upper-class mothers, already stripped of any significant role as economic producers, of one of their most demanding and respected domestic functions."[13] For women like Stowe, Hoffert suggests, the death of a child was a double loss, a loss of child and of self. This "peculiar sorrow"[14] is the one to which *Uncle Tom's Cabin* primarily addresses itself. Surely, Stowe would ask, any woman who had a true mother's heart could not stand by while a child was taken from a mother's loving arms.

Moreover, Hoffert points out, most "literary discussion of infant death in stories and poems published during the 1840s and 1850s was designed to offer solace to bereaved parents by confirming their belief

11. Hoffert, *Private Matters*; Dorothy C. Wertz and Richard Wertz, *Lying-in: A History of Childbirth in America* (New York: Shocken, 1979); and Ryan, *Womanhood in America*.
12. Hoffert, *Private Matters*, 170.
13. Ibid., 176–77.
14. Ibid., 180.

that their children preceded them to heaven,"[15] and many middle-class parents believed that these child-souls would act in heaven on behalf of the whole family. Like their mothers, then, children were often represented as particular agents of moral perfection. William Lloyd Garrison, when he lost his own baby daughter, had daguerre-otypes taken of her corpse, the better to remember the influence of her providential innocence.[16] Anti-slavery propaganda frequently fo-cused on the death of children, not only to prove the "humanity" of the slave but also to arouse white, middle-class empathy, as well as an apocalyptic Christian fear. Suggesting that African Americans, as the "lost children" of slavery, were the moral responsibility of their white "parents," abolitionist rhetoric created an atmosphere of both domestic and millennial responsibility. Emphasizing the sundering of child from mother as the ultimate scene of ethical depravity, aboli-tionist literature suggested time and time again that only total ruin would result if the healing union of parental affective bonds—specif-ically, maternal bonds—were either broken outright or misused as in the fiction that slavery provided such parental care for slaves. And, as Hoffert observes, the connection between this private, domestic un-ion and the public integrity of the domestic Union of the States was, on a rhetorical level, quite immediate. Not only could babies "awaken moral sensibilities in others," but they served "as a reminder of the need to preserve and perpetuate traditional ethical values that were deemed important to the survival of the American republic."[17] As Stowe has St. Clare remark, "Your little child is your only true dem-ocrat" (UTC, 273).

Furthermore, as mothers toward mid-century bore an increasingly large responsibility to socialize children properly—to raise good, con-tributing, and properly behaved American citizens, as Lydia Maria Child wished—it is not hard to understand why the abolitionist move-ment became, in large part, a white, middle-class woman's venue. Providing a language that directly linked the "private" family to the "public" country, placing morality in the political sphere, the aboli-tionist movement offered many middle-class women a way to stake a claim in their country's future without abandoning but in fact en-hancing and expanding the essentially conservative position of mother that restricted them to the domestic sphere.

15. Ibid., 170.
16. Ibid., 171.
17. Ibid., 187.

Stowe, in particular—exploiting and inverting the gendered emphasis in the sentimental, patriarchal political rhetoric of antebellum discussions that sang praises to the Founding Fathers and reverted to their authority with regard to slavery—attempted to reorient the familial-political structure around what she saw, and what antebellum maternal ideology reinforced, as its proper center. As Ann Douglas remarks in her introduction to the novel, "Stowe was astute in comparing herself writing *Uncle Tom's Cabin* with a mother entering a burning building in order to rescue her child" (*UTC*, 31). With young America in danger of becoming forever blasted by the "sins of the Fathers,"[18] it was not just her duty but, as a good mother, her imperative cultural and religious function (according to Lincoln) to come to the rescue.

Stowe often said that her novel was a faithful reproduction of God's words. In His words she revealed America's particular sin, and like the Bible—which Augustine St. Clare emphasizes as his mother's book (*UTC*, 280)—*Uncle Tom's Cabin* would redeem. Moreover, if God had dictated this book, it was through Stowe's maternal agency that God's conception was brought forth. Indeed, she continually metaphorized her writing as a bodily fruitfulness. Her authorial destiny was as a (sanctified) mother, and in some quarters her evident and proven dedication to maternity made her writings all the more authoritative. Stowe figuratively placed herself in that position to which Fuller had earlier claimed all American women might be heir: she was an American Madonna. Yet if, as an American Madonna, Stowe (like many nineteenth-century women writers in both Britain and America) imagined her function with regard to writing as essentially passive; or if, as Margaret Homans says of Victorian ideology, "from Mary comes the repeated figure of a woman who gives birth to or carries a child who represents language,"[19] thus making Mother anterior to Logos, nevertheless, Stowe's rhetorical challenge was emphatic and immediate. Particularly in America, it was precisely through such imperative maternal iconography that women like Stowe could imagine a way for Woman to minister actively to the needs of an erring nation. Bound to their children in a nearly symbiotic relation, as well as spe-

18. This biblical phrase, often used in the nineteenth century, reflected the widespread view that slavery was an inherited sin, handed down by the Founding Fathers. See also Frederick Crews, *The Sins of the Fathers* (New York: Oxford University Press, 1966).

19. Homans, *Bearing the Word*, 7–13.

cifically and relentlessly bound to be good mothers, American women, if they were to be good Americans, were thus also bound to an ideology of maternal salvation—or as Ammons names it, to the icon of the Mother-Savior who was both mother and redeemer.[20]

In the novel George Harris proclaims that for "free, enlightened America . . . to wipe from her escutcheon that bar sinister which disgraces her among nations, and is truly a curse to her as to the enslaved" (*UTC*, 610), Lady Columbia will have to conceive a new democratic order symbiotically bound to the true Christian morality of a mother's love. Thus, when Stowe has Harris justify the creation of Liberia, she has him imagine this new African nation as a republic of an even "higher" moral order than America. The secular revolutions she saw beginning in 1848 were "but the birth-pangs of an hour of universal peace and brotherhood" (*UTC* 611), and the most perfect fruit of this birthing would be Columbia's new-born daughter, Liberia.

Recall that Lincoln's *Gettysburg Address* began as follows: "Fourscore and seven years ago, our *fathers* brought forth *upon* this continent a new nation, conceived *in* liberty and dedicated to the proposition that all *men* are created equal (emphasis added). Had Stowe devised a similar speech, it might have read something like this: "Fourscore and seven years ago, our *mothers* brought forth *within* this continent a new nation, conceived *by* Liberty and dedicated to the proposition that all *her children* are created equal."

Cassy and Marie

Of course, there were other and decidedly less sanguine views of what would happen to the United States when and if the mothers of America flocked to the redemption of their enslaved "children" and brought forth a new nation—and, perhaps, a new "race." Several early reviewers of *Uncle Tom's Cabin* slyly suggested that Harriet Beecher Stowe's interest in her mulatto character George Harris was far more than a pious one.[21] Meanwhile, African-American freedwomen such as Harriet Jacobs and Sojourner Truth struggled not only with accusations of inherently improper sexuality but also with the agony of maternal ties to children who were often born of rape, or sold away,

20. Ammons, "Stowe's Dream," 160.
21. Cited in Yellin, *Women & Sisters*, 29–52; and Walker, *Moral Choices*, 244–48.

or identified by the so-called Christian culture in which they were enslaved as mongrel bastards because they were legally (for the most part) "fatherless."[22]

Was Woman savior or fiend? Would Eve, the sinning first mother, or Mary, the redeeming virgin mother, prove the more accurate representation of American Woman, American Mother? President Tyler's inflammatory outburst (noted earlier) that Woman was "to be made the instrument of destroying our political paradise" conjures up the anger and fiery power of trespass inherent in the dichotomy of the Christian Eve/Mary, or the Whore/Madonna split. Pure angels, after all, must have their opposites in order to substantiate their purity. Stowe's belief that Christian, feminine morality would triumph over the masculinized marketplace and that moral suasion could abolish a traffic in human beings is written out in *Uncle Tom's Cabin* as a relatively benign conquest, a gradual dawning of righteousness. She was wont to assert that a motherly religion would prevail where a paternalized politics had failed.

But what lies behind these images of passive resistance? Despite the perfection and placid unity Stowe writes into her Quaker paradise, it is described not as the New World but rather as utopian Eden, the lost country; Rachel Halliday is likened not to Mary but to Eve, "the original mother" (*UTC*, 222). When Eliza Harris dreams of safety there, what she imagines is obviously a dream landscape, a space dependent upon the strong, protecting arms of her husband. And, in order to guarantee such a paradise, Stowe supplies her passive resisters with a store of brute strength and pistols. In other words, looking to the New Testament, one cannot help but note how Christ himself reacted to the marketplace; his fury and direct action with regard to the money changers in his Father's house suggests that Stowe's maternalized Christian politics are not fueled by the tears of passivity alone. Whether *Uncle Tom's Cabin* makes politics subservient to typology, as Tompkins insists,[23] or whether this novel in appealing to the heart rather than the head is "apolitical" or perhaps depoliticizing, as David Leverenz and Richard Yarborough have both suggested,[24] it

22. Harriet Jacobs's struggle to own her children, despite the fact that in the eyes of her northern friends they were illegitimate, is a good example of the problem (see Chapter 5 below).

23. Tompkins, *Sensational Designs*, 126–28.

24. David Leverenz, *Manhood and the American Renaissance* (Ithaca: Cornell University Press, 1989), 196; and Richard Yarborough, "Strategies of Black Characterization in

does not *wholly* hinder active revolution. Lurking behind the maternal, Christian ideology of resigned, dogged docility are fires of passionate rage. Note Aunt Chloe's reaction to having her "old man" stolen. "Aunt Chloe shut and corded the box, and, getting up, looked gruffly on the trader, her tears seeming suddenly turned to sparks of fire" (*UTC*, 168). Tears as sparks of fire? It is hardly coincidental that Haley the slave trader has earlier been described as a man who'd "sell his own mother at a good percentage" (*UTC*, 68). In Margaret Fuller, female electricity improperly channeled may cause electrocution; in Stowe, motherhood may be a vale of tears, but those tears may prove as caustic as pure lye, a kind of domestic vitriol.

Of course, as David Leverenz has shown, it is clear that Stowe often naïvely recast "incipient sectional and racial conflicts as a sex-role struggle that any woman can win. . . . At the most obvious rhetorical level, *Uncle Tom's Cabin* insists that what white men do to black people can be changed if men can be brought to feel what any mother feels."[25] Moreover, the novel demonstrates that although maternal feelings are supposed to be forever and always benign, the maternal heart is also infused with a potentially destructive rage. The Victorian iconography of the "Angel in the House" insists that angels have their opposites in devils, and although Stowe attempts to keep the two separate, the dividing line is never entirely clear. Add the Old Testament imagery depicting angels as the fiery instruments of God's vengeance, and "mother" begins to look anything but domestic or benign. Thus, if *Uncle Tom's Cabin* seeks to demonstrate that nothing less than the survival of republican democracy itself rested in the mother's hands, it less obviously chronicles the full-blown vengeance such a motherhood—defined by a Christianized patriarchy as the tender regulator and gentle scourge of God the Father—can command when thwarted. As Stowe wrote, if slavery should continue, "the country will have reason to tremble, when it remembers that the fate of nations is in the hands of One who is very pitiful, and of tender compassion" (*UTC*, 625). The One is Jesus, but Stowe's identification of motherhood with godliness makes the One an ambiguous agent. In short, as Leverenz notes, "Stowe's ideology of empowering women through their role as mothers holds together a contradictory mixture of rage, empathy and

Uncle Tom's Cabin and the Early Afro-American Novel," in Sundquist, *New Essays on "Uncle Tom's Cabin,"* 72.

25. Leverenz, *Manhood,* 190–91.

accusation under the broad umbrella of a conversion-oriented theology, one obviously indebted to her father."[26]

But is this mixture of rage and empathy, in the context of antebellum cultural logic, truly contradictory? Leverenz names the image of the Tender Avenger a "duplicitous paradox" and points to the book's tragic mulatta figure, Cassy, as one emblem of that duplicity: "At the heart of this book about motherly love," he says, "Stowe's strongest female character is twice a mother murdering her child."[27] And indeed, much feminist commentary too has focused on Cassy (as well as Topsy) as a possible figuration of a supposedly subversive, if murderous, female power.[28]

Certainly, Cassy's liberating use of the "madwoman in the attic" scenario for her own ends has its appeal, for although Cassy is responsible, in her position as slave-mother and ghost-mother alike, for the deaths both of her own unnamed son and of Simon Legree, she does not pay for this "infanticide" with her life. She is, in fact, exonerated and rewarded: she is textually exonerated because she had been stung to moral madness by the cruel loss of her first two children; she is eventually rewarded by being reunited with those children after she has been "saved" from her moral depravity through Uncle Tom's martyrdom. There is something undeniably refreshing—and "strong"—in the mere fact of Cassy's survival. But Stowe's Gothic development of Legree's plantation, Karen Halttunen has argued, casts Cassy in the dubious role of a dark Medusa, or of Henry Ward Beecher's "Strange Woman." She may be a betrayed mother, but she is also clearly a prostitute and something of a witch, that "fallen woman [who] was an 'empowered outcast' whose freedom from the restricting bounds of domesticity endowed her with demonic magical powers, including the power to mesmerize and paralyze men."[29] Furthermore, as Yarborough argues, Cassy's power and force are racially ascribed to her Anglo-Saxon

26. Ibid., 203.

27. Ibid., 198.

28. See Douglas, Feminization, 293–309; Elizabeth Ammons, "Heroines in Uncle Tom's Cabin," American Literature 49 (May 1977): 66–79, rpt. in Ammons, Critical Essays on Harriet Beecher Stowe (Boston: G. K. Hall, 1980); Gillian Brown, "Getting in the Kitchen with Dinah: Domestic Policies in Uncle Tom's Cabin," American Quarterly 36 (Fall 1984): 503–23; and Tompkins, Sensational Designs, 123–39.

29. Karen Halttunen, "Gothic Imagery and Social Reform: The Haunted Houses of Lyman Beecher, Henry Ward Beecher, and Harriet Beecher Stowe," in Sundquist, New Essays on "Uncle Tom's Cabin," 116.

forebears. No character designated as a "full black" in the panorama of *Uncle Tom's Cabin* revolts against "fate" the way Eliza Harris, Cassy, and George Harris do.[30] Stowe thus equates female desire with the witchery and depravity assigned to overtly sexual women, and "Afric" denotes a dependency and malleability associated with children. Pro-slavery advocates did the same.[31] Cassy is both literally and figuratively "dark"—a mad creature who is not in control of herself. This "darkness" distances her from acceptance into the American republic, as her ultimate "removal" to Liberia shows. Although Stowe later regretted her decision to move her "redeemed" black characters to Liberia, their emigration signals Stowe's own culturally ingrained prejudice. Cassy's fate and the depiction of Eliza illustrate their author's inability to imagine a positive sexual power for women beyond the patriarchally defined realm of legitimate Christian motherhood, as Mrs. Shelby and her "good child" Eliza Harris demonstrate.

Nevertheless, Stowe's depictions of the slave mother do illustrate the schizophrenia inherent—and still endemic—to that state named "maternity," a difficulty that Harriet Jacobs's *Incidents in the Life of a Slave Girl* more forcibly addresses (see Chapters 4 and 5). To be respected and accepted as a woman was to be both sexually passive and reproductively abundant, restricted to the home yet responsible for the creation of an obedient and vigorous citizenry. In other words, Woman was to be active and passive at once, to play the role of what late twentieth-century slang, significantly, often refers to as "bitch."[32] Although Stowe's own race, class, and sectional prejudices set up stereotypes that serve as blinders to this maternal paradox and allowed her, as an author, to ascribe the energetic, cruel hysteria of Marie St. Clare and Cassy's murderous fury to supposedly wholly different sources, it is interesting to note how these two different representations of Woman share oddly parallel sexual biographies. After all, both characters thought they were married to "white" men who loved them, when neither Cassy's "husband" nor Augustine St. Clare does, in fact, love his wife. Both Cassy and Marie suffer the loss of their children, and both women's excessive behavior can be ascribed to a radical perversion of maternal love. Stowe's rhetoric demands that Cassy be read as redeemable victim,

30. Yarborough, "Strategies," 48–50.
31. Ibid., 61.
32. Bitches, it should be noted, breed.

Marie as unredeemable victimizer. But the portraiture also suggests that the patriarchal paradigm of the maternal creates, fosters, and condones a sexual and psychological violence that denies women—particularly as mothers—both self-interest and self-determination. Slavery, race prejudice and class divisions reinforced by a mystified madonna/whore split allowed white, middle-class women to claim the madonna while denying the basic fact that both "madonna" and "whore" were not only women, but that both had the reproductive potential to be mothers.

The madonna/whore paradigm, however, denied the enslaved African-American woman both femininity and motherhood. It required her to be an erotic sexual object without having an eros of her own and to bear child after child without the considerable benefits associated with being acknowledged, in the culture, as a mother. The paradigm also required of many "white" mothers a denial of personal desire coupled with a willingness to bear repeatedly, although clearly under less direct compulsion. This was often a killing combination, particularly for any woman trapped by slavery, poverty, or an abusive husband. African-American mothers who actively resisted their enslavement through murder, infanticide, or escape were condemned as "unnatural" mothers despite the fact that they were not supposed to have maternal feelings at all. And for those who were freedwomen, maternal iconography made it extremely difficult to claim their children or their homes, particularly if either they or their children were of a "mixed" racial heritage. Unmarried women who had children and who worked outside the home to try to support those children ran the risk of being defined as not-women—or, in the case of prostitutes, literal demons—and of having their children taken from them.[33]

Women who could not bear or did not bear were seen as tragically doomed, pathetic, frivolous, or useless. For instance, the only childless white woman in *Uncle Tom's Cabin* is Aunt Ophelia, who is repeatedly ridiculed as an old biddy. She has a rather ominous name in light of the popularity of *Hamlet* to the nineteenth-century imagination, though she is neither as beautiful nor as tragic as her Shakespearean namesake. Aunt Ophelia—Topsy's "Miss Feely" (Miss Sentimental?)—is represented as narrow and foolish, a figure of loss and dep-

---

33. See Hoffert, *Private Matters*; Ryan, *Womanhood*; and Grossberg, "Who Gets the Child?"

rivation. It is not until she can be trained to become Topsy's "good" mother that her life has any meaning. In the case of slave women, the "uselessness" of childlessness could have murderously devastating results, as slave narratives bear out and as Stowe's character Prue shows.

The paradoxical or contradictory duplicity of Woman is, of course, yet another manifestation of the standard device Madonna/ Whore or Dark Lady/Light Lady. But what is seldom noted about this twinning is the way in which the Dark Lady/Light Lady opposition is related to woman's primary cultural function as the mother of a future citizenry. On the surface, as previously noted, it is apparent that the "good" Christian, asexual, white, middle-class mother is the Light Lady while the "bad" sexualized mother is the Dark Lady, a role connoting all ethnic, cultural, and moral variations on darkness.[34] The coherence of the opposition, however, is particularly friable at the hinge of reproduction. For how can Woman become Mother without sexual intercourse? To conceive implies desire and pregnancy denotes it, no matter how much Madonna may divert that energy.[35]

Moreover, the paradox of female reproduction and desire in the mid-nineteenth century generated class and race divisions among women as they struggled to fulfill, resist and in some cases redefine their role. The image of Pregnant Woman—a sight that an increasingly professionalized medical establishment urged should be kept private, hidden in the bedroom or parlor[36]—or that of Woman-and-Child, disrupted the neat separation of Light from Dark Lady. Both the original George Thomas illustrations for *Uncle Tom's Cabin* (1852), and the later James Daugherty illustrations (1929, in the Coward-McCann edition) point to the sorts of continuing confusions the mother-and-child figure could raise. Thomas creates a beatific

34. See Dorothy Dinnerstein, *The Mermaid and the Minotaur* (New York: Harper Colophon Books, 1977); and Claire Kahane, "The Gothic Mirror," in *The (M)Other Tongue: Essays in Feminist Psychoanalytic Interpretation*, ed. Shirley Nelson Garner, Claire Kahane, and Madelon Sprengnether (Ithaca: Cornell University Press, 1985).

35. The allusion to the 1980s and 1990s singer and popular icon Madonna is deliberate, particularly given her vexed and politically confused involvement in/with/ against African-American culture, as evidenced by the lawsuits arising from her video *Truth or Dare*, and in the questions raised by *Paris Is Burning* with reference to her appropriation of voguing. Briefly, see bell hooks, "Is Paris Burning?" in *Black Looks* (Boston: South End Press, 1992).

36. Hoffert, *Private Matters*, 183–85.

Figure 3. Harry's Breakfast, George Thomas's 1852 illustration of Eliza and Harry in a typical, iconic mother-and-child pose.

madonna-and-child icon for Eliza and Harry (Fig. 3), but his vision of Eliza on the ice suggests fright on Harry's part and a kind of witchy flight on Eliza's. Her grip on him seems rather tight, and indeed Harry seems taken aback by his mother (Fig. 4). Is Mama Eliza a heroic savior or a madwoman? Daugherty offers visual aids to clarify interpretation: Eliza now has the benefit of a lifting archangel to explain her witchy flight; she needs the help because devilish white hands reach up out of the ice to stop her (Fig. 5). In both sets of illustrations these African-American characters are depicted as "white," so far as black and white illustration techniques can make the distinction.

Another way to look at such confusions is to note that if Cassy's "liberation" to Liberia and her moral redemption are, as Leverenz

Figure 4. George Thomas's 1852 illustration of Eliza and Harry on the ice: "With one wild cry and flying leap, she vaulted sheer over the turbid current to the shore."

Figure 5. James Daugherty's 1929 illustration of the same scene. Note how the nineteenth-century depiction offers no clue as to what mother and child are flying from—or into?—or whether they themselves constitute a threat. The twentieth-century version depicts angelic protection and attributes menace to supernatural ice hands.

states, defined by the Laws of the White Father's House, so are Marie St. Clare's cruelty and hysteria. Both end up as outsiders. Cassy remains a sexual and ethnic "outcast," despite the power of her "redemption," if Stowe will not find a home for an empowered Cassy in her homeland; and Marie St. Clare's self-absorption makes her a moral outcast, even though she wields an actual, if despotic, worldly power to determine the fate of her own "fortune." Thus empowerment per se became demonic in a female form because the "strength" or "activity" of that "power" was determined by patriarchal definitions that had welded masculinity to power. Energy—sexual, political, social— could not be gendered female, no matter how Stowe tried in *Uncle Tom's Cabin* to make maternity powerful, since her own definition of the maternal and thus her matrifocal utopia, as Leverenz has pointed out, rested "on a paternalistic base."[37] When Cassy initiates her escape plan, Emmeline—toward whom Cassy has been developing a maternal relation—nearly faints (as the good woman ought to do). Cassy's response is to pull a knife on her "daughter." This portrait of strength requires the derangement and sundering of domestic and most specifically, maternal bonds as defined by white antebellum imagery: a woman cannot be "dark" and a good mother, too. Only as Cassy's "darker" nature is redeemed can she become the good mother and the good grandmother—and in that process she becomes "whiter," a more demure figure, her rage and knife-wielding strength leeched away.

Ironically, however, Marie St. Clare's portrait shows that the "whiteness" of cultural approval is also often merely a cover, like the sheet Cassy wears to help Legree's hallucinations along. The solution for both of Stowe's characters would be to become the Madonna. But this, of course, is no solution at all. However much Stowe believed in the mystery of the Virgin Mary, she knew as well that being Madonna was impossible. *That* hour—the Virgin Mary's sacrificial moment of her Son's death—was over. The Madonna solution also clearly deactivates any power of self-determination. Mary accepted her fate without anger or resistance; both Cassy and Marie St. Clare each briefly exhibit a certain resistance. And however much Stowe would identify their power as "evil," there is still a sense of delight in the text about the way both characters shrewdly, if cruelly, exercise their desires to get their way.

37. Leverenz, *Manhood*, 195.

A Different Sort of Bounteous Lap?

In the end, what Stowe's monument to maternal iconography cannot address is that the only evident source of power within legitimate,
patriarchal motherhood is the power of negation. Death—the eternal
death of damnation, as the most extreme representation of negative
power—becomes the only legitimate threat that Woman can bring to
bear, as it were, in *Uncle Tom's Cabin*. No matter how benign, the
persuasive arguments Stowe's women characters use on their families,
or on those they love, are invariably veiled death or suicide threats.

Moreover, as Hoffert remarks, much antebellum literature "con-
veyed the idea that infant death was an instrument through which
traditional values vital to the American republic could be perpetuated,
implying that the demands of the cult of motherhood could be ful-
filled as much by the death of an infant as by the birth of one."[38]
Ironically, then, infanticide becomes nearly a logical mandate for
mothers who would do best by their children and their country. Indeed, as Hoffert goes on to suggest, the mother who would become
truly strong and dutiful, most Christian toward her family and patriotic to her nation, is the mother who urges death upon her children.
The rhetoric of Civil War enlistment, urging mothers to urge their sons
into the ranks, bears this out.[39]

Thus, in a cultural economy where death, as Stowe wrote, was "a
better country" (*UTC* 416), Mother and Home, as St. Clare tells us,
become defined as outside of and the opposite to daily life. Stowe's
supposed celebration of motherhood is, in many ways, a requiem
mass. It would seem, in fact, that the most enduring paradox of sentimental maternity is not that it reveals Woman to be empowered
through duplicity—promising life yet delivering death as Leverenz
argues—but rather that woman's reproductivity, her supposedly
sacred ability to conceive, was both required and yet denied. Conception, her essential function, was also a de facto condemnation, represented as a death-dealing stasis rather than as a life-oriented action.
The paradoxical logic of mid-nineteenth-century patriarchal motherhood not only deemed that Woman must be defined by a sexualized
function—mother—yet behave as if nonsexual; it also insisted that a

38. Hoffert, *Private Matters*, 170.
39. Douglas, *Feminization*, 198–240. That American mothers should urge their sons
to lay down their lives for the "cause" of democracy remains a popular notion, as
evidenced by the rhetoric surrounding both the Vietnam War and the Gulf War.

mother's real power, and her gift to her nation, was not to reproduce and proliferate but to restrict, deny, and perhaps kill. Given this logic, the surprise is not that Stowe had Cassy kill one of her children but rather that Cassy had not killed them all. Like Margaret Wilkins Freeman's "Old Woman Magoun," who chooses to murder her granddaughter rather than see the child bartered off and sexually abused as payment for her drunkard father's gambling debt,[40] Cassy's choice of murder ironically becomes the rational, moral, and laudable choice: better dead than used and violated. Indeed, Cassy's attempt to frighten Legree to death might be read not as a malicious act of rebellion but rather as a good "mother's" sworn duty to move her son quickly into a better world. Images of child death were frequently invoked as narrative set pieces of illustrative morality. One framed by Lydia Maria Child for *The Mother's Book* showed the beauty of a faith that promised—particularly to the slave—that the hard things in this world would be righted in the next:

A friend, who had resided some time in Brazil, told an anecdote, which was extremely pleasing to me, on account of the distinct and animating faith it implied. When walking on the beach, he overtook a negro woman, carrying a large tray upon her head. Thinking she had fruit or flowers to sell, he called to her to stop. On being asked what she had in her tray, she lowered the burthen upon the sand, and gently uncovered it. It was a dead negro babe, covered with a neat white robe, with a garland around its head, and a bunch of flowers in the little hands, that lay clasped upon its bosom. "Is this your child?" asked my friend. "It *was* mine a few days ago," she said; "but it is the Madonna's now. I am carrying it to the church to be buried. It is a little angel now." "How beautifully you have laid it out!" said the traveller. "Ah," replied the negro, "that is nothing compared to the beautiful bright wings with which it is flying through heaven!" (*TMB*, 82)

In this sentimental economy, a woman's only legitimate form of passionate, creative expression is in the arrangement of death; as Jane Tompkins has noted, death is, for Stowe, where Christian power is most truly active and revealed.[41] "What may look . . . like an ideology

---

40. Mary Wilkins Freeman, "Old Woman Magoun," in *Short Fiction of Sarah Orne Jewett and Mary Wilkins Freeman*, ed. Barbara H. Solomon (New York: New American Library, 1979), 485–502.

41. Tompkins, *Sensational Designs*, 127.

of passionlessness," says Leverenz, "is really [a] return to the older Christian meaning of passion: intense suffering, symbolized by Christ's passion and crucifixion."[42]

Yet because this passion is coded not as "life" but as "death," fears about Woman's fiendishness were also justified. Making Uncle Tom an African-American male Madonna—a "white" antebellum woman voguing, as Elizabeth Ammons's reading of him suggests[43]—or representing Little Eva as a "white" female Christ may have challenged traditional antebellum narrative constructions of race and gender roles. The sacrificial deaths of these characters, however, also fulfill traditional antebellum assumptions. Says Hortense Spillers, "The *requirements of sacrifice* which Stowe's critics inevitably point out as death's *raison d'être* in the novel and which Stowe herself reinforces in the narrative's habits of pathos, seem to galvanize the murderous instincts of a patriarchal, phallogocentric synthesis rather than effectively challenge them."[44]

And yet, Spillers goes on to argue, the relationship between Little Eva and Uncle Tom, while designed to evade picturing adult heterosexual desire, also allusively underscores it as pervasive and indeed interracial. Antebellum cultural taboos regarding miscegenation (taboos particularly intense and potentially explosive where the relations between "white woman" and "black man" were concerned) preemptively disengage sexuality from this relation: "The relationship between the pre-pubescent 'white' female and the adult 'black' male is shrouded from the start by a past history," for the prohibition against seeing Eva and Tom's relation as anything but innocent "was already vividly in place for Stowe's generation of readers."[45] But not only does Eva utter what Spillers calls "an astonishing sequence of lines" with regard to Tom, a sequence that marries money to an active female desire—" 'Papa, do buy him! it's no matter what you pay,' whispered Eva, softly, getting up on a package, and putting her arm around her father's neck. 'You have money enough I know. I want him' " (*UTC*, 236)—but the descriptive attributes Tom acquires in the course of his "courtship" of Little Eva endow him with a far more sexualized image

---

42. Leverenz, *Manhood*, 203.

43. Ammons, "Stowe's Dream," 155–90.

44. Hortense J. Spillers, "Changing the Letter: The Yokes, the Jokes of Discourse, or Mrs. Stowe, Mr. Reed," in McDowell and Rampersad, *Slavery and the Literary Imagination*, 20–21.

45. Ibid., 23–25.

than has been generally ascribed to him. After all, Stowe does call Tom "a very Pan in the manufacture of whistles of all sizes and sorts. His pockets were full of miscellaneous articles of attraction" (*UTC*, 232). Spillers remarks dryly that "a captive person with his pockets full of play toys strikes a perfectly ludicrous image to my mind . . . but if the seductive resonance of 'Pan,' 'cunning,' the 'pockets' is allowed to do its work, then we come to regard aspects of this *persona*— 'sweet-tempered,' Bible-toting, *Uncle* Tom—as a potentially 'dirty old man,' 'under wraps.' " During Reconstruction, in fact, racist depictions of African-American men as rapists would exploit the image of powerful, heavyset Tom as a molester of angelic white girls.[46] All this casts a rather different light on illustrations of Tom as Madonna.

Spillers's angle of vision deftly uncovers one of the culturally forbidden, supposedly errant pathways of consenting desire which antebellum strictures attempted to repress and deny, and her resexualization of "Uncle" Tom also points to the variety of ways in which this figure unravels apparently stable social relations. That is, granting Spillers her rereading of Eva and Tom's relation as revelatory with regard to racial taboos surrounding "white woman" and "black man," one might also note that such a reading reveals the extent to which the cultural taboo supposedly forbidding father-daughter incest was hardly writ in stone, particularly, as Spillers notes, when such incest was not in fact forbidden at all but rendered invisible, under the slavocracy.[47] Further, though, the problematic concatenation of imagery Stowe uses to create Uncle Tom briefly makes him over not just into Ammons's white, moral savior-mother, or into Leverenz's Christian "beaten-down self" transformed "into triumphant power for both sexes;"[48] using Spillers as a guide, one might also read Tom as a fleeting image of fertility, an affirmation of proliferating reproductivity—the "dark" mother of reproductive capability—whose "pocket" produces a whole world. The scenario of Uncle Tom sitting contentedly with Eva on his lap or holding her in his arms was, indeed, disturbing enough to have been consistently presented on the popular stage and in illustrations as benign and desexualized in a variety of attempts to domesticate and reduce that relation.[49] Tom, still captive

46. Ibid., 26–27.
47. Ibid., 27.
48. Leverenz, *Manhood*, 195.
49. Sundquist (introduction to *New Essays on "Uncle Tom's Cabin"*) and Yarborough ("Strategies") both mention how Uncle Tom and Little Eva were popularized on the

and still alive in this scene, has not yet achieved the role of paternal liberator, "Father" Tom, which his martyrdom will secure for him. Nor is he, after all is said and done, fully identifiable as a "mother" redeemer. Stowe's representation of him as a site of confusion concerning traditional gender and racial markings points to an elusive and unrepresentable conceptual energy that is neither precisely male nor precisely female, and certainly not precisely legitimate; to a conceptual sensuality that might exist without becoming either sinful or destructive. Might "Tom" then be an attempt to construct an image for the power of Eve without having to make that power either sexually Evil or virginally Eva?

Certainly Tom is a "man" in Stowe's depiction of him, yet as a captive he does not possess a fully empowered masculinity as traditionally narrated. By the same token, being a black Christian with the heart of a white man, as Stowe denominated him, the figure cannot be read unproblematically as either "black" or "white." Indeed, Stowe makes him into an odd source of an unidentifiable yet vital, almost palpable, creativity. To echo Spillers, where *did* all those toys in his pocket come from? The image of Tom with Eva on his bounteous lap, his pockets stuffed with Pan's toys just for her, seems both to mimic and yet to disrupt what the mother-and-child icon supposedly signaled in Christian terms—that is, the legitimate potency of paternal genealogy—and shift it into something like the potency of potentiality.

Uncle Tom's Cabin, with its emphasis on death and martyrdom, feeds into antebellum gender mores and racial stereotypes. Nevertheless, by taking Christian, patriarchal logic to its extreme and accepting death as a better country, a Motherland, Stowe's imagery also reveals the denied crux of a patriarchal system's paradoxical death wish. In other words, the loss of Uncle Tom and of Little Eva ironically demonstrates that by denying legitimacy to a conceptual creativity culturally coded as "maternal," antebellum patriarchal logic invoked, rather than forestalled, its own annihilation. Forcing its children to prefer the "better home" of death to living in the bitter prison house it had built for them, the paternalized state subsidized a project that condemned its own offspring.

---

stage and in the movies. Sundquist (5) theorizes that these spinoffs may have been popular attempts to recontain the power of Stowe's novel. See also Harry Birdoff, *The World's Greatest Hit: "Uncle Tom's Cabin"* (New York: S. F. Vanni, 1947); and Gunning, "Facing 'A Red Record.'"

4

Frederick Douglass's
Strategic Sentimentality

Anything dead coming back to life hurts.
—Toni Morrison, *Beloved*

"America," wrote Frederick Douglass in an 1846 letter to William Lloyd Garrison, "will not allow her children to love her."[1] Sketching here a sentimental scenario that genders an enslaving nation and places the enslaved in an apparently benevolent—desiring-to-love—familial economy, Douglass also attacks the "heartland" by describing "her" as a vampire whose "most fertile fields drink daily of the warm blood of my outraged sisters" (*MB/MF*, 225). America would not simply kill its own, as Stowe's vision might suggest; the state would also eat its own. Despite such a picture of Gothic horror, however, Douglass envisions a time when the demon will yield milk instead of exacting blood. To him, America was not by nature so heartless; how could she be, if she were true to the "great law of liberty, written on every human heart" (*MB/MF*, 279)?

In other words, how could a nation, repeatedly personified as Lady Liberty and favored by, if not an emblem of, Mother Nature continue to endure slavery's perversions?[2] Liberty was Mother Nature's body language; a "birthright," it "looked from every star, smiled in every calm, breathed in every wind and moved in every storm" (*MB/MF*, 101). Enslavement was an unnatural convulsion of a (maternal) homeland's heart.

Douglass manipulated antebellum sentimental ideology thus, to

1. Frederick Douglass, *My Bondage and My Freedom*, ed. William L. Andrews (Urbana: University of Illinois Press, 1987), 225 (hereafter cited as *MB/MF*).
2. On Douglass's use of nineteenth-century angel/demon conventions, see Carby, *Reconstructing Womanhood*, 28–29. On America depicted as a woman, see Banta, *Imaging American Women*, 45–221; and Yellin, *Women & Sisters*, esp. 113–17.

make a mother's heart emblematic of an ideal social body, an America who could embrace all her children.[3] That Douglass should also imagine a horrific perversion of maternal love as an analogy to American slavery is not surprising. Although slave women were not placed in the role of demon, a desecration of familial ties was a central feature of nineteenth-century African-American narrative, as previously noted, and a staple of abolitionist texts.[4] Tableaux of familial disorder were used to demonstrate that to sunder the natural bond of love between mother and child was to incur irrevocable loss.[5] As critics have claimed, in 1845 Douglass made his own maternal loss an image for slavery. In her article "The Punishment of Esther: Frederick Douglass and the Construction of the Feminine," Jenny Franchot argues that a striking aspect of Douglass's writing is the use of the female per se as a synecdoche for slavery, a device that gives him the rhetorical means to "master the subject" of a feminized slavery.[6] Thus Douglass aligns his identity with the white patriarch's, she argues, particularly in his "paradoxical exploitation of the very feminine which [he] seek[s] to rescue."[7]

Although it is clear that Douglass did endorse an Emersonian self-

3. Although it is clear that Douglass often advocated "union" rather than "separation," his investment in assimilationist policies shifted over time. For his changing thoughts on being an "American," see Wilson J. Moses, *The Golden Age of Black Nationalism, 1850–1925* (New York: Oxford University Press, 1978), 83–105; Waldo E. Martin, *The Mind of Frederick Douglass* (Chapel Hill: University of North Carolina Press, 1984), 200–223; David W. Blight, *Frederick Douglass' Civil War: Keeping Faith in Jubilee* (Baton Rouge: Lousiana State University Press, 1989), esp. 65–115.

4. On the emblem of maternal loss in slave narrative and abolitionist discourse, see Yellin, *Women & Sisters*, 88–96; Jacobs, *Incidents in the Life of a Slave Girl*, 91–96, 141; Carby, *Reconstructing Womanhood*, 20–40; Ammons, "Stowe's Dream," 155–95.

5. Harriet Beecher Stowe's is perhaps the easiest voice to cite with regard to the connection between millennial apocalypse and maternal separation (see *KUTC*); see also Blight, *Frederick Douglass' Civil War*, 70–73, on millennialism in nineteenth-century American culture.

6. Jenny Franchot, "The Punishment of Esther: Frederick Douglass and the Construction of the Feminine," in *Frederick Douglass: New Literary and Historical Essays*, ed. Eric J. Sundquist (New York: Cambridge University Press, 1990), 141. Regarding the figure of the slave woman in general, see William Andrews, *To Tell a Free Story* (Urbana: University of Illinois Press, 1986); Houston Baker, Jr., *The Journey Back: Issues in Black Literature and Criticism* (Chicago: University of Chicago Press, 1980); Baker, *Blues, Ideology, and Afro-American Literature* (Chicago: University of Chicago Press, 1984); Carby, *Reconstructing Womanhood*; Jacobs, *Incidents in the Life of a Slave Girl*; Robert B. Stepto, *From Behind the Veil: A Study of Afro-American Narration* (Chicago: University of Illinois Press, 1976); Valerie Smith, *Self-Discovery and Authority in Afro-American Narrative* (Cambridge, Mass.: Harvard University Press, 1987).

7. Franchot, "Punishment," 158–59.

reliance congruent with the configurations of antebellum white masculinity,[8] I argue that a detailed examination of his revisions of his
own rhetoric of mastery reveals just how complex and equivocal his
use of that self-reliance was.

Flesh and Text

Under Emersonian self-reliance, to have authority means to be transcendent, "free"; still, as Douglass's earliest narrative of his life shows,
this independence is structured on an ability to induce ignorance and
fear: "I would keep the merciless slaveholder profoundly ignorant of
the means of flight adopted by the slave. Let him be left to feel his
way in the dark, . . . let him feel . . . he is running the risk of having
his hot brains dashed out by an invisible agency."[9] Here the positions
of slaveholder and slave are neatly reversed, inverting what constitutes and who controls the hinge between knowledge and ignorance.[10]
Authority is welded not simply to self-reliance but to an active ability
to produce an "invisible [punitive] agency." A signal aspect of that
agency, as the passage above makes clear, is a murderous control over
the body—a control assured in slavery by the whip. Under the whip,
a body trembles, weeps, and may have its brains dashed out. In lacking (mind) control, the body is identified with hysteria and thus with
the feminine, as it was predominantly constructed.[11] Douglass's *Narrative*, to evoke sympathy, literalizes this identification in Aunt Hes-

8. Smith, *Self-Discovery*, 26–28, points out how rhetorically indebted Douglass was
to Emersonian self-reliance as an ideology; however, she also carefully notes how Douglass's voice "supercedes the power of ancillary documents" (Garrison and Phillips) to
contain it. On Douglass's investment in and rhetorical use of paternalism, see also Baker,
Blues; Leverenz, *Manhood*, 128–32; Walker, *Moral Choices*, 213–54; Eric J. Sundquist,
"Frederick Douglass: Literacy and Paternalism," *Raritan* 6 (Fall 1986): 108–24.

9. Frederick Douglass, *The Narrative of the Life of Frederick Douglass, an American
Slave, Written by Himself*, ed. Houston A. Baker, Jr. (New York: Penguin American Library, 1982), 38 (hereafter cited as N).

10. Henry Louis Gates, Jr., described this phenomenon in Douglass's work; see his
"Binary Opposition in Chapter One of *The Narrative of the Life of Frederick Douglass, an
American Slave, Written by Himself*," in *Afro-American Literature: The Reconstruction of
Instruction*, ed. Robert B. Stepto and Dexter Fisher (New York: Modern Language As-
sociation, 1978).

11. On the association of hysteria with femininity, see Cott, *The Bonds of Womanhood*,
and Smith-Rosenberg, *Disorderly Conduct*.

ter's beating.[12] Such logic requires, however, that (feminine) flesh, open to domination, must be transcended.

Thus the *Narrative* appears to define conceptual cognition in opposition to the corporeal: to be trapped in the physical is to lose the ability to conceive abstraction. As Douglass wrote, the *idea* of liberty, a concept he had acquired through reading the Bible and the *Columbian Orator*, was nearly lost in mind-numbing plantation labor: "In thinking of my life, I almost forgot my liberty" (*N*, 135) he wrote, suggesting that one's physical life and one's concept of liberty are mutually exclusive.[13] Therefore, to be under the rule, and the education, of a phallicized whip was to be trapped by the concrete. The most immediate alternative to being educated in this fashion would be to hang on to the mind and forget about the body. In the often cited fight with Edward Covey, Donald B. Gibson has argued,[14] Douglass physically resists Covey's attempt to whip him, but what the *Narrative* validates is his (masculinized) ability to conceptualize the resistance: "This resistance revived within me a sense of my own manhood. It was a glorious resurrection, from the tomb of slavery, to the heaven of freedom. *I did not hesitate to let it be known of me*, that the white man who expected to succeed in whipping, must also succeed in killing me" (*N*, 112–1-3). In this scene's apotheosis Covey is "enslaved" to a feminized body, "trembl[ing] like a leaf," his mind "taken aback" (*N*, 112).

Therefore, to achieve manhood in these terms was also to embrute physicality, denigrating whatever was associatively female. This transcendence of (manly) spirit over (womanly) flesh witnesses to Douglass's investment in a masculinized, punitive rhetoric. Yet Douglass's description of his "resurrection" in the passage above also displays a

12. I want to emphasize the widespread rhetorical conflation of the feminine with victimhood, to indicate that Douglass was using a system of rhetorical and cultural codification regarding femininity which was already deeply embedded in abolitionist thinking. On the complexities and conflicts within abolitionist and suffragist discourse, see Carby, *Reconstructing Womanhood*, esp. chap. 2; Angela Y. Davis, *Women, Race, and Class* (New York: Random House, 1981), chaps. 2–4; Ellen Carol DuBois, *Feminism and Suffrage: The Emergence of an Independent Women's Movement in America, 1848–1869* (Ithaca: Cornell University Press, 1978); Sánchez-Eppler, "Bodily Bonds," 28–59.

13. Harriet Jacobs expresses the same notion when she claims that her brother "did not mind the smart of the whip, but he did not like the idea of being whipped" (*Incidents in the Life of a Slave Girl*, 19).

14. Donald B. Gibson, "Reconciling Public and Private in Frederick Douglass' Narrative," *American Literature* 57 (December 1985): 567–68. Gibson makes a persuasive argument for Douglass' validation of intellectual over physical control in the *Narrative*.

rhetorical awareness of the cost of transcendence. If being a man means learning dominance, then becoming a man invokes death. To control the flow of knowledge—*"I let it be known of me"*—means courting death, for choosing death in lieu of a whipping implies that only one "man" would survive such a confrontation.

If Douglass's 1845 *Narrative* provides the reader, as Valerie Smith wrote, with "a profound endorsement of the fundamental American plot, the myth of the self-made man,"[15] it also reveals the murderous consequences. In Douglass's writings mastery, masculinity, and agency are often linked to death, so that, rhetorically, to gain a manhood guaranteed by violence, no matter how liberating, was to incur fracturing penalties that could tear "life" from "liberty" and replay slavery's painful separations. The fusion of abstract "liberty" with concrete "life," which Douglass saw as Mother America's best promise to her children, would be impossible to achieve under the rule of a punitive, gendered authority.

This impossibility bespeaks severe ramifications. If flesh and spirit, female and male, are fixed opposites structuring knowledge, then a social system dependent on that oppositional logic for its stability could never offer black and white—also scripted as opposites—a means of reconciliation. In a nation where "white" equals "value," such logic could force a black person into the acrobatics that W. E. B. Du Bois described as "doubleness"[16] in his or her attempt to validate both sides of what twentieth-century terminology calls an "African-American" heritage, for that of logic militates against any such dual validation. Without a revision of the logical structure defining knowledge, an African-American heritage predicated (in part) on a maternity made ironically prominent as a historical result of the slave code would be placed at the triple remove of race, class, and gender from culturally validated sources of power, memory, and political efficacy.[17] Before a woman such as Douglass's mother, Harriet Bailey, could signify something other than loss or lack, the punishing cleavages of black/white, master/slave, body/soul, angel/demon had to be

15. Smith, *Self-Disovery*, 26.

16. W. E. B. Du Bois, *The Souls of Black Folk* (1903; New York: Signet, 1969), 45.

17. The law that "a child shall follow the condition of its mother" makes the mother paradoxically visible as parent; slave children, when engaged in a project akin to Douglass's, would have had to reckon parentage through the mother. See Carby, *Reconstructing Womanhood*, 24–25, 38–39; and Hortense Spillers, "Mama's Baby, Papa's Maybe: An American Grammar Book," *Diacritics* 17 (Summer 1987): 65–81.

altered. And unless this logic of discontinuity was undone, an America scripted as a white "mother" would remain a blood seeker rather than a milk giver. She would never fulfill her promise to her natural (African) children. A different discursive frame for agency was needed, one that could enable a new politics. But how?

One means with which Douglass experimented was that of the sentimental (white) maternal because, theoretically, it insisted upon continuities of the heart as potentially liberating. Yet Douglass's canny use of the sentimental is not generally considered a positive factor in his work. Most appraisals single out the *Narrative* as "classic" and thus do not contend with the "sentimental" revisions of his later autobiographical work. Why is the 1845 *Narrative* repeatedly invoked as the "classic" text? In asking this question I do not mean to elide the struggle that has occurred over whether slave narratives should be taught as literature; such a struggle structures the way Douglass is treated. Despite critical praise for the *Narrative*, however, the implication has been that *My Bondage and My Freedom* (1854) and *The Life and Times of Frederick Douglass* (1881) are *not* classic. As William Andrews has noted, a combination of publishing pragmatics (the *Narrative* is short) and "the politics of academic scholarship" have left Douglass shorn, "a one-book author."[18] Indeed, Andrews demonstrates that those who see the *Narrative* as more authentic, as having "the terseness so appropriate to describing life under the hardships of bondage,"[19] pass over what he calls a "dialogue of sentiment," preferring the "punchy" *Narrative* to the "self-indulgent," "flabby," presumably inauthentic revisions.[20] I would not claim that in revising, Douglass escaped a tight-lipped self-reliance, but his sentimental revisions do deauthorize the dominant logic that to be a free American citizen required the attainment of a punitive (white, male) agency.

While it is not difficult to read gender bias in the complaints about

18. Andrews, *To Tell a Free Story*, 266.
19. James Matlock, quoted in ibid., 266–69.
20. Andrews, *To Tell a Free Story*, 273–74, 266–69. Although Eric J. Sundquist, in his introduction to *Frederick Douglass: New Literary and Historical Essays* (New York: Cambridge University Press, 1991), 4, stresses that reevaluations of Douglass's corpus as a whole are ongoing and relevatory, he too judges *The Life and Times* a self-indulgent work. Likewise, Franchot ("Punishments," 143) claims that Douglass's later writings categorically display a "loss of literary power. As story, Douglass's autobiography threatens to stop at the punishment of Esther, unable to rival the aesthetic power achieved in the indictment of slavery's iniquities." She does not explain what this loss of aesthetic power entails beyond the halting quality of the punishment scenario. Aesthetic loss is treated as self-evident.

flaccid writing, it is less obvious that (with an almost *invisible agency*) such a gendered aesthetic enables twentieth-century criticism to reenact what Garrisonian abolitionism did on the basis of racial prejudice masked as political need: that is, restrict Douglass's voice to the *Narrative*. In validating the 1845 tale to the active exclusion of his other works, the later critics eerily echo those abolitionists who tried to hold Douglass to this earliest version of himself. He obviously chafed under the patronizing attitude of those who saw only the *Narrative* as authentic, since his stated impulse for the 1854 revision was in part that he was tired of being a "text" with knowledge whipped into his flesh, "a graduate from the peculiar institution with my diploma written on my back" (*MB/MF*, 218–19). As Eric Sundquist writes, if Garrisonian politics would have had Douglass remain a slave, his revisions insist on breaking that image.[21] Douglass did exploit rhetoric that conflated (feminized) flesh with text and (masculinized) pen with whip, he also explored another logic, one that did not so easily equate pen and whip. "My feet," he said, in a now-famous passage, "have been so cracked with the frost that the pen with which I am writing might be laid in the gashes" (*N*, 72). Robert Stepto called this an image of "fusion," an emblem of "travail transcended."[22] But why does such of fusion require transcendence? Might this image also be read as a metaphoric refusal of an identity bound to a logic requiring that bodily wounds be forgotten? Taking Stepto's term "fusion" as a guide, might one say that Douglass, in calling attention to the cracks in his flesh, also remembers the pain supposedly transcended? He did seek to heal his wounds, but not wholly in order to achieve transcendent mastery. Rather, Douglass used an image of wounded flesh to insist that whatever imaginative closure time and change might permit, the cold facts of the past shape the present and future. By 1854 he had also begun to interrogate, through revision, the representational logic that had so deftly allowed for the equation of pen and whip. If Doug-

---

21. Sundquist, introduction to *Frederick Douglass*, 4–5. On the gendering of textuality, see Susan Gubar, " 'The Blank Page' and the Issues of Female Creativity." in *Writing and Sexual Difference*, ed. Elizabeth Abel (Chicago: University of Chicago Press, 1982), 73–94. I am indebted to Anne Goldman for discussions concerning text and flesh in Douglass.

22. Stepto, *From Behind the Veil*; I must stress that it is no easy task, historically, to place slave narrative per se within the realm of the "literary," since to do so often results in a deauthorization or deauthentication of the experience related; see Houston Baker, Jr., introduction to *N*. See also Yellin's introduction to Jacobs, *Incidents in the Life of a Slave Girl*.

lass revised so that his identity would not remain in the stasis of just-escaped-slave and so that he would not be a one-book author, he also revised so that his story would not be a mere reiteration of hard-won (white, masculinized) transcendence.

Finally, while part of the role-playing Douglass manipulated involves the text-flesh dynamics I have traced here, another related aspect concerns the filial; as Douglass himself says, Garrison acted as a father and mentor to him (*MB/MF*, 216). Through the *Narrative's* impact and lean efficacy, he had gained access to the "father's" ears. In writing *My Bondage and My Freedom*, however, he found that despite such entitlement he was still caught in a hierarchy demanding that he be a good boy. This filial placement recalls the familial metaphorics with which I opened this argument: if Douglass was a "son," it meant he could claim to be one of Mother America's natural children—yet did it mean as well that he must remain a boy?

Historically, the use of "boy" as denigrating epithet is enough evidence to indicate the painful situation Douglass faced when using the rhetorical formulations available to him. America might be appealed to as a mother, but if "she" herself could not be invested with an agency other than a punitive one, dependent upon the whip of the "father's" primacy, she would yet be a (white) demon to her (black) children. Given the meshing of parental and political authority in abolitionist rhetoric, Douglass had to try revising the familial dynamics so that America did not require a whip to underwrite the stability of her family.[23] Thus, as he shifted away from a manly rhetoric of transcendence, he concentrated on examining the stasis of a silenced feminine. Using a strategic sentimentality, Douglass attempted the creation of a logic that allowed a fleshly diploma to signify something other than abject (feminized) embrutment. The so-called literary impact of the *Narrative's* terse rhetoric muted a potent defiance that he saw in a place of supposed degradation: that is, the potentially signifying defiance of wounded (feminized) flesh.

---

23. Child's revision of advice in *The Mother's Book* can illuminate how urgently Douglass had to fight off being restricted to the role of Mother America's boy: in the *New-York Herald Tribune*, December 24, 1845, Child states that she no longer considers whipping necessary to child rearing ("I believe this can never be done without injury to the child")—showing that the practice of whipping as disciplinary action had been generally accepted. The whip was not only a slaveholder's educative device or even just the father's rod; white maternity also wielded it to ensure obedience. For antebellum cultural ideology's manipulation of sexuality and power with regard to black and white women, see Carby, *Reconstructing Womanhood*, 20–26.

Aunt Hester to Queen Esther

Even though the *Narrative* sympathizes with Aunt Hester, the text appears to make punitive or masterly judgments about her by offering a justification for the master's anger: that is, Captain Anthony's fury, if roused by paternal concern to shield Hester's "innocence" from promiscuity, might be laudable. But as a "master," Anthony has aborted his paternal authority; a sotto voce, incestual desire for Aunt Hester erupts when the proper rule of a benign, Christian patriarch is removed, freeing illicit passions. In fact, the scene of Hester's punishment might be read as a Freudian parable for the disrupting discovery of sexual intercourse, particularly given Douglass's euphemism for this whipping, a "spectacle" that he calls a "bloody transaction" (*N*, 51).[24] Yet if this scene is such a parable, it must be read as an inverted one: if the father, in antebellum slavery, is powerful, he is (because unknown as father) an illegal and unnatural tyrant; the observing child is not, as in Freud, given a knowledge that helps to institute autonomy. This spectacle crams an emerging Douglass backward into a near fetal position, through a bloody gateway into a "womb" of slavery. What such a child is supposed to learn is a passivity culturally associated with the feminine. Silenced, he knows that it could "be [his] turn next" (*N*, 51)—essentially, to be raped.

It is not a surprise, then, to see Douglass's *Narrative* reverse the gendering trajectory of Hester's punishment, enabling the "I" to move out of the bondage of (female) passivity into what the logic of the *Narrative* suggests is agency. This reversal, a two-staged process, bears close analysis because in it a suggestive difference is quietly made betweem forms of femininity.

Although hardly in congruence with Anthony's whipping of Aunt Hester, Master Hugh Auld's punishing prohibition of his wife's teaching is also a gendered "spectacle" that has much in common with Hester's punishment. Douglass's own rhetoric links the two scenes when he claims that Auld had opened another gateway: he "called into existence an entirely new train of thought. It was a new and special revelation, explaining dark and mysterious things" (*N*, 78). Drawn through this gateway as an inarticulate participant (like Aunt Hester, neither Douglass nor Sophia Auld speak against the master's

---

24. See George P. Cunningham, " 'Called into Existence': Race, Gender, and Voice in Frederick Douglass's *Narrative* of 1845," *Differences: A Journal of Feminist Cultural Studies* 1.5 (1989): 108–35.

voice), Douglass finds himself briefly placed beside Sophia Auld[25] in
that he learns precisely the same thing she is compelled to know—
that if one designated a "slave" were educated, "there would be no
keeping him" (N, 78). Sophia, like Aunt Hester (and the child Douglass), is silenced. Though her desire, unlike Hester's, wears the robes
of maternal affection—in her Christian wish to help the manchild
Fred—it is still illegal. The possible legitimacy of that Christian impulse, however, allows Douglass, identifying with her at this first
stage of gender reversal, a partial path to agency. Even he is muted
by the feminized silence he shares with Sophia Auld, some mysteries
have been explained, and he has gained partial title to a masculine
pronoun. Hugh Auld may deny Douglass, but when he says "there
would be no keeping *him*," he acknowledges the child's gender. The
later scene of Covey's thwarted effort to whip him (the second stage
of gender reversal) gives Douglass a fuller title to active use of masculinized power.

Thus to track out a gender reversal in Douglass's position, however,
is to overlook a significant slippage between forms of femininity.[26]
Unlike Sophia Auld, Hester Bailey must be forced to obey the master's
command. She is far less submissive and far more dangerous. Indeed,
just as slippage is evident in Douglass's uneasiness about an agency
gained through dominance, as previously demonstrated, there is a
slippage in the "female" between Hester Bailey and Sophia Auld. If
Hester's disobedience results in the flow of warm blood, Sophia's obedience freezes hers in her heart. Douglass may be shown as punitive
toward a feminine object in the *Narrative*, but he also slyly asks, what
is female?

Thus, even if Douglass does use a rhetoric of punitive agency to
define himself against feminized passivity, he has opened up a meaning for "female" that may not be clearly visible in the *Narrative* but is
locatable. This interpretation holds when he returns to Hester's punishment in *My Bondage and My Freedom*, in which his use of sentimental rhetoric refines the presence of such subcutaneous 1845 resistance.
What he is witness to in 1854 is no longer a "bloody transaction" (N,
51) between Hester and Anthony but rather a "tempest of passion"

25. Franchot notes that the mulatto status Douglass occupied was structurally similar
to the status of a white woman ("Punishment," 147). For a more detailed and complete
discussion of the mulatto, see Berzon, *Neither White Nor Black*.

26. Franchot's argument depends on seeing Douglass's movement into subjectivity
as a gender reversal.

on the part of "old master" alone (*MB/MF*, 57–58) the "chief offence" (*N*, 51) is no longer Aunt Hester's desire for a slave but Aunt *Esther's* "woman's love" (*MB/MF*, 58) for a man, Edward Roberts. As Douglass writes, "Edward was young and fine looking, and he loved and courted her. He might have been her husband . . . .but WHO and *what* was this old master?" (*MB/MF*, 58). In the *Narrative*, Aunt Hester's sexual "innocence" is at issue; in *My Bondage and My Freedom*, Esther's disobedience is honorable. She is no longer a daughter running after a slave but a woman and a bride.

Therefore, if the *Narrative*'s scene of Hester's punishment situates the torn, objectified female body at the site of the abject,[27] Douglass's later accounts redefine that placement and outline a rebellion potent *within* what was first written as a narrative of submission transcended. Taking into account Douglass's later work, one can see that it is his maternal aunt's willful *desire* for the man Ned—as well as the possible result of that desire—which is the chief offense to the white patriarch. To Captain Anthony, Hester's desire for one other than himself makes her both disobedient and dangerous.

That danger is made clearer by glancing again at Sophia Auld's situation. Hugh Auld's prohibition halts his wife's maternal desire to see Fred as like any other manchild. Could this prohibition mean that her desire granted the boy too much agency? I would suggest that Sophia's enthusiastic compliance with her husband reveals the man in manchild. Hester's desire locates Ned as a man and thus as potent; should Sophia likewise move from boy-Fred to man-Frederick, might her "innocent" desire to mother seem less so? What might happen to Sophia Auld's maternity if she saw her boy Fred as a fully grown man?[28] Although the 1845 account is oblique, what is at stake for "mastery" here is its own paternalized basis of entitlement. If a woman could own an active desire that needed prohibition, and was capable of directing that desire toward one who was supposed to be "only" a slave, it must have meant that all "slaves" were born

27. On the fleshly as a site of the abject, and on abjection, see Kristeva, *Powers of Horror*.

28. McFeely, *Frederick Douglass*, notes that Douglass's presence in the Auld household may have had unsettling implications for Sophia Auld; however, the slavocracy's fears about possible desire—and its consequences—between white women and black men is more fully explored in Carby, *Reconstructing Womanhood*, 20–40; and in Gunning, "Facing 'A Red Record.' " I am in debt to Sandra Gunning for many long and provocative discussions about the interconnections between class, race, and gender in the nineteenth century.

(hu)man. And indeed, the ways in which Douglass revised his 1845 account reveal not only the potency of female desire to occupy and locate agency but also the danger that this power had always been to the stability of both the southern slavocracy as a political system and the northern patriarchy as a system of logic that defined agency as punitive and invisibly gendered.

One striking instance of Douglass's sentimental strategy is the way in which he grants his once inarticulate aunt vocal agency. In the *Narrative*, the only speaker at Aunt Hester's punishment is the master, who says, "Now you d——d b——h, I'll learn you how to disobey my orders!" (*N*, 52). In *My Bondage and My Freedom*, however, it is Esther who speaks: "Have mercy! Oh! have mercy . . . I won't do so no more" (*MB/MF*,59). In this text Master Anthony remains mute, his words "too coarse and blasphemous to be produced" (*MB/MF*, 59). The sheer content of Esther's speech hardly invites a reading of defiance; in fact, Douglass's veiling of the "punchier" 1845 "d——d b——h" seems contrived. Yet is it not significant that by using a sentimental strategy, Douglass gives his mute aunt a voice while robbing Anthony of his?

Still, the 1854 rescripture does not erase the rhetorical definition of "femininity" as a position against which Douglass had to struggle. Not only does Esther remain a "suffering victim," but Douglass is linked to this victimization: "I was hushed, terrified, stunned and could do nothing and the fate of Esther might be mine next. The scene here described was often repeated in the case of poor Esther, and her life, as I knew it, was one of wretchedness" (*MB/MF*, 59). Douglass does not specify whether he was stunned by Esther's passivity or by the implied tenacity of her rebellion; in either case, she and he remain "wretched."[29]

---

29. Franchot's argument dismisses this sudden eruption of Aunt Esther's voice, claiming that its brevity and the subsequent elision of women, black or white, as figures in Douglass's work indicate both his failure to "uncover women's voice" ("Punishment," 151) and his uneasy disaffiliation with black women—especially denoted by his silences regarding his first wife, Anna Murray Douglass, and by his second marriage to Helen Pitts Douglass. My argument stresses rather the difficulty Douglass faced in his attempt to represent what he knew as the potency of women, particularly black women, given the entrenched structure of paternalistic logic that repeatedly militated against locating the female as anything but lack. To "uncover women's voices" is, as the politics of contemporary feminist theory indicates, hardly a simple matter of mimesis. On Douglass's marriages and his relation to anti-slavery women, see McFeely, *Frederick Douglass*; and Ida B. Wells, *Crusade for Justice: The Autobiography of Ida B. Wells*, ed. John Hope Franklin (Chicago: The University of Chicago Press, 1970), 72–78.

In *The Life and Times of Frederick Douglass,* Esther's story changes again, and oppressive victimization as a representational category is stunningly altered. In 1881, Esther and Edward are described as a proper Victorian couple who "were true and faithful to each other."[30] Douglass concludes: "I was terrified, hushed, stunned and bewildered. The scene here described was often repeated, for Edward and Esther continued to meet, notwithstanding all efforts to prevent their meeting" (*LT*, 49). In this version of "Esther's Punishment," it is hard to tell what the punishment accomplishes or who suffers the most diminishment from it. Douglass is hushed, but he is not next in line to be beaten; and the couple, against all odds, continue to meet. Who, by silent implication, is impotent here? Further, Esther's refusal to be separated from Edward is now linked to a stubborn and "honorable perpetuation of the race" (*LT*, 48–49).

Indeed, Douglass's sentimental revisions seek to rescript a politics of community so that the ties that bind the flesh do not mean enslavement. For example, even though "Hester" to "Esther" seems a mere spelling variation, given the patterns of naming in slave culture, this shift ought to be telling.[31] Esther brings to mind that Judaic queen who saved her enslaved kindred from death. Rising to her place as queen through a passivity the former Queen Vashti had denied, Queen Esther took on an identity dictated by her captors—until her community was threatened with erasure. Then, using the tools she had acquired in passivity, Esther employed an active resistance that circumvented a genocidal plot. Her combination of resistance and obedience ensured her own survival and the political survival of her people.[32] Aunt Hester's people are likewise trapped by a slavery that demands both obedience and defiance. Douglass's 1854 script ennobled his aunt; by 1881 her ennobled desire results in the hereditary continuance of the people. Indeed this later story, read in conjunction with its earlier versions, completes the outline of rebellious female potency indicated both in the *Narrative* and, more fully, in *My Bondage*

30. Frederick Douglass, *The Life and Times of Frederick Douglass* (London: Collier, 1962), 48 (hereafter cited as *LT*).

31. On naming in slave communities, see Walker, *Moral Choices*, 255–59; Cunningham, "Called into Existence," 128–31; Sidonie Smith, *Where I'm Bound: Patterns of Slavery and Freedom in Black American Autobiography* (Westport, Conn.: Greenwood Press, 1974), 18–22; and particularly Sterling Stuckey, *Slave Culture: Nationalist Theory and the Foundations of Black America* (New York: Oxford University Press, 1987).

32. On the use of the biblical Esther as abolitionist emblem, see Yellin, *Women & Sisters*, 134.

and My Freedom. Using sentimental rhetoric, Douglass maintains an emotional connection with Esther without entailing his own victimization or requiring her to remain a victim. As the last line of the 1881 version shows, Esther is left not in the "wretchedness" specified in *My Bondage and My Freedom* but in a position of continued and potentially fertile rebellion.

Home Is Where the Heart Is?

One of the most sentimental scenes Douglass wrote is that of his grandmother's death, an incantation of slavery's attempt to force African-American motherhood to signify loss. Her death is a "climax of . . . fiendish barbarity" (*N*, 92) revealing the absolute labor that slavery exacted. Betsy Bailey's progeny were the Auld's fortune, her usurped motherhood the hidden source of their plenty. Therein lay one of the slavocracy's most revealing riddles. As slaves, Betsy Bailey and her daughters were not allowed to be "mothers," yet they *had* to be mothers in order for slavery to function. Betsy had to be fantasized as fertile and passive, desirable but not desiring, absent and present. She had to perform as mammy without being a mother.[33] She was necessary to the system but denied, because her power, if acknowledged, might cause total systemic disjuncture. Who had the right, in the logic of slaveholding, to produce children without visibly reproducing? The answer to this riddle is, of course, the master.

This answer offers a logical clue as to the potential for black maternity to signify something other than pure loss. For instance: Douglass's original name was the one his mother gave him, Frederick Augustus Washington Bailey. The patronymic is identified as not paternal but maternal and, according to William McFeely, may also be of African derivation.[34] Douglass renamed himself in order to reject the material dispossession of slavery.[35] Without diminishing that dispossession, I would point out that although "black" maternity supposedly represented loss, Harriet Bailey's ability to usurp the space of

33. On the power of black maternity, see Carby, *Reconstructing Womanhood*, 20–39; Elizabeth Fox-Genovese, *Within the Plantation Household* (Chapel Hill: University of North Carolina Press, 1988), 292–320.

34. McFeely, *Frederick Douglass*, 5.

35. For alternative readings of Douglass's name change, see Cunningham, "Called into Existence," 128–31; and Walker, *Moral Choices*, 255–59.

the patronymic suggests that a "black" mother might possess title to that which the (white) master claimed.

Moreover, since antebellum culture clung to the sentimental fantasy that "mother" was an iconic index of humanity, it became a useful discursive place to attack the inhumanity of slavery. When Harriet Beecher Stowe cited Douglass as a source for *Uncle Tom's Cabin*, she rewrote a portion of his 1845 tale in sentimental terms to promote natural motherly tenderness: "When he was three years old his mother was sent to work on a plantation eight or ten miles distant. . . . after her day's toil she would occasionally walk over to her child, lie down with him in her arms, hush him to sleep in her bosom, then rise up and walk back again to be ready for her field work by daylight. Now, we ask the highest born lady in England or America, who is a mother, whether this does not show that this poor field-laborer had in her bosom, beneath her dirt and rags, a true mother's heart?[36] Douglass, definitively reclaiming himself from Stowe, would write his own sentimental version, which shrewdly exploited a language proven expedient in promoting abolitionist goals. By appealing to the truth revealed in a mother's heart, he could appeal to a sentimental culture; and by using the sentimental skillfully, he would prove *himself* cultured—an effective writer, more than a one-book author. Thus, when Douglass composed *My Bondage and My Freedom*, he chose *not* to revise those few sentimental scenes already in the *Narrative*—such as the death of Betsy Bailey.[37]

Sentimental maternity as it existed in antebellum culture, however, was primarily a white woman's model. To ascribe it to black women was to risk ascribing something other than a true heart; it was to invoke an image of possible demonization (Sophia Auld) as well as to inscribe an ideology of docile martyrdom that some were already fighting.[38] Therefore, although Douglass used sentimental paradigms

36. *KUTC*, 17.

37. On Douglass's use and retention of sentimental discourse, see Andrews, *To Tell a Free Story*, 265–91; and Gregory S. Jay, *America the Scrivener: Deconstruction and the Subject of Literary History* (Ithaca: Cornell University Press, 1990) 236–62.

38. Douglass's involvement with the women's rights movement was long and often bitter; see *Frederick Douglass on Women's Rights*, ed. Philip S. Foner (Westport, Conn.: Greenwood Press, 1976). It is clear that the postbellum issue of black (male) suffrage splintered the alliances made during the abolitionist movement and caused bitter invective on both sides of the "race" line. For a discussion sympathetic to the white suffragists, see DuBois, *Feminism and Suffrage*; for a discussion sympathetic to black suffragists and black suffrage, see Davis, *Women, Race and Class*; on Douglass's role, see Martin, *The Mind of Frederick Douglass*.

to revise (black) motherhood, his revisions accomplish something other than a simple transposition of (white) sentimental motherhood to (black) slave women. Just as Aunt Hester's rescripture reveals how a strategy of sentimentality enabled Douglass to embody an empowered space where both self and community could survive, his revision of African-American motherhood shows how he used sentimental maternal icons to create an ideal American homeland, one structured by reciprocal relation rather than predicated on a vocabulary of separation.

In 1854 Betsy Bailey is portrayed, as she was in 1845, as Douglass's shielding home and as the locus of loss. Yet she has also become a clear source of fertility. Douglass's birthplace, Tuckahoe, is in barren country known for its "truly famine stricken" nature by "all Marylanders, black and white" (*MB/MF*, 27). Yet Betsy Bailey grows both an abundance of food and a family.[39] Thus Douglass begins to rescript African-American motherhood as a sentimental emblem of home in a way not found in the *Narrative*. Still, Betsy Bailey remains a troubling source of betrayal insofar as her provident maternal home is subject to the master. Leaving her grandson at Anthony's house, she abandons him to a demonized mother, Anthony's whip-by-proxy, Aunt Katy.

The story Douglass then tells of Harriet Bailey, however, serves to heal the betrayals forced upon "motherhood"—exemplified by both Betsy and Katy—under slavery. On one of Harriet Bailey's infrequent (and previously anonymous) night visits, she finds that her son has been punished by Aunt Katy, who "meant to *starve the life out of* [him]. ... The friendless and hungry boy, in his extremest need—and when he dare not look for succor—found himself in the strong, protecting arms of a mother; a mother who was, at the moment (being endowed with high powers of manner as well as matter) more than a match for all his enemies" (*MB/MF*, 40–41). Harriet Bailey possesses *both* manner and matter here. She is doubly endowed, able to *read* "Aunt Katy a lecture which she never forgot" and to provide Douglass with "a large, ginger cake" (*MB/MF*, 41) instead of parched corn. Douglass

39. Unlike the magical (masculinized) root that Douglass's betrayer Sandy will later give him as protection against the white man's whip, Betsy Bailey's root is useful in and of itself; it is edible and does not need magical properties to perform a kind of salvation. On Betsy Bailey, see Sterling Stuckey, " 'Ironic Tenacity': Frederick Douglass's Seizure of the Dialectic," in Sundquist, *Frederick Douglass: New Literary and Historical Essays*, 24–25.

gives his mother an aura of the extraordinary while insisting that such maternal endowment is ordinary: like any good mother she protects her child—but she doesn't just scold; she reads a lecture. Like all good mothers, she provides her child with food—but her provision isn't just nourishment; it is a " 'sweet cake' . . . in the shape of a heart, with a rich, dark ring glazed upon the edge" (MB/MF, 41). She is clearly everything that Aunt Katy is not, and she eclipses Grandmother Bailey, her own mother, by being more than a match for all enemies. And here Douglass makes literacy, too, a "black" maternal attribute: "I learned, after my mother's death, that she could read, and that she was the only one of all the slaves and colored people in Tuckahoe who enjoyed that advantage. How she acquired this knowledge, I know not, for Tuckahoe is the last place in the world where she would be apt to find facilities for learning. I can, therefore, fondly and proudly ascribe to her an earnest love of knowledge." (MB/MF, 42).

Without question, the basic motivation of this revisionary strategy was apparent to many of Douglass's contemporaries. James M'Cune Smith wrote in his 1855 introduction to My Bondage and My Freedom that Douglass's new maternal portrait had the political agenda of ascribing naturalized capabilities to blacks.[40] In Moral Choices: Memory, Desire, and Imagination in Nineteenth-Century Abolition, Peter Walker notes that Douglass renounced the primacy of "white" paternity in My Bondage and My Freedom by equi-vocating about his white father and, as M'Cune Smith said, by disavowing as well the Garrisonian abolitionists who had patronized him. So, as Walker argued, Douglass, having lost his black mother twice—first in slavery and then again in the silences of the Narrative—sought in 1854 to reclaim her as a means of claiming a black heritage.[41]

But here I want to point out that Douglass inadvertently lost "black motherhood" a third time in 1854. The first loss occurred when Douglass as a slave was forbidden access to kinship and to a language of maternal tenderness. The second came when in seeking to make himself "a man and a brother" to the white abolitionists, he allied himself with a cultural philosophy that silenced the female. The third loss occurred in the reception of My Bondage and My Freedom, a discourse of literary evaluation that left little room to acknowledge either the

---

40. On Douglass and his relation to an African-American heritage, see also Martin, The Mind of Frederick Douglass; McFeely, Frederick Douglass; Blight, Frederick Douglass' Civil War; Walker, Moral Choices.

41. Walker, Moral Choices, 257–58.

political efficacy or the aesthetic power of sentimentality. In 1854 Douglass was clearly addressing the earlier losses through a manipulation of antebellum sentimental maternity. Because that ideology has since been read as a simple script of martyrdom, and belittled aesthetically, the power he saw in this ideology has been obscured.[42] Douglass sought to reclaim his mother in order to redefine himself as "black" through a popular language effective against the slavocracy. As Walker says: "through the continual development and refinement of the autobiographical mother, Douglass was also developing and refining his own conception of self. He was driving himself deeper and deeper into a proud identification with Harriet Bailey who above all else was a black slave."[43] If, as Walker's reading suggests, he saw her as "above all else" a black and a slave—but not as a woman— the sentimental choice Douglass made caused him to lose a part of Harriet Bailey once again. Douglass did seek to empower the categories "black" and "slave," but what happened to the category "woman"? Walker's emphasis obscures gender.

A far more startling indication of this gender invisibility is evident in the way Walker reads Douglass's claim that: "there is in *Prichard's Natural History of Man* the head of a figure . . . the features of which so resemble those of my mother, that I often recur to it with something of the feeling which I suppose others experience when looking upon the pictures of dear departed ones" (*MB/MF*, 39). Walker argues that Douglass's choice displays his never satisfied need to recapture a lost white patrimony: "For most of his life, Frederick Douglass apparently found his black mother in the form of a princely man who, as far as the picture showed, may have been white."[44] A number of critics cite Walker's analysis as indicative of Douglass's allegiance to the rhetoric

42. Most critical discussions of nineteenth-century sentimentality focus on it as a specifically political discourse, in opposition to the category of the aesthetic following Jane Tompkins's question, "But is it any *good*?" (*Sensational Designs*). My argument reorients a discussion about sentimentality around questions of aesthetics; see also Harris, "But Is It Any *Good*?" As Ann Douglas (*Feminization*) rightly points out, sentimentalism is a complex phenomenon, particularly with regard to how it might be, as a discourse, implicated in its own "victimization." Still, to harp on the complexities of sentimental discourse is to ignore the fact that aesthetic theory on "greatness" is in part based on the perception that (a) the sentimental and the nostalgic are congruent categories of memory and desire, and (b) that politics and aesthetics are de facto separable and distinct categories. These assumptions enable aesthetic judgment to bypass the historical and cultural specificities that Tompkins so eloquently argues for.

43. Walker, *Moral Choices*, 252.

44. Ibid., 254.

of mastery. For instance, although she grants that Walker oversimpli-
fies Douglass's affiliations, Franchot claims that: "when Douglass sin-
gled out the portrait of Rameses the Great . . . as that most like . . . his
mother, he . . . chose an image of royal manhood [that] . . . reveals
again the impediment of the masculine in any recovery of the feminine
and in so doing, the presence of the punitive within any imagined
redemptive space. As a primary Christian symbol of racial and religious oppression the Pharoah . . . is a dual figure: Douglass's selection
of 'him' to impersonate 'her' reimposes the slave-holder onto the figure of the mother. The recovery of origin would always speak of duplicity rather than union."[45]

Why did Walker see Prichard's image as "white," while Franchot's
analysis privileges "Pharoah"—and both, in any case, would have us
see a "man"? The figure is mute; Walker sees a "white" person there;
and Prichard's text gives it a gender and class. How did Douglass see
the portrait? His 1854 text tells us it reminds him of a woman "of
deep black, glossy complexion [who] had regular features" (MB/MF,
38). M'Cune Smith's introduction focuses attention on the racial "mixture" that the Egyptian represented to nineteenth-century ethnology,
and both Walker and Franchot do concede Douglass's use of Egyptian
as mixed. Yet these concessions do not hinder their claims that Douglass identified with white (masculinized) mastery.

Why should Douglass's choice of "white" Pharoah as meet emblem
of his "sable" mother not suggest that Douglass rescripted his origin
so that it could mean both "duplicity" and "union"? Why not read
this picture as multidirectional—for if one can claim that "he" is im-
personating "her," does not Douglass's sentimental text also make
"her" impersonate "him"? In other words, why do critics assign an
authority to Prichard that overrides that of Douglass's text? Why not
insist that it is the combination of the picture and his memory that
completes the portrait? It is, after all, that combination which allows
for an identity that does not require the "her" to be passive and the
"him" to be punitive, which seeks a way for both to be human but
not white, to be powerful but not a punitive ruler-master. I do not
mean to suggest that Douglass's choice of Rameses as Mother is not
ambiguous. It is. What I would emphasize instead is that most critics
ignore the complexity of Douglass's revisions—in this instance, his
insistence upon both picture and text.

45. Franchot, "Punishment," 159.

If Douglass appropriated the voice of white mastery in writing the *Narrative* and then, in *My Bondage and My Freedom*, revised that strategy with a sentimentality that had its own pitfalls, what happened when he wrote *The Life and Times of Frederick Douglass*? Hester's full revision into Esther suggests a way to understand what Douglass did to his mother's portrait. By 1881 a new Douglass struggles to emerge along with a new definition of the female, one that does not lend itself readily to a reading of "feminine" as silenced "object." This later voice tells a story that does not make the definition of the individual antipathetic to the communal. Moving away from a masculinity predicated on the punishment of femininity, it seeks a definition of "mixed" union that encompasses both without lessening either. Criticism seldom follows Douglass that far.

In his 1881 portrait of Harriet Bailey, Douglass rescripts the dubious, silenced heritage of a white sentimental maternity. He modifies the 1854 statement that his mother was mute (*MB/MF*, 42) grieving that he had so *few* of her words to remember (*LT*, 36). As McFeely recounts, in 1854 Harriet Bailey ends in a grave that was "as the grave of the dead at sea, unmarked, and without stone or stake" (*MB/MF*, 43); in 1881 her portrait leaves out such melancholia, ending rather on her love of literacy.[46] To end here rather than in the grave is remarkable enough, but Douglass's 1881 revision also casts into deep shadow any whiteness tainting such a love. He is now "happy to attribute any love of letters [he] may have, not to [his] presumed Anglo-Saxon paternity, but to the native genius of [his] sable, unprotected, and uncultivated mother—a woman who belonged to a race whose mental endowments are still disparaged and despised" (*LT*, 36). By 1881 Douglass has made literacy Harriet Bailey's primary attribute and, in so doing, made literacy into a native black genius far more than in 1854.

Further, when one reads this final portrait in conjunction with previous versions, the trajectory of Harriet Bailey's palimpsest describes an arc of identity that, if traced backward, illuminates an obscured but never absent force. Through a strategic use of sentimental maternal iconography, Douglass was able to make visible and vocal a black maternity that *had always been present* to him but obscured by the representational politics of paternalism. In developing his mother's portrait, Douglass found a means to empower her without lessening

---

46. McFeely, *Frederick Douglass*, 7.

himself, a way to have agency without having to erase hers to get it. His revisions sketch out an agency that balances at the tension point between polarities. Rather than either cleaving to or being cloven by fractions, Douglass sought a "mixed" personhood, a way to imagine Egyptian without becoming primarily Pharaoh or primarily white. Through sentimentality, Douglass found a way to temper his *Narrative's* voice so that in 1881 neither mother nor self is lacking.

Of course should "lack" determine what critics see as "female," then slavery, as a position of loss, would function as such. Yet the nuances of Douglass's revisions make flexible the rigid antebellum concepts of "masculine" and "feminine" or "black" and "white"; to see him as primarily beholden to paternalism is to miss the point. In 1861 Douglass wrote, "All subjective ideas become more distinct, palpable and strong by the habit of rendering them objective . . . .This weapon can be potent in the hands of the bigot and fanatic or in the hands of the liberal and enlightened."[47] Obviously, Douglass valued an "objective" vocabulary of mastery. But objectivity is a tool that depends on the user's motivation—and, I would add, the interpreter's. Aesthetics that obscure the sentimental as a powerful if troubling route to knowledge ignore how Douglass used sentimentality to enable the survival of his own selfhood while allowing for a female potency. Indeed, his process offers a blueprint for imagining an agency that both is and is not autonomous, a way to conceive of identity that does not require liberty to be divorced from life, mother from child, male from female, subject from object. What Douglass tried to map was a definition of "American" that did not require one to wield a whip.

Douglass's rescriptures do not always hold the balance between polarities; they oscillate uneasily. The ambiguity of "Rameses" as "Mother" is a symptom of such an oscillation; it allows one to claim that Harriet Bailey was not, after all, a Pharaoh. And despite his work on maternal rescripture, for Douglass a genealogical tree seeded in the soil of slavery always needed a *paternal* root. Indebted to a definition of male presence that depends on female absence, he could not wholly discard patriarchal logic. Though he tempers the *Narrative's* paternalism with sentimental maternity, a "voice" that mixes the two can result in an unstable oscillation between penetration and emanation.

47. Frederick Douglass, "Life Pictures" (1861), quoted in Blight, *Frederick Douglass' Civil War*, 12.

Douglass had, in part, accepted that power was paternal. For instance, in trying to ascribe literacy to the maternal, he made it an inherent "love of knowledge" and so naturalized literacy as a kind of genetic quantity. Harriet Bailey did not teach her son to read (never mind that neither did his presumed Anglo-Saxon parent), and natural proclivities, particularly when wed to the maternal, bespoke passive inheritance. Douglass's work could not wholly construct origin without father. As he wrote in 1881, the mark of a "civilized country" is to make the father a "person of some consequence" (*LT*, 27). To progress was then—as it is still, given contemporary legal battles over the "problem" of female-headed households—to have a patrimony.[48]

The directional logic of the "progressive" is revealing, since it actuates a critical aesthetic that would block a multidirectional reading of Douglass's work in toto. If one believes that only linear progress can represent stable and identifiable gain, then cycling through Douglass's revisions is to circle back to no end. The pull of linear logic is illustrated by his seesaw frustration, in *My Bondage and My Freedom*, about how he should depict his mother, the problem being that to speak of his mother is "to return, or rather, to begin" (*MB/MF*, 38). In fact, accurately fixing any moment of beginning, or any moment of conception, is almost by definition a vexing discursive project. A concept may be open, changeable, in flux, but linear interpretation seeks to foreclose on its possibilities, particularly in a gendered system of value where flux is often defined as leakage, a possible conduit of changes that might disrupt the status quo. Flux questions the system's notion of positive value. If the iron gate of slavery may be penetrated with, in Douglass's terminology, "one gallant rush,"[49] the change thus wrought cannot guarantee that the gateway will be any less bloody. To invite change invokes risk, and although he wished to locate power at the hinge of the gate, Douglass worried. Who would sway meaning in a system that valued progress more than process?

Such an interpretive crisis occurs in *My Bondage and My Freedom* when Douglass describes the instability of his presumed Anglo-Saxon parent. Aaron Anthony behaved at times as if he were "a kind old man, and, really, almost fatherly," but he frequently raved aloud, proving he was "a wretched man, at war with his own soul, and . . .

48. See Carby, *Reconstructing Womanhood*, 20–39.
49. Frederick Douglass, *The Life and Writings of Frederick Douglass*, vol. 3 (New York: International Publishers, 1953), 123: "The iron gate of our prison stands half open. . . . one gallant rush . . . will fling it wide."

he little thought that the . . . black urchins around him could see, through those vocal crevices, the very secret of his heart" (*MB/MF*, 54–55). Benevolent patriarch or deranged madman? Douglass's account suggests that because slavery had perverted the civilized role of father, Captain Anthony became vulnerable to appropriation. Ignoring his children, he lost control of his voice and became penetrable. A "vocal crevice" opened up to reveal the mute secret of his heart: wretchedness. This emotional disarray is revelatory, but the gender reversal implied by the image of a crevice suggests that without the securing authority of paternal identity, who knows what dangerous secrets might escape the perimeters of the heart? Vocal crevices are fine if they reveal the slavocracy's weakness. But what about the heart's vulnerability? Douglass claimed that when Harriet Bailey saved him from Katy, she gave him a sweet cake shaped like a heart. Such a memorable gift begs a question Douglass never asks—where did a fieldhand *get* such a thing?[50] Daring in its defiance of the expected, boldly extravagant yet inexplicable, the heart may symbolize love, but this brief, unique connection between mother and son is also marked by loss: the child ate the cake, and his mother disappeared. To open one's heart is to be vulnerable, and yet, as Douglass repeatedly insisted, such vulnerability could be a daring attack.

50. William McFeely writes that Harriet Bailey ousted Aunt Katy from the kitchen and baked the cake right then and there. That would certainly solve the mystery, but I find no evidence of such a scene in any of Douglass's own discussions.

5

The Tender of Memory: Restructuring Value in Harriet Jacobs's *Incidents in the Life of a Slave Girl*

Surely there must be some justice in the man.
—Harriet Jacobs, *Incidents in the Life of a Slave Girl*

In declaring that the "war of [her] life had begun," Harriet Jacobs, speaking as "Linda Brent," describes this war as a consequence in part of her ripening ability to "read the characters" and so "question the motives" of those around her—particularly those who call themselves her owners.[1] Brent's first mistress, her mother's "whiter foster sister," had taught Linda how to "read and spell" (*ILSG*, 7–8)—rare skills for a slave, skills upon which Frederick Douglass's 1845 *Narrative of the Life of Frederick Douglass* places an extremely high value.[2] This boon of early literacy, however, and Linda Brent's later, self-taught ability to write do not grant her access to freedom in North Carolina. Nor does literacy motivate her as much as another form of lived understanding. "I had not lived fourteen years in slavery for nothing" (*ILSG*, 19), she says, by way of explaining how she came to her war. Indeed, it is only through combining the powers of her literacy, her lived knowledge, and her retention of what she describes as the unruly "sparks of [her] brother's God-given nature" that Brent formulates heroism: "I resolved never to be conquered" (*ILSG*, 19).

Still, this militant vocalization evokes an immediate sentimental lament of unspecified woe: "Alas for me!" she says (*ILSG*, 19). That foreshadowing, formulaic cry indicates the manifold, inevitable losses she will face. Yet she does not dwell on sorrow. Rather, she sets up a

---

1. Harriet Jacobs, *Incidents in the Life of a Slave Girl* (Cambridge: Harvard University Press, 1987), 19 (hereafter cited as *ILSG*).
2. For selected work on the importance of literacy in Douglass, see also Baker, *Blues*; Leverenz, *Manhood*, 128–32; Walker, *Moral Choices*, 213–54; Sundquist, "Frederick Douglass: Literacy and Paternalism."

scene of noble conflict, highlighted by a clash of willpower between Uncle Benjamin (Jacobs's Uncle Joseph) and his master, a story that prefigures her own struggles with Dr. Flint (Dr. James Norcom).[3] As she will say, "My master had power and law on his side; I had a determined will. There is might in each" (*ILSG*, 85). Thus, through her language and in the narration of key "incidents," Brent's story promises to be a tale of thrilling moral uplift, similar to many mid-nineteenth-century American abolitionist narratives. These works, whether deemed fictional (like Harriet Beecher Stowe's *Uncle Tom's Cabin*), or authentic (like Stowe's later *Key to Uncle Tom's Cabin*), a distinction to which I will return, functioned as Books of Revelation. As Jacobs says, the "adventures" of Linda Brent's life might sound too thrilling to be true, but they were true and were meant to arouse the moral indignation of "the women of the North to a realizing sense of the condition of two millions of women at the South" (*ILSG*, 1).

Liberty or Death?

Strangely, Linda Brent's early declaration of a "girl's" war is made in a chapter of Harriet Jacobs's *Incidents in the Life of a Slave Girl* called "The Slave Who Dared to Feel like a *Man*" (*ILSG*, 17; emphasis added). Indeed, Brent's declaration is not followed by an opening salvo from her own battle. Rather, she offers the account of her Uncle Benjamin's escape to the Free States, a story that follows what has often been called the classic slave-narrative quest pattern of fight-and-flight, perhaps most famously enacted by Douglass's *Narrative*.[4] Linda Brent allies her own experiences with her uncle's as thoroughly as they were twins. Uncle Benjamin, she says, was more "like my brother than my uncle" (*ILSG*, 6). He was "a bright handsome lad, nearly white" (*ILSG*, 23)—so fine, in trade parlance, and yet such a spitfire that a slave trader "said he would give any price if the handsome lad

---

3. For the purposes of my argument, it is important to maintain an acute awareness, following Yellin's approach as Jacobs's editor and her appendixes, that Jacobs used "characters" to embody the "historical" figures in her autobiographical narrative; see *ILSG*, 223.

4. Yellin notes on the basis of arguments such as Stepto's *From Behind the Veil*, Gates's "Binary Opposition," Baker's *The Journey Back*, and his *Blues* that "this genre has been characterized as dramatizing 'the quest for freedom and literacy' " (*ILSG*, xxvi). See also Smith, *Self-Discovery*.

was a girl," since Benjamin's reputation as rebellious made him an unsuitable masculine investment. In keeping with a popular image of the manly heroic slave,[5] Brent reports that the family "thanked God" he was not a girl (*ILSG*, 23). Of course, within the context of *Incidents* such thanks sit awkwardly, silently begging the question of Linda's condition as a high-spirited slave who *does* have the unfortunate fate of being a girl.

In aligning her "war" so closely with her uncle's in this instance and in others throughout her narrative, Harriet Jacobs structures Brent's impulse for liberty as parallel to, if not the double of, a masculinized martial exercise. At the same time, she genders the narrative so clearly as to question the applicability of such a masculinized exercise to a slave woman's experience. Brent cannot physically "tackle" Dr. Flint, the way her uncle does his opponent; as she soon reveals, physical "contact" between a slave and a master has different (often reproductive) consequences when the slave is a "girl" and not a "man." Yet liberty appears to require both men and women to foster those rebellious sparks Brent describes as God-given only to men, an emotional state of "dar[ing] to feel like a man."

But not just any man. When Brent starts "upon this hazardous undertaking" of emotional daring, she chooses to quote Patrick Henry: "Give me liberty or give me death was my motto" (*ILSG*, 99). In 1861 Jacobs has Brent revoice Henry's 1775 speech to the Virginia Convention. On the verge of a second American Revolution—or, as the nascent Confederacy would soon name it, the Southern War for Independence—Brent appropriates an ennobled cultural sentiment about liberty taken from the mouth of an already mythologized, white, male American rebel—a sentiment the slavocracy was attempting to manipulate for its own purposes.

But further, in her use of Patrick Henry she invites her audience to a reading of the character of the revered rebel in order subtextually to question the motives[6] of those who, like Dr. Flint and his wife, would argue that a Linda Brent's situation is incommensurate with a Patrick Henry's. While conjoining Brent's desire for liberty with a masculinized pattern of fight-and-flight, Jacobs also mobilizes an increasingly urgent critique of how this "will" to liberty has been log-

5. See Richard Yarborough, "Race, Violence, and Manhood: The Masculine Ideal in Frederick Douglass's 'The Heroic Slave,'" in Sundquist, *Frederick Douglass: New Literary and Historical Essays*, 166–88.

6. See Nelson, *Word*.

ically structured. After all, if Patrick Henry's rhetoric offered a potentially suicidal choice, the historical fact óf the matter is that Patrick Henry himself did not die in the Revolution. His either/or was— and still is, if more recent displays of American nationalism are any indication[7]—deemed heroic. But this choice of liberty or death, an Enlightenment scenario that also fueled Transcendentalist romanticism, falls curiously in line with the slavocracy's repeated claim that African-Americans were made to be slaves merely because they endured slavery. The romance of white supremacism insisted that the will of a true man would not allow him to put up with enslavement. A real man would rather die. Jacobs has even Brent voice such romantic logic when she and her family say to one another approvingly, "He that is *willing* to be a slave, let him be a slave" (*ILSG*, 26).

Yet the way Brent's family uses the verb "willing" in this textual moment follows upon a story of survival *within* slavery. Jacobs redefines such culturally revered terms as "will" and "liberty," upon which antebellum notions of identity ride. Contrary to a logic insisting that one's survival as a slave denotes a cowardly lack of will, the various histories Jacobs relates represent intermeshed, complex patterns of living, survival, and strength revise the two-dimensional, simplified, one-way, masculinized liberty-or-death logic that antebellum cultural mores associated with nobility, willpower, and selfhood. By repeatedly demonstrating that liberty, within the context of racial slavery, can also mean separations that both resemble and replay the definitive, deliberate ones that slavery tried to force upon African-Americans, Jacobs uses Brent's story to show that a wholesale restructuring of the value of individual liberty is necessary. The validity of the American democratic experiment depends on such a restructuring; otherwise, northern "freedom" will be no better than southern "slavery."

Such an assertion is clearly a staple of abolitionist texts. Anti-slavery politicians often warned that the slavocracy's unbridled authorities produced aristocratic, undemocratic tyranny.[8] Jacobs's rendition of

---

7. Rhetoric concerning the "liberation" of Kuwait during the 1990 Gulf War and the U.S. depiction of Chinese students dying for an effigy of Lady Liberty in Beijing (1988) bear witness to a resurgence of American nationalist idealism wherein a heroic willingness to die is repeatedly juxtaposed with the abstract but transcendent value of democratic freedom.

8. Walters's early essay "The Erotic South" demonstrates this anti-slavery claim clearly. For further references, see Walker, *Moral Choices*; and Yellin, *Women & Sisters*.

this abolitionist warning, however, demonstrates that it does not apply simply to the community that imagined itself as white but impinges on future generations of African-Americans as well. Therefore, and not surprisingly, Jacobs will show that Brent's reading of "liberty" is more accurate than the readings of those who claim to be the inheritors of Patrick Henry's legacy. Jean Fagan Yellin sees Jacobs as creating "a new kind of female hero . . . yok[ing] her success story as a heroic slave mother to her confessions as a woman who mourns that she is not a storybook heroine" (*ILSG*, xiv). As both Yellin and Beth Maclay Doriani have demonstrated, early African-American authors such as Harriet Jacobs and Harriet Wilson, the author of *Our Nig*, could neither adopt the "conventions of personhood as they were reproduced in the male slave narrative" nor "wholeheartedly embrace the definitions of womanhood that the popular genres of women carried to the American reading public in the 1830s, 1840s, and 1850s."[9] Their projects necessitated narrative strategies of adaptation. In fact, using antebellum concepts of masculinized self-reliance very much as Douglass does, Jacobs equates antebellum slave women who display resourcefulness—who, Doriani claims, "take responsibility for the welfare of their children"—with "the white, male Emersonian hero—shapers of their own destinies and responsible for their own survival."[10]

But why did Yellin use the term "female hero"? What of Doriani's syntactic frame that places the "personhood" of male slave narratives and the "womanhood" of Jacobs's text into such pro forma structural opposition? Why compare Jacobs's story to a narrative of Emersonian self-reliance? What do the repeated terms "hero" and "heroine" denote? These words track a potential interpretive paucity similar to those that Jacobs herself points to when she descants on the anomaly of the concept of "virtue" for a slave girl. Just as "virtuous slave girl" and "slave mother" linguistically display the hypocritical violence of mid-nineteenth-century heterosexual ideology,[11] so does "female

9. Beth Maclay Doriani, "Black Womanhood in Nineteenth-Century America: Subversion and Self-Construction in Two Women's Autobiographies," *American Quarterly* 43 (June 1991): 203.

10. Ibid., 219.

11. "Mockery" (*ILSG*, 62) is the word Jacobs applies to the way slavery, that "cage of obscene birds" (*ILSG*, 52), devalues Christian virtue and motherhood. As Carby notes (*Reconstructing Womanhood*), "Slave women gave birth to the capital of the South and were therefore, in Linda Brent's words, 'considered of no value, unless they continually increase their owner's stock' [*ILSG*, 49]."

hero" indicate a twentieth-century paradox that continues to shape the way Jacobs's narrative is read and the questions a reader might ask of it.

This is not to say that the critical focus on Jacobs's attempt to formulate a new, racially specific definition of "true" womanhood has not been vital. But designating Linda Brent a "new form of female hero" and a "black heroine" can occlude considerations of how this text also revises the character of such gender and race designations. That is, comparisons of *Incidents* with either "classic" African-American male slave narrative or "classic" Anglo-American female domestic or seduction fiction have generally noted the ways in which it deviates from one or the other without significantly questioning the gendered and racial assumptions made about those narrative patterns. Nor do such comparisons tend to grapple with how critics use their own historically-determined language, a literary terminology that constructs the character of both narrative patterns and that may obscure the extent of Jacobs's revisions.

Early commentary about this text invalidated its authenticity by declaring it to be too melodramatic to be a real slave narrative.[12] Likewise, designating Brent a "female hero" allows a reader to envision her decked out in Patrick Henry's conventional breeches, rather than to come to terms with how Jacobs may have, in fact, redesigned the garment. And if my image of a cross-dressing Brent decked out in breeches is meant to confuse gendered readings of this text, I would also point out that even when Jacobs stresses the consequence to lived social relations of racial identity, she questions "race" as a category. In her picture of two sisters, one of whose lives will be blighted because she has been designated a slave, Jacobs quietly makes the only difference between these children rest squarely on the designation "slave" and not on appearance, character, or familial role, thereby reinforcing the idea that race is a "legal fiction"[13] determined by economic conditions, a commodity relation.[14] And what happens to the

12. As Yellin, Carby, and Andrews all point out, *Incidents* was for many years discounted as too melodramatic, most infamously by John Blassingame's assessment in *Slave Testimony: Two Centuries of Letters, Speeches, Interviews, and Autobiographies* (Baton Rouge: Louisiana State University Press, 1977), xvii–xv.

13. I borrow the phrase from Mark Twain, *The Tragedy of Pudd'nhead Wilson* (New York: Penguin, 1987), 25.

14. This is to say not that the sorts of class distinctions developing during the antebellum years and the concomitant race relations stemming from race slavery operated alike but rather that they were shaped by similar logic and indeed shaped the dimen-

supposed purity of the term "white" if Brent's first mistress is, as Brent describes her, merely a little bit "whiter" than her foster sister, Brent's mother? In moments like this, while Brent insists that both "African" and "Anglo" have meaning, her text severely complicates a clear definition of either term.

Indeed, Jacobs's restructuring of mid-nineteenth-century racialized, gendered logic rescripts that logic in such a way that the basis on-which narrative identity or any constructed "character" accrues cul-tural value must change. As William Andrews claims, her process of linguistic retribution strives to appropriate "language for purposes of signification outside that which was privileged by the dominant cul-ture."[15] If the identifying, relational, gendered terms mother or sister, father or son have been bankrupted by the violence of slavery, so too have words such as hero, liberty, and patriot; all these words, those bearing specific gender or racial definitions and those that some would claim are neutral, will have an impact upon Jacobs's construc-tion of that self named Linda Brent. Brent's value will ride on how these words signify. Clearly, Jacobs was interested in making gen-dered and racial identities the special subjects of her narrative, and much twentieth-century commentary focuses on "gender" and "race" as her subjects. Those commentaries, however, tend to use these words primarily as simple synonyms for "woman" and "black." As Andrews writes: "To facilitate the enslavement of people, the ideology of slavery must first master the potential meanings of key words in the language of the oppressing culture. Slavery must construct the free play of meaning that normally informs words like mother, home, lady or freedom so as to reduce the multivalent to the univocal"[16] I would add this question: Doesn't using "gender" as a signifier for "woman," or "race" as a signifier for "black," also perform a reduction of the (Bakhtinian) multivalent to the univocal?

In his excellent study of *Incidents*, Andrews makes clear Jacobs's own interest in "signifying" when he demonstrates how her use of southern dialect, when put in a "dialogic relationship with standard-

---

sions of each other. One cannot speak of how class is constructed in the middle to late nineteenth century without understanding how racial myths were intertwined with class and vice versa. Jacobs made plain that the prejudice she experienced outside of slavery was embedded in that commodity economy which had allowed people of one class arbitrarily to designate others as legally purchasable objects.

15. Andrews, *To Tell a Free Story*, 290.
16. Ibid., 289.

ized usage that has become morally bankrupt or emotionally bogus," attains a new linguistic vitality.[17] Still, in concentrating on those dialogic moments in the text that allow Linda Brent to "talk her way out of the most abject forms of humiliation,"[18] Andrews does not fully explore Jacobs's revaluation of standard English, her translation of bankrupted terms that turns them back into a means of exchange valuable for her and her family. Such translations retool the process of narratively structuring character per se in cultural productions. Andrews's analysis does focus on those incidents—such as the invasion of Grandmother's home by "feral white trash"[19] or Brent's command of the word "love"—that turn on domestic exchanges, and it is clear that Jacobs's interest did lie heavily within the antebellum sphere of "woman." But what this analysis misses is the way these revisions of the so-called private (fantasized as feminine) connect sharply to a revision of how an antebellum public (masculine) could be legitimately construed.

In other words, if familial dependency, culturally scripted as "private," must be abjured so that a "self" can rise to an individual liberty, isn't the resulting liberated self simply another form of the disfiguring disempowerment that slavery's logic has already enforced? Doesn't such a logic of masculinized solipsism threaten to undermine the ground of all personhood? If what antebellum mores claimed as most "human" was represented by a kinship tie—the tie between mother and child—what would happen if such bonds were as little regarded in the North as in the slavocracy? What conceptual stay remained to keep "person" from being translated into "property"—or, to use Jacobs's terms, to keep citizens from becoming nothing more than "God-breathing machines" (*ILSG*, 8)?

Ultimately, what Jacobs throws open to revision is the whole framework of individuality that supported the value of "liberty" in nineteenth-century American culture. Freedom, *any* American's freedom, she will show, hangs in the balance of her revision. If Linda Brent's character, formulated as a result of strong interdependencies, can be read, interpreted, remembered, and valued as if she were a Patrick Henry (that is, if Linda Brent's name can signify a trope for Liberty) all justifications of enslavement, racial discrimination and gendered degradation become more than simply points of sophistic debate.

17. Ibid., 289.
18. Ibid., 278.
19. Ibid., 279.

They become ludicrously hypocritical and, above all for that time and moment, dangerously unpatriotic, threatening to debase the valuable tender underwriting Patrick Henry's cultural memory.

Translations and Relations

When Uncle Benjamin finally attains his liberty, he says to his brother Philip (Mark Ramsey), whom he meets by chance in New York, "Phil, I part with all my kindred." Jacobs has Brent remark dolefully, "And so it proved. We never heard from him again" (*ILSG*, 26). Benjamin disappears from the family as completely as if he'd been sold down river to a Georgia trader. Above all, Benjamin is lost to his mother, Aunt Martha (Molly Horniblow). Given the extreme emphasis that abolitionist rhetoric and antebellum narrative in general placed on the mother-and-child bond, this last separation is the most telling.[20] Without directly comparing Benjamin's new-found liberty in the North to his slavery in the South, Jacobs has pointed to their structural similarity. Although she rejoices that her uncle has escaped the condition of white man's property, Brent shows that Benjamin still loses what the slavocracy insisted a slave had no real cognizance of (outside, of course, the bonds in the "peculiar institution")—a family. All those kin ties or affective terms upon which "white" identity and moral worth supposedly rested—in Benjamin's case, the words uncle, husband, brother, father, and son—but which have been rendered theoretically invalid (or sarcastically comic) by the volatile situation of slavery are then made materially insubstantial. Should Linda go, she too would part from her kin.[21]

20. Jacobs reports that in one of Dr. Flint's elaborate letters of persuasion to Linda Brent, he claimed (writing under a pseudonym) that the "heartfelt tie . . . between a master and his servant" was the same as that "between a mother and her child" (*ILSG*, 172). Further, Flint repeatedly refers to his desire for Linda as based on such a familial model—"I consider you as yet a child" (*ILSG*, 83)—begging questions of incest and pedophilia. On maternal loss as a widely used emblem in antebellum discourse, see Ammons, "Stowe's Dream," 155–95; Carby, *Reconstructing Womanhood*, 20–40; Yellin, *Women & Sisters*, 88–96.

21. Linda Brent's ambivalence about "freedom," given its relation to familial loss and death, is emphasized again when her brother William escapes: "If you had seen the tears, and heard the sobs, you would have thought the messenger had brought tidings of death instead of freedom. Poor old grandmother felt that she should never see her darling boy again. And I was selfish. I thought more of what I had lost, than of what my brother had gained" (*ILSG*, 134).

Therein, of course, lies one of the most striking features of *Incidents in the Life of a Slave Girl*: Jacobs's insistence that Brent retain the material reality of familial ties (which did exist, slaveholding fictions to the contrary), while also seeking and at last attaining freedom from enslavement. To allow Brent to do so, as more than a few critics have demonstrated, Jacobs's 1861 narrative negotiates several forms of nineteenth-century discourse.[22] Many (if not most) evaluations of this text focus on how Jacobs had patiently to cross-stitch elements from what has often been read as a primarily masculine fight-and-flight slave narrative to the feminine rhetoric of domesticity, in order to pattern a voice out of the "spoken and the silenced"[23] pieces of both a "slave's" narrative and a "girl's" story. As Jean Fagan Yellin writes, "The resulting text is densely patterned. Although slave narrative has been likened to the 'rootless alienated' picaro, Jacobs's Linda Brent locates herself firmly within a social matrix" (*ILSG*, xxvii). And as William Andrews declares, the narrative skirmishes most prominent in Jacobs's work show "graphically the discursive nature of male-female power relationships."[24]

Still and all, in Jacobs's narrative as in Douglass's, the concept of American "liberty" is most often concretely realized—if also consistently challenged—in masculinized representations.[25] The equation "liberty = masculinity" is made evident in such moments as the graveyard scene in which Linda Brent consolidates a determination to take Patrick Henry's motto for her own and to follow her Uncle Benjamin's course. Note how Jacobs ties her resolution to heroic images of traditional, Americanized male courage:

22. For various claims concerning Jacobs's use of "traditional" discursive patterns, particularly sentimental tropes, see Yellin's introduction (*ILSG*, esp. xxvi–xxxiii); Andrews, *To Tell a Free Story*; Carby, *Reconstructing Womanhood*, 20–24; Doriani, "Black Womanhood," 199–221; Foreman, "The Spoken and the Silenced," 313–24; Karcher, "Rape, Murder, and Revenge"; Mills, "Lydia Maria Child"; Laura E. Tanner, "Self-Conscious Representation in the Slave Narrative," *Black Literature Forum* 21 (Winter 1987): 415–25.

23. I borrow Foreman's title, "The Spoken and the Silenced." For more detailed arguments concerning Jacobs's rhetoric, see Andrews, *To Tell a Free Story*; Carby, *Reconstructing Womanhood*; and Yellin, *Women and Sisters*.

24. Andrews, *To Tell a Free Story*, 278.

25. Although I have argued (see Chapter 4 above) that the evolution of Douglass's representations demonstrates a changing view of the equation liberty = masculinity, his 1845 *Narrative*, as Valerie Smith (*Self-Discovery*) has demonstrated, often turns that equation to his advantage.

The graveyard was in the woods, and twilight was coming on. . . . A black stump, at the head of my mother's grave, was all that remained of a tree my father had planted. His grave was marked by a small wooden board bearing his name, the letters of which were nearly obliterated. I knelt down and kissed them and poured forth a prayer to God for guidance and support in the perilous step I was about to take. As I passed the wreck of the old meeting house where before Nat Turner's time the slaves had been allowed to meet for worship, I seemed to hear my father's voice come from it bidding me not to tarry till I reached freedom or the grave. (*ILSG*, 90–91).

Brent's deceased mother's "voice" has spoken to her at this same spot earlier, but now, in the hour of crisis regarding an overt bid to escape, only her father's "voice" is heard. The dead mother is mute. Moreover, the paternal voice emanates not from her father's grave, as one might expect, but rather erupts from the house of God, a sacred meeting hall desecrated by slaveholders out of their fear of rebellion—or the fear of a righteous and noble revolution? Neatly conflating political freedom and rebellion (Nat Turner and Patrick Henry), morality (the wrecked but sacred meeting hall), and the written word (her father's grave marker) with paternal sanction (her father's voice crying "liberty or death"), Jacobs multiply authorizes a fight for freedom in the "Name of the Father" and thus validates a heroic course of action using traditionally paternal emblems that have very specific references to a rebellious African-American context.[26]

Yet even as this passage upholds the validity of an ennobled, masculinized fight-and-flight bid for liberty or death, it also scrutinizes the logic that has produced such a pattern. Why does the passage mention Brent's dead mother? Why the comment that the tree her father had planted to mark her slave mother's grave had become nothing but a black stump? Might this dead tree be a submerged reference to those (father-lacking) "genealogical trees [that] do not flourish in slavery" (*MB/MF*, 28) of which Frederick Douglass wrote in 1854?[27] Read in such a way, Brent's black stump insists that the eventual survival of African-American family trees will depend on remembering

26. See Spillers, "Mama's Baby, Papa's Maybe," for a fuller consideration of how the historical condition of patronymic loss in American slavery affects African-American representation.

27. See also Andrews's introduction to Douglass, *My Bondage and My Freedom*, xi–xxvii.

both mother's and father's narratives. Indeed, what this moment fore-grounds is just how much the heroism of "give me liberty" owed its density and the desiring urgency of its conceptual power not only to the other half of the cry—"or give me death"—but to the culture's dichotomous gendering of the either/or logic that associates liberty with masculinity and death with femininity.[28] Of course, Brent's slave father has literally died, but his death is figured as heroic and his voice reanimated as the sacred, rebellious, defiantly liberatory pater-nal. The mother, by contrast, has been silenced—not mute but muted, her grave bearing a blasted and unfertile symbol. Thus does Jacobs's scene subtly question the value of "rising" to a liberty that has been defined through a muting or outright denial of the feminine. The ge-nealogical paternity that Douglass wrote of as vital to "civilization"[29] cannot, for Jacobs, be fertile if rooted on a feminized and silent grave.

Hazel Carby called Jacobs's graveyard scene a moment of "transi-tion from death as preferable to slavery, to the stark polarity of free-dom or death." Further, the narrative "disrupt[s] conventional expectations of the attributes of a heroine ... by transforming and transcending the central paradigm of death versus virtue."[30] Indeed, Brent's revision of virtue is marked by her own claim that slave women ought not to be judged by standards of morality the denial of which is a constituting factor of enslavement (*ILSG*, 56).

Yet isn't it precisely in understanding that her children are not (as Carby says) "the fruits of her shame" but "her links to life"[31] that Brent does not, in fact, choose *any* stark polarity? However much her narrative endorses "freedom or death," it also shows that such an endorsement threatens to debase the "black" motherhood Brent is in the process of making more legitimately valuable than "white" purity. Separating herself from her children by making the classic slave nar-rative break for freedom might put her outside a definition of "mother" that she intends to claim. When Aunt Martha warns, "No-body respects a mother who forsakes her children; and if you leave them, you will never have a happy moment ... and your suffering would be dreadful. Remember poor Benjamin" (*ILSG*, 91), the word

28. The associative links between femininity and maternity, maternity and death is pervasive and well-documented in a wide range of antebellum narratives. See Hoffert, *Private Matters*, 170–87.
29. On Douglass's lasting belief in the need for paternity, see *LT*, 27.
30. Carby, *Reconstructing Womanhood*, 59–60.
31. Ibid.

"nobody" reminds Brent that she risks damaging both her reputation (as she has already done once, in sacrificing her virtue) and the respect her children have for her. Losing her own virtue is one thing; losing her children's respect is quite another. Brent's voluntary desertion treads very shaky narrative ground, given anti-slavery rhetoric's stressed or the immorality of slavery's involuntary separation of mother and child. Risking no one's sanction might mean that her story would become unintelligible, perhaps aphasic.

Moreover, heeding Aunt Martha's injunction, Brent does remember her uncle—all too well. His "rememory"[32] is always painfully before her, doubly resonant with liberation and loss. And unlike Uncle Benjamin, who has no children and who is remembered with a love that makes the day he was captured "seem as but yesterday" (*ILSG*, 21), Linda may be forgotten by her family if she cannot create for them a story of self-liberation worth remembering. This is loss terribly compounded. As she says, she does not wish to leave her children, and quite particularly her daughter—who is herself about to go, ironically and tellingly, to the Free North, "without a mother's love to shelter her from the storms of life; almost without memory of a mother! I had a great desire that she should look upon me, before she went, that she might take my image with her in her memory" (*ILSG*, 139). In this Brent shares Aunt Martha's morality: in freedom, former slaves such as Linda and her daughter may incur what predominant cultural traditions have described for women as a fate worse than death. But unlike Martha, Linda Brent also knows, through her experience of Dr. Flint's degradations, that slavery in and of itself is a fate worse than death. Escape must remain a risk worth taking, not only for men like her uncle but also for women like herself and her daughter.

The storyteller's trick that Jacobs must pull off, then, is to tell a tale of freedom for herself and for her children that activates a new narrative economy, one in which what some (say, Aunt Martha) read as desertion will translate into devotion—a narrative where liberty does not require death.[33] Such a trick inevitably brings Brent back to her

32. In *Beloved* (New York: Knopf, 1987), Toni Morrison uses "rememory" to signify the way the past comes back despite efforts to keep it "at bay": Sethe says of Paul D, "Now he added more: new pictures and old rememories that broke her heart" (95).

33. As Carby notes, "In order to save her children, Linda Brent apparently had to desert them" (*Reconstructing Womanhood*, 60). Carby's analysis, however, is concerned with how Brent's desertion finds validation in its acceptance by her daughter, Ellen (Louise Matilda Jacobs). That acceptance as narrated, writes Carby, "exclud[es]

central dilemma: how to be a Patrick Henry, or how to activate the cultural respect associated with the liberty his story has symbolized for the Uncle Benjamins of Brent's world, without either devaluing Uncle Benjamin's memory or weakening the value of Brent's. How can she validate the choice made by Uncle Benjamin and cry, "Give me liberty or give me death," without discrediting female experience and maternity? How can she *adapt* his choice without *adopting* it? Clearly, Brent is not a white man—nor would she desire to be one; Dr. Flint and Mr. Sands (Samuel Tredwell Sawyer) both illustrate the axis of revulsion Jacobs associates with being a white man. Indeed, she is not male at all, no matter how much her story is prefigured by Uncle Benjamin's. This means that the most locatable narrative models for heroic liberty available to Jacobs in 1859 would not fit. Whether they told of white Revolutionary folk heroes or of the manly, heroic slave escaping north, following them would exact a price that Jacobs could not pay.

But those narrative patterns that *were* deemed appropriate to Brent's gender role required frailties Jacobs could not condone. As Yellin and Carby aptly point out, the pattern of the betrayed, passive white heroine of domestic ideology demanded the woman's death with as much force as the Patrick Henry model would demand death for those men who did not attain liberty. Meanwhile, the tragic mulatta-and-child image of Eliza and Harry Harris in *Uncle Tom's Cabin* made a "black" mother's character just as hysterical as her whiter foster heroine-sister's. These patterns offered little upon which to value the lived stoicism Jacobs saw daily expressed in those around her. As Carby dryly notes, the Cult of True Womanhood represented not a "lived set of social relations" but rather "a racist, ideological system."[34]

What to do, then, asks Carby's analysis, with an Aunt Martha who manages to endure enslavement while nurturing a family tree in the very jaws of slavery—a "rememory" that anticipates as much as Uncle Benjamin's, Brent's own tale? Despite a cultural mythology that would

---

the need for any approval from the readership. Jacobs bound the meaning and interpretation of her womanhood and motherhood to the internal structure of the text, making external validation unnecessary and unwarranted" (61). I agree with Carby that "judgement was to be passed on the institution of slavery and not on deviations from conventions of true womanhood" (61). Still, Jacobs's awareness that she might speak to future generations of African-Americans would make it imperative that she take some account of external (readers') judgments as influenced by the circulation of cultural narratives, in order to change those narratives' valuation.

34. Carby, *Reconstructing Womanhood*, 49–50.

insist otherwise, Aunt Martha has her freedom without breaking with all her kin—though a freedom severely compromised by racial slavery. She has a potency of sorts: at least she owns her own house; she feeds and protects her starving grandchildren; she can remind Dr. Flint, with visible effect, that he will go to hell (*ILSG*, 82). She may be circumscribed by his economic privilege to sell those grandchildren, by his patriarchal power to claim them, and by his legal immunity from the consequences of his cruelty, but she is not at his mercy as much as Jacobs is. If such "incidental" female models, circumscribed as they are, still display personal dignity and loyalty, how are they *not* noble?

Denoting a will that has not taken the heroic liberty-or-death stance is clearly not an easy task. Even when depicting a woman's potency, Jacobs resorts to paternal, masculinized emblems. Her grandmother was "a woman of a high spirit. . . . I had been told that she once chased a white gentleman with a loaded pistol, because he insulted one of her daughters" (*ILSG*, 29). Grandmother's pistol-packing does not strictly resemble the heroic liberty for which a Patrick Henry stands, but then again, it is a culturally approved model of courage— most often for a sentimental father. Doesn't this story rely, in part, on countless depictions of wronged fathers defending the good name of their daughters? In pointing out such an image, I am not disputing that Jacobs sought alternative narratives with which to combat the antebellum Cult of True Womanhood, alternatives that describe what Carby calls an evolving "discourse of black womanhood."[35]

As Frederick Douglass would show during the bitter suffrage debates within abolitionist-feminist circles, the particularity of gender was a vexing issue. Those abstract New England ideals he had adopted, which had supported his own right to freedom, could wither in the face of gendered political expediencies and lived animosities separating "Americans." At the 1869 Equal Rights Convention he advocated support of the Fifteenth amendment despite its lack of provision for women.

> MR. DOUGLASS: When women, because they are women, are hunted down through . . . New York and New Orleans, . . . when their children are torn from their arms, . . . then they will have an urgency to obtain the ballot. . . ."

35. Ibid., 184, n. 14.

A VOICE: Is that not all true about black women?

MR. DOUGLASS: Yes, yes, yes; it is true of the black woman, but not because she is a woman but because she is black.[36]

Therefore, though Brent's story, as Valerie Smith writes, "is not the classic story of the triumph of the individual will [but] . . . more a story of a triumphant self-in-relation,"[37] her tale nevertheless has to work inside and outside that classic language of individuality: she can denounce neither the validity of Douglass's *Narrative* nor his later pained perception of how racial identity crosscuts gender roles in the politics of national identity and citizenship. Jacobs shows how Brent's racial identity has been formed in the masculine context of her uncles and son. She will not deny them. But then again, such narratives can disavow hers. For of course Douglass's statement reveals that he was willing, for expediency's sake, to downplay the importance of an African-American woman's experience.

Thus, although Linda Brent's alterations of classic narratives—whether the tale of the heroic slave or of the tragic heroine—may be specifically aimed at delineating and revising a black mother's role, *Incidents* does not speak only to women; these stories must alter the roles for African-American men, if not for *the man* as well.[38] When her Uncle Benjamin determines to escape, Linda Brent's first remark to him is a reproach: "Go," she says, "and break your mother's heart" (*ILSG*, 21). Silently she repents of the statement, yet she has verbalized it, lending those words the narrative impact of direct quotation. Her reproach does not alter his determination, but it does serve as an emotional check on the upcoming scene of heroic escape. Then, in recounting Uncle Benjamin's heroism, she tells the story of Philip, who does not follow the course of the "heroic slave" to freedom but opts to return home. He may be returning voluntarily to bondage but he is also going home to his mother and his family. He calmly tells Benjamin that "it would kill their mother if he deserted her in her trouble. She had pledged her house, and with difficulty, had raised money to buy him" (*ILSG*, 25). Benjamin will not allow his mother to buy *him*—and Brent approves of the decision, for "the more my mind had be-

36. Proceedings of the American Equal Rights Association Convention, Steinway Hall, New York City, May 12, 1869, in Foner, *Frederick Douglass on Women's Rights*, 87.
37. Smith, *Self-Discovery*, 27.
38. The allusion to 1960s American slang for those in control, particularly white men, is intentional.

come enlightened, the more difficult it was for me to consider myself an article of property" (*ILSG*, 199). She thus acknowledges the bravery of a freedom gained through an Enlightenment narrative of individual will.

Still she validates Philip's story:

> The brave old woman still toiled on, hoping to rescue some of her other children. After a while she succeeded in buying Philip. She paid eight hundred dollars and came home with the precious document that secured his freedom. The happy mother and son sat together by the old hearthstone that night, telling how proud they were of each other, and how they would prove to the world that they could take care of themselves, as they had long taken care of others. We all concluded by saying "He that is *willing* to be a slave, let him be a slave" (*ILSG*, 26).

Without giving up the rhetoric of a self-determination that grants Benjamin his heroic status, she manages to laud Uncle Philip, whose course might otherwise be described—particularly in antebellum terms—as passive, indeed as feminine. Jacobs's rhetoric suggests as well that Philip and Martha in conjunction constitute an alternative definition of identity, one that acknowledges, relies on, and is structured through relation and dependence—an intermeshing that makes taking care of oneself mean taking care of others. Pride as well as independence—we can take care of ourselves—emerges from the rhetorical collectivity "we all." And it is out of this translation that an alternative version of national identity begins to emerge.

Strange Words in a Strange Land

Who is this composite being, Philip-Martha? Can Yellin's term for Linda Brent, "female hero," apply to Philip as well as to Martha? Philip's story is not like that of Stowe's Uncle Tom, whose caretaking role leads to his martyrdom. Nor is Uncle Philip a figure for Mr. Self-Reliance. Besides, as Jacobs has shown, what sort of identity is self-reliance, if those who embody it have been compelled, like Uncle Benjamin, to deny mother and brother? If being accepted as a freeman means denying family ties, then slave and (free)man are clearly not the complete metamorphic opposite that Douglass's famous statement would have them: "You have seen how a man was made a slave; you shall see how a slave was made a man" (*N*, 107). Slave and freeman are two sides of the same coin of a patriarchially determined identity. And if the most obvious lack in such a coin can be characterized as the absence of the African-American woman, what Jacobs makes clear is that Uncle Benjamin loses too. The narrative of heroic manhood as a tale worth telling, that stuff which Hawthorne extolled in 1862 as the "pristine value" upon which true poetry "broods," becomes a debased fiction.[39] Only in narratives that stress mutuality, where the many can speak in the same voice without a "we" to cannibalize the one, will freedom ring clear.

Indeed, the younger Benjamin's revision of his namesake's history demonstrates this new logic. "Some of the apprentices were Americans, others American-born Irish; and it was offensive to their dignity to have a 'nigger' among them, after they had been told that he *was* a 'nigger,' " says Jacobs of Benjamin Brent's (Joseph Jacobs's) experiences as a Boston laborer (*ILSG*, 186). This moment underscores the northern "prejudice against color" (*ILSG*, chap. 35). It also demonstrates how the noun "nigger" produces an unquestioned narrative of insult that translates relations of favor into their opposite. Abuse is substituted for praise: Benjamin had been "liked by the master and was a favorite with his fellow apprentices" until that word "transformed him into a different being" (*ILSG*, 186).

But what sort of a different being is a "nigger"? The searing, restrained irony of Jacobs's tone in this passage is made all the more palpable by her previous redefinition of that racial insult. For instance, much earlier, Brent's friend, Betty, who has helped her, hide from her master, pronounces "anathemas over Dr. Flint and all his tribe, every now and then saying, with a chuckling laugh, 'Dis nigger's too cute for 'em' " (*ILSG*, 103). A process of redefinition based on the speaker's position is evident here: Betty compliments herself for the cleverness that the term "nigger" does not—for some—mean.[40] Young Benjamin's tale takes Betty's compliment further by showing that the force of the supposed insult "nigger" is based on blatant contradictions, since Benjamin could "pass" for a man who had no genealogical connections to an African heritage. His "being" thus is masked not by

39. Hawthorne, "Chiefly about War Matters," 59.

40. With thanks to June Jordan's teaching and her work, esp. "Problems of Language in a Democratic State," in *On Call: Political Essays* (Boston: South End Press, 1985), 27–36.

his history but by the inconsistent "seeing" of his fellows and his master, who had previously regarded him as a favorite.[41]

Here, as well as in other works where the light-skinned mulatto or mulatta is placed on the cusp of an imagined racial binary,[42] the cultural racism that has tried to force "nigger" to carry a negative connotation is shown up as a meaningless shame even in the culture's own system of adjudication, if Benjamin can so easily be judged "white." The antebellum fantasy that racial characteristics were inherent is quietly scripted as just fantasy; in turn, "nigger" loses the smack of insult. In fact, Jacobs has made the material content of that insult boomerang to its source. For if "family values"[43] truly underwrote the strength of mid-nineteenth-century northern conceptions of individual merit, a northerner could not justify any cultural script of being that would demand a man to have, in order to be free, so little regard for his family. Should young Benjamin choose to deny the name "nigger," he would be agreeing with his master's reading of that term and would therefore have to deny Linda Brent. Since she is the only one of his acknowledged parents to give the parental tie any evident positive, material consequence, to deny her would be to betray those virtues that so-called Americans had assigned such high value. And if Benjamin should deny Linda's maternity by refusing to be identified as a "nigger," he would simply repeat the loss that abolitionist rhetoric situated as southern slavery's deepest horror, the separation of mother and child.

Thus *Incidents* makes it clear that Benjamin's own self-worth relies on his identification with a heritage that others would try to disparage. He has learned that his mother's value cannot be reduced to a sheer commodity relation; Brent has demonstrated that her "worth" is not measurable two-dimensionally in the terms that slaveholders set down—that is, "by dollars and cents" (*ILSG*, 196). Thus Benjamin knows, through his mother's narrative example, that his own "worth" as an apprentice cannot be reduced either to a commodity relation or by a word whose meaning is, after all, subject to interpretation. Hence, Benjamin does not deny his being as a nigger, despite the insults of

41. I borrow from Carolyn Porter, *Seeing and Being: The Plight of the Participant Observer in Emerson, James, Adams, and Faulkner* (Middletown, Conn.: Wesleyan University Press, 1981).

42. On the figure of the mulatto, see Chapter 1.

43. This reference to the rhetoric of the 1992 United States presidential campaign is intentional.

"the Americans and American-born Irish" who require such contradictions as props to their own status. His refusal, focusing attention on the repeated terms "American" and "nigger," not only highlights his familial loyalty but also points to the indissoluble linkage between private family and public or national identity. Jacobs has already posited that link when she has Brent say of her former lover and the acknowledged father of her children, "Surely there must be some justice in *the man;*" (ILSG, 42; emphasis added). Their son Benjamin's refusal to abjure his mother underscores the link that his father, U.S. Congressman Sands, has denied.

Which of these "American-born" men, then, Sands or his denied son, truly embodies justice? The choice is clear. Jacobs has made justice, one of the founts of national pride, depend on a refusal to deny family relations. Such a refusal will infuse those supposedly private affectional ties with the political value and legal consequence they should—by virtue of the morality preached in a Christian democracy—already contain.

Of course, Jacobs has proposed similar questions about legitimacies earlier in her text, and certainly they are central to most abolitionist work. Still, in outlining such inconsistent logic in this late chapter of her narrative, Jacobs not only reiterates how slaveholding has made for moral, cultural, and political bankruptcies ; she also makes young Benjamin's story an emblem of mutuality that defines a way around those losses. His example of a fierce tender feeling (for his mother) translated into a public identity (as proud to be a "nigger" in the face of insult) will explore a semiosis of agency that proposes a new means of signification based on tenderness and dependency, or on the continuities of memory, rather than on false occlusions, silencing mutations, and Self-Reliance.

Cannily, Jacobs has used the word "master" in this incident to designate Benjamin's Boston employer. Of course, the word is literally appropriate; the skilled-trade apprenticeship system in the Free States named employers "masters."[44] But Jacobs's application of it here cannot help but figure young Benjamin's freeman status as a northern version of his former southern condition. Given just how pejorative the word "master" has become over the course of its narrative association with Dr. Flint's public (legally supported) and private sexual

44. Ironically, the feudal master-apprentice system was common in publishing and printing, a trade in which, Yellin reports, blacks were routinely denied apprenticeship (*ILSG*, 287 n.1).

perfidy, the word now shudders with negative meaning. Southern hierarchical bankruptcies are imbricated in the language of the northern work ethic. Where the accumulation of associative, experiential meanings behind such words as "master" and "nigger" redefine the way those words signify, especially for her northern audience, Jacobs's exposures threaten the narrative surety of tradition. She unseats the anchors of cultural reference that have disallowed value to interracial intercourse (except as a hidden commodity relation) or have allowed a northern master to see himself as a different being from a southern slaveholder: any man who was "originally a Yankee peddler" could easily become "a slaveholder" (*ILSG*, 197).

Moreover, it is precisely in activating this threat to unmoor traditional referentiality that Jacobs's narrative asserts the need for a new value system to underwrite meaning. If it takes a baseless insult to validate "white" worth, then the favor of being white is no favor at all; if it takes death to make freedom ring, then freedom has a tinny sound. One might say here that Jacobs's logic, unlike the cry "give me liberty or give me death," does not see change as suicidally oriented. The logic within the *Incidents* shows how the deterministic narrative of mastery has overwritten the vital flux of potential meanings. Prefabricated plot lines that have cut off "American-born" Benjamin will map America as manifestly destined to be exclusive. If such a map—incommensurate with America's own utopian, idealistic sense of itself as inclusive—should stand, then *belonging* to America will mean just that: citizens will be slaves to a system of government that views them as dead things.

Uncle Philip's obituary is a good case in point. When the newspaper notice names the deceased Philip "a good man and a useful citizen," Jacobs has Brent cry, "So they called a colored man a citizen! Strange words to be uttered in that region!" (*ILSG*, 201). Yet what *Incidents* has already shown is that those words are as strange as they are familiar. If, as Emerson wrote, America was the "asylum of all nations,"[45] then why was Uncle Philip denied the name citizen until he was dead? Such idealism scripted American value as based on

---

45. Ralph Waldo Emerson, quoted in Martin, *The Mind of Frederick Douglass*, 223. Emerson goes on to write of America as that place where "the energy of Irish, Germans, Swedes, Poles, and Cossacks, and all the European tribes—of the Africans and the Polynesians, will construct a new race, a new religion, a new literature which will be as vigorous as the new Europe which came out of the melting pot of the Dark Ages."

those "free" associations that would allow for previously unseen or devalued histories.

And yet, as Jacobs has Linda Brent describe her stay in New York, "oppressed Poles and Hungarians could find a safe refuge in that city . . . but there I sat, an oppressed American, not daring to show my face" (*ILSG*, 198). When abolitionist Theodore Parker claimed that America had but "one series of literary productions that could be written by none but Americans and only here—I mean the Lives of the Fugitive Slaves,"[46] Jacobs heard a Mr. Thorne, who justified revealing Brent's whereabouts to Dr. Flint by saying, "I am a patriot, a lover of my country, and I do this as an act of justice to the laws" (*ILSG*, 179). Which one of these stories about Americanness will determine the shape of American citizenship? Is either version adequate? The various "incidents" Jacobs has related all point to a condemnation of any narrative of agency empowered to such an extent as to require the exclusion (death) of others, whether northern or southern. Where inferiority and superiority are assigned by narrative fiat so that embodied practices are discounted, ignored, or rendered invisible, there lies violence.

Indeed, for Jacobs the word "father," as defined in a system that would empower that role through the systematic disempowering of others, more often than not functions as the very blade that slices off the roots of African-American genealogical trees. While Douglass often sought to establish a genealogical root and so restore a paternity the slavocracy had rendered invisible or legally inconsequential, Jacobs's situation gave her a different view: "What tangled skeins are the genealogies of slavery!" (*ILSG*, 78). Where Douglass sees paternal loss as emblematic of a lost genealogy, Jacobs sees a networking of genealogical inheritance extant. By pulling at these skeins, she shows how laughable are complacent beliefs in the staying logic of (pa-tri)lineal fictions, such as the one claiming that paternity is not of consequence across racial lines. Jacobs recounts how one slaveholding papa's world was shattered by just such a revelation. Slaveholders like the father of Brent's children could regularly "take" African-American women and then sell their (own) children only if they could maintain the fiction that an indissoluble bar of difference existed between black and white, a bar that, among other things, produced the

46. Theodore Parker, quoted in Houston Baker, Jr., introduction to *N*. Both Parker and Thomas Wentworth Higginson expressed such views (*ILSG*, xxxiii); see also Margaret Fuller, review of Douglass's *Narrative* in the *New-York Tribune*, June 10, 1845, 1.

differential structures of erotic desire evident in antebellum concepts of sexuality. When Jacobs tells of the wealthy white slaveholder's daughter who "took" a slave lover and subsequently gave him free papers, a story of inherent difference shreds to reveal that what is at issue is not simply "race" or "sex." The issue is authority. As Brent observes, a slaveholder's daughter knows that the inmates of a patriarchal household, including herself, are "subject to their father's authority in all things" (*ILSG*, 52).

Commentary on Jacobs's famous chapter 21, "Loophole of Retreat" (*ILSG*, 14–18) has shown that using the master's tool of authority may not entirely dismantle the master's house, but it can shake the foundations.[47] White daughters who "exercise the same authority" (*ILSG*, 52) as their papas may not overthrow the father, but their replication of the fathers' behavior is disruptive in "shameful" and revealing ways. Linda Brent, captive in a domestic space, uses the (father's) tool of literacy to unsettle Dr. Flint. Indeed, Jacobs's "loophole of retreat," as Smith and Yellin note, is a version of a "madwoman in the attic" trope,[48] and although such a trope can not entirely succeed in rewriting domestic ideology, it does loop Dr. Flint into a scene that makes him as impotent as that master "whose head was bowed down in shame" (*ILSG*, 52) over his daughter's mimicry.[49] Further, such a doubling-back exemplifies what northern anti-slavery politicians feared, that "slave power" would endanger their own liberties.[50]

Jacobs describes her confined state as a "living grave" (*ILSG* 147), which can double for a description of slavery itself. Yet by the very act of doubling her condition, Jacobs converts that tomb into a womb. She has found a way to "part with all her kin" without actually departing. She has "died" out of slavery while remaining inside the system, in a sort of suspension between being and not-being that allows the formerly silent grave of the maternal female to speak out for

47. I borrow from Audre Lorde: "The master's tools will never dismantle the master's house," in *Sister Outsider* (Trumansburg, N.Y.: Crossing Press, 1984).

48. See Smith, *Self-Discovery*, 33–40, and Yellin's introduction to *ILSG*, 5. Both critics identify this scene as a form of the scenario that Gilbert and Gubar traced out for British fiction in their *Madwoman in the Attic*.

49. My argument is informed by ongoing feminist debates as to the political usefulness or effectiveness of linguistic parody and mimicry, particularly as these debates relate to French philosophy. See Luce Irigaray, *Ce sexe qui n'en est pas un* (Paris: Minuit, 1977); Hélène Cixous and Catherine Clément, *La jeune née* (Paris: Union Générale d'Editions, 1975); Judith Butler, *Gender Trouble* (New York: Routledge, 1990).

50. Walters, "The Erotic South," 80.

liberation. And this suspension, while painful, allows Brent to remake "self" and her children into free beings. Manipulating the space of the "feminized," Jacobs engineers the same metamorphosis (from brute to man) that Douglass (and Uncle Benjamin) staged with physical force. But she has done it without fisticuffs and without separation from the kin, through a strategy of doubling or looping.

Indeed, the words "loop" and "loophole" have similar meanings. As Hortense Spillers notes, a loop is emblematic of "coiling and re-coiling and rotation upon rotation"; it indicates both the crack in for-tifications from which a cannon protrudes and a closed, magnetic circuitry. It is, as well, a term used in knitting. Thus it pulls together, as it were, a number of moments in the narrative, connecting the fist-icuffs in masculinized modes of freedom to feminized forms, making both say "rebel."[51] For instance, a narrative loop reveals the closed circuitry of meaning when the slaveholder's daughter takes what she can get as a white woman. Paternal authority is both replicated and shot to pieces spectacularly here, by the way this story locates in a woman three attributes that a woman supposedly could not have: legal power, willfulness, and erotic desire. Claiming that this brief story shows how "slavery is a curse to the whites as well as to the blacks" (ILSG, 52), Jacobs also locates a potency where none had been thought to exist. And even if this white daughter is as cruel as Mrs. Flint in brutalizing those "over whom her authority could be exercised with less fear of exposure" (ILSG, 52), the daughter's action has a curious consequence: she gives her lover the free papers that will end his brutalization.

It is not, then, a "father" whose name represents "freedom." Ja-cobs's insistence upon deflating inherent paternal privilege is evident when Brent says, "I loved my father, but it mortified me to be obliged to bestow his name on my children." Such patronymics have been proposed to her by the "mistress of my father," who later "clasped a gold chain around" her daughter's neck: "I thanked her for this kind-ness; but I did not like the emblem. I wanted no chain to be fastened on my daughter, not even if its links were of gold" (ILSG, 78–7). Here, Jacobs has Brent connect the abstract power of the Father—no matter that the father, in this case, is her own, his last name has been handed down through the patriarchical system of slavery—to the material wealth and self-sustaining fictions of mastery.

51. Spillers, "Changing the Letter," 40.

In the end, what *Incidents* performs is indeed a revision of the master-slave relation very different from that of the classic slave narrative. As Valerie Smith has emphasized, Linda Brent refuses to be robbed of her maternity, her kinships, or her sexuality.[52] In these refusals, she succeeds in making "potency," so often attributed to masculinity, signify for a woman. But she also succeeds in changing the way masculinity should be narrated. At stake here, as I have suggested earlier, is how *Incidents* itself, as a form of private memory, will come to be valued publicly. Will the "feminine" tenderness of familial dependencies become legal and cultural tender? The story involves cultural disapprovals and shames, yet it must become a sustaining fiction. As Brent says about her loss of the cultural virtue of passive virginity, "I have shed many and bitter tears to think that when I am gone from my children they cannot remember me with such entire satisfaction as I remembered my mother" (*ILSG*, 90). Yet as her later interactions with her children show, in the act of remembering this "shame" for them she will set into motion a new narrative economy of satisfaction. Though she must recount the likely debasement of her memory in an economy underwritten by purity, she manages to trace that devaluation of the pure back to its denied source: patriarchal fictions of mastery. When she says of Dr. Flint's death, "The man was odious to me while he lived, and his memory is odious now" (*ILSG*, 196), that "now" is the time of her narrative, whose potency has made the memory of him, not of her, reek.

Still, Jacobs is well aware that the looping circuitry of narrative can loop back at her. So, she brings Linda Brent's story to a close, she introduces several documents to prevent a negative loop. The first is a legal bill of sale for Linda Brent; the second, a private letter relating Aunt Martha's death; and the third, another black-bordered letter accompanied by her Uncle Philip's newspaper obituary. Together these documents provide a reified recapitulation of the whole narrative, showing the hidden connections between public and private histories. The bill of sale, on public record in New York for "future generations," is legal evidence "that women were articles of traffic" (*ILSG* 201); the private letters of grief echo the various familial losses Brent has suffered as a result of the public institution of slavery; the obituary returns private loss fully to a public sphere, Philip's death having been an occasion to contemplate citizenship. She may be as free "as the

52. Smith, *Self-Discovery*, 33.

white people of the north," Brent comments, but that "is not saying a great deal" (*ILSG*, 201). These documents resonate with legal, social, and cultural connections occluded not just by the "peculiar institution" but by a logic the North shares with the South, a cultural logic that can make the still potentially valuable word "liberty" not say "a great deal."

Harriet Jacobs's 1981 editor, Jean Fagan Yellin, notes that no obituary notice for Mark Ramsey (Uncle Philip) can be found but assures her readers that other such notices, worded similarly, do exist (*ILSG*, 292). That Yellin felt the need to write this footnote points to that bedeviling conundrum "authenticity" and is tellingly apt for this text, which bears a literary history of confusion and which, I have argued, troubles the waters of cultural referentiality. Did Harriet Ann Jacobs write Linda Brent's story herself, as her subtitle (*Incidents in the Life of a Slave Girl, Written by Herself*) claims? Yellin's discovery of official legal data documenting Jacobs's story has given Brent's historically muted voice a louder literary and cultural hearing—especially since the text was attributed previously to an author whose work many literary critics saw as dubious: that is, Lydia Maria Child. But does it matter if these (tender) memories cannot be given the official, reified gloss of supposedly objective history? Is not Jacobs's "rememory" of Uncle Philip a valuable telling of history?

Part III

Paternal Return

6

Melville, Monstrosity, and Euthanasia: Pierre's Mother and Baby Budd

In Ramah there was a voice heard—weeping, and lamentation, and great mourning; Rachel weeping for her children, and would not be comforted.

—Jeremiah 31:15

On the second day, a sail drew near, nearer, and picked me up at last. It was the devious-cruising Rachel, that in her retracing search after her missing children, only found another orphan.

—Herman Melville, *Moby-Dick*

It may seem as odd to speak of maternity and Herman Melville in the same breath, as to speak of predominant nineteenth-century concepts of maternity without invoking Stowe. It is equally unremarkable to say that Stowe wrote about the sanctity of mothers and that Melville did not. In defining the scope of an "American" literary tradition, most critics place the two writers at opposite ends of an aesthetic framework, like counterweights on a seesaw: Stowe, the most widely read sentimentalist of her time, wrote (in excess) about maternity; Melville, the most abjured and ignored of American authors, wrote of paternal anxiety. Eric Sundquist succinctly locates the traditional critical view of these two authors and their best-known works:

Melville's novel [*Moby-Dick*] went largely unrecognized by readers and critics until this century; Stowe's novel [*Uncle Tom's Cabin*], although retaining a popular audience, was progressively lowered in scholarly estimation almost in exact proportion to Melville's ascent—in part because it lacks the complex philosophical intent and dense literary allusiveness of *Moby-Dick* and in part because it is in direct opposition to the rich American tradition of masculine confrontation with nature (the frontier tradition of the "American Adam") that Melville helped to define.[1]

1. From Sundquist's introduction to *New Essays on "Uncle Tom's Cabin,"* 2.

Indeed, if one takes Sundquist's assessment as definitive, then Stowe and Melville were telling very different "tales": one complex, the other presumably simple; one dense, the other presumably thin; one rich with tradition, the other, I would guess, poor in or even lacking tradition. But are they so unrelated? If Melville helped to define the "American Adam," then Stowe, I have argued, was working within a tradition of the "American Eve." And if Genesis is lurking around these definitions as a paradigmatic story, the history of Adam and Eve was a shared one.

Moreover, if *Moby-Dick* reflects a complex philosophy and dense literary allusiveness, surely *Uncle Tom's Cabin* reflects an equally dense biblical allusiveness and a driving Christian philosophical intent, as Jane Tompkins argues.[2] They are perhaps separated by a specific sort of complexity (if Christian orthodoxy is not philosophical), but, it can be argued, they are equally intent—separate but equal, as it were. Yet Melville and Stowe are often used to denote "different" literary heritages, one for Adam and one for Eve. Seldom are their works read as cultural partners. And just where the figures of Uncle Tom and Daggoo, Cassy and Eliza, or Sambo and Queequeg are supposed (figuratively) to sit on this critical seesaw with Adam and Eve—a question that both Stowe and Melville at least *asked*—is conveniently, seldom an issue. There is apparently only one seesaw, on a playground that has been carefully tended and fenced in to keep the riffraff out.

Traditional categorizations do not allow for an examination of the cultural heritage Melville and Stowe might share, or of how and where their works might intersect. Yet Herman Melville's *Pierre*, written not long after *Uncle Tom's Cabin*, demonstrates such an intersection, one of imagery and thematic concern.

Mother's Milk or Death Milk?

At the time of its publication, critics found *Pierre* either incomprehensible or, as one reviewer said, "mad as a March hare—mowing, gibbering, screaming like an incurable Bedlamite, reckless of keeper or strait waistcoat."[3] It has been read most frequently as a philosoph-

2. Tompkins, *Sensational Designs*, 123.
3. Hershel Parker, *The Recognition of Herman Melville: Selected Criticism since 1846* (Ann Arbor: University of Michigan Press, 1967), 62.

ical failure, an exercise in imaginative futility, and focused, if it focuses at all, on the traditionally Gothic horrors of incest and parricide.[4] Co-incidentally, *Pierre* is one of the few Melville works in which women play a heavily significant part, with the exception of the earlier (and often unread) *Mardi* and *Oomo*, named and identifiable women char-acters are relatively scarce. Otherwise, women—and, by extension, mothers—do not participate in Melville narratives. If named at all, they are generally named as absent, as is Ahab's wife in *Moby-Dick*.

Yet Woman is curiously pervasive in Melville. As Annette Kolodny might note,[5] Melville's "she" figuratively haunts his landscapes, ob-jects, and creatures. In *Typee*, Tommo "looked straight down into the bosom of a valley, which swept away in long, wavy undulations to the blue waters in the distance."[6] In "Benito Cereno," a "strange ship," the *Saint Dominick*, "wimpled by . . . low creeping clouds showed not unlike a Lima *intriguante*'s one sinister eye peering across the Plaza from the Indian loophole of her dusk saya-y-manta."[7] And "suspended in those watery vaults" described in *Moby-Dick*, "floated the forms of the nursing mothers of the whales, and those that by their enormous girth seemed shortly to become mothers" (*MD*, 497).

In using the female body as a metaphor, Melville uses Woman as Emerson does: "she" is an emblem, not surprisingly, of Mother Na-ture and of "her" prodigious reproductivity; she is, as well, the mute vessel/vassal/slave, the dark exotic who is as destructively seductive as totemic Woman was feared to be.[8] She is a lady-ship, a wave-girl, a fish-wife (pun intended). Always figured as a hybridized monster, then—from the disheveled, anorexic *Saint Dominick*, to the cannibal-istic Marquesan mermaid Fayaway, from the automatonic statuette Lucy Tartan to the hauntingly aphasic Isabel Banford—she can sel-dom be identified because Melville's feminine is that which can no longer speak for itself. This speechlessness, however, struggles; apha-sia, after all, implies a loss, not a lack. Just as Harriet Jacobs's narrative

4. John T. Irwin, *American Hieroglyphics: The Symbol of the Egyptian Hieroglyphics in the American Renaissance* (Baltimore: Johns Hopkins University Press, 1983), makes the novel's primary motivation a form of parricide.

5. See Annette Kolodny, *The Lay of the Land: Metaphor as Experience and History in American Life and Letters* (Chapel Hill: University of North Carolina Press, 1975).

6. Herman Melville, *Typee* (Evanston, Ill.: Northwestern University Press and the Newberry Library, 1978), 49 (hereafter cited as *T*).

7. Herman Melville, "Benito Cereno," in *Selected Tales and Poems* (New York: Holt, Rinehart & Winston, 1963), 4.

8. Dinnerstein, *The Mermaid and the Minotaur*, 5.

moves in various directions to avoid threats of culturally enforced silence and of becoming incomprehensible, so too does the female in Melville while revealing an antebellum cultural mandate for aphasia, bespeak the possibility that erotic plenitude might exist in the space of the aphasiac—as in the "universal verdure" and "rich profusion" of the Polynesian valley that "ravishes" Tommo.

Yet for Melville this erotic abundance is figuratively monstrous. Ultimately, such pregnancies are often figured as the burgeoning agent of death, similar to the beauteously overpowering Sirens whose enigmatic, unintelligible, and seductive songs led Odysseus's sailors to their execution from surfeit. As Dorothy Dinnerstein suggests in *The Mermaid and the Minotaur*, feminine sexuality is the "treacherous mermaid, seductive and impenetrable female representative of the dark and magic water underworld from which all life comes and in which we cannot live, [who] lures voyagers to their doom."[9] A cup that runneth over may drown those who try to quaff.

Although the mermaid is pervasive in Melville's metaphoric language in general, it is in *Pierre* that he confronts femininity and maternal reproduction most directly, since it is in *Pierre* that he deliberately attempts a close exploration and explosion of the nineteenth-century, Anglo-American fictional conventions that determined the popular figuration of heterosexuality. These conventions required gentrified, sentimentalized, and gendered oppositions that would clearly identify such things as virtue and vice according to the rigid determination of social, moral, and political norms. Ann Douglas views *Pierre* as a book that operates very much like *Uncle Tom's Cabin* being "profoundly concerned with sentimentalism and self-hatred."[10] Of course, her statement begs the question of why the sentimental is necessarily a mode of self-hatred, a problem with which *Pierre* as a text is, in fact, profoundly concerned.

The book opens with bitterly sarcastic, parodic versions of the romantic hero, Pierre Glendinning; his blond ladylove, Lucy Tartan; and the raven-haired temptress, Isabel Banford, who stands between them. Their stories move at a snail's pace, the plot impeded by the hothouse psychological conundrums of the assumed hero, in what has often been called a deliberate and malicious attempt on Melville's part to

9. Ibid.
10. Douglas, *Feminization*, 364.

frustrate those readers looking for yet another comforting, conventional romance. As Douglas suggests, this romantic "fiction is, in a sense, Melville's way of imitating and punishing his fiction-hungry audience," an audience that demanded a steady diet of treacle and was composed primarily of women.[11] Melville's parodic voice attacks the sentimental with the sentimental, using an overdetermined, baroque vocabulary that hopelessly enwebs the narrative. In what appears indeed to be a deliberate inversion of Stowe's model of how Christian maternity would bring about moral and emotional authenticity, Melville locates the unreal in a maternal authority (Mama Glendinning) which, allied to a masculinity enervated by Christianity, co-opts the "natural" and the "authentic."

Pierre begins within the confines of Mary Glendinning's martial empire. She is—like the missionary consul's wife, the English matron Mrs. Pritchard of *Typee*—a keeper of the patriotic standard. Mary Glendinning's world is ordered, pastoral, and figured as highly artificial. Saddle Meadows, the family seat, is Nature contained: a tamed stallion with Mary Glendinning astride, whip in hand and spurred with the paternal authority she has seemingly "usurped" from her dead husband. She is supported by her infantilized, and untried son, Pierre, as well as by the likes of such dandified gentlemen as the Reverend Falsgrave. She is also supported by such weak replications of herself as Mrs. Tartan and her daughter Lucy.

Lucy Tartan, at first, seems but an exceedingly pale shadow of Mary Glendinning, hardly a replica at all. Yet they are alike; Mrs. Glendinning herself notes their similarity: "Yes, she's a very pretty little pint-decanter of a girl; and I—I'm a quart decanter of—of—Port—potent Port! Now, Sherry for boys and Port for men—so I've heard men say; and Pierre is but a boy; when his father wedded me—why his father was turned of five and thirty years"[12] Although this description is offered as a telling differentiation, what Mary Glendinning's analogue shows is that both she and Lucy are intoxicants bottled up and constrained. And although both women appear accessible to Pierre, the truth is that he can only handle the decanters; he can never quaff the wine. As an adult, he cannot "have" his mother, even though their

11. Ibid.
12. Herman Melville, *Pierre*, ed. Harrison Hayford, Hershel Parker, and G. Thomas Tanselle (Chicago: Northwestern University Press and the Newberry Library, 1971), 66 (hereafter cited as *P*).

relationship is figuratively eroticized. By keeping Pierre tempted but sober, Mary Glendinning maintains a paternalistic authority over him. Sentimentalism screens this sexual power play as they very prettily call each other brother Pierre and sister Mary. Ironically, however, such wordplay reveals that legitimate, patriarchal authority in an economy of absolute restraint turns inevitably toward the Gothic topos of incest as a kind of familial conservation pattern, a protection of the familiar against uncontrollable or alien influences.

If Pierre marries Lucy, as is planned, he will be allowed to sip at the intoxicant, but the rules of antebellum decorum and order prevent any drunken frenzies. With Lucy, Pierre would in effect be safely replicating his parents' marriage—committing incest without committing incest. The controlling domestic proprietary laws would then govern the erotic. Such legalities keep Nature groomed, the children legitimate, and the potent port of the mother/*mater* safely bottled, while the sherry is carefully decanted in small measure. In other words, the generative power of the sexualized mother remains subject to the controlling "Name of the Father."

In fact, the domesticated order of antebellum patriarchal mores can remain legitimate only if reproductive sexual energy is contained by rigidly determined gender distinctions which in turn structure morality, social order, and racial difference. These binary, gendered determinations require, as Pierre knows, "that ere promising forever to protect, as well as eternally to love his Lucy, he must first completely invigorate and embrawn himself into the possession of such a noble, muscular manliness, that he might champion Lucy against the whole physical world" (*P*, 16). To be the patriarch, he must embody the physical, the muscular, the "masculine"; she must be an ethereal "feminine" creature in need of a champion. Together they will create and sustain the social cage that keeps sexualized energy and appropriate reproduction strictly within legitimate bounds.

Ann Douglas reads this restrictive social cage as a direct result of sentimental feminization. Although she notes that "Mrs. Glendinning has all the authority usually associated with the man of the family," Douglas does not see her as an emblem constructed by the "father" but claims instead that Mrs. Glendinning uses paternal authority only "to keep Pierre in innocent and amiable ignorance of the real world— her rival. Melville," Douglas continues, "seems to be cynically suggesting that the Victorian lady, and reader, will use all her influence to keep her men, and her authors, as feminine and as restricted as she is supposed to be."[13]

Reading Mrs. Glendinning more sympathetically, however, one might also note that Pierre's social power, as well as that of his father, is partially constituted by the perpetuation of such "feminizing" restrictions. If a father cannot identify his son as completely his own, how can he legitimately pass on the family fortune or name? Without Douglas's Victorian ladies all sons would be potential bastards; the antebellum patriarchal social order that in effect also kept the man readable as (reproductively) masculine would perish in a fear of illegitimacy complicated and inflamed by installed class and race boundaries. Without Mary Glendinning's use of patriarchal authority, and without her as emblem, a character like Pierre's cousing Glendinning Stanley would have nothing to inherit—neither his father's name, his aristocratic privilege, nor perhaps even the surety of his bloodline. The order of meaning regulating the patriarchal universe would be threatened by an illegitimacy so bewilderingly mixed that all might become absolute chaos.

In fact, Saddle Meadows *is* rocked and undermined by the catastrophic existence of that illegitimate catastrophe Isabel Banford, Pierre's supposed half-sister. From the moment Pierre first encounters her, the order of things as he has known it is threatened. Her existence deranges the artificially constructed, gender-polarized social order that has given Pierre his name.

Ann Douglas claims that Isabel's presence is unsettling because she allows Pierre "to conceive of virility": "We never really hear anything detrimental about Mr. Glendinning beyond the fact of his illicit liaison and its fruit. Pierre recalls his father's death-bed remorse, his calling for 'my daughter'; Isabel remembers his kindness and generosity with her. What Pierre has learned is not that his father was 'bad' so much as that he was not altogether satisfied to live a prisoner in his wife's home and mind."[14] But this claim fails, strikingly, to attend to a number of problematic factors. For instance, as Douglas tells Melville's narrative, Pierre recalls his father's remorse but seems to take no note of Mr. Glendinning's death-bed madness, as he so clearly does in Melville's text. And since, as Melville states through Dorothea Glendinning, Pierre's father had his liaison *before* he entered Mary Glen-

13. Douglas, *Feminization*, 374.
14. Ibid.

dinning's home, he could hardly have been using the affair to escape it. Further, the fact Mr. Glendinning was content to abandon Isabel's mother and allow his daughter to grow up in a madhouse is surely "detrimental" information about him, Douglas to the contrary. Melville does have Isabel remember her father's generosity, but he also has her register the grief of her abandonment by him; Pierre does recall his father's remorse and attempt to uphold his father's reputation, but he also recalls his father's disordered dying condition and understands that the man's social reputation rested upon a pack of illusions—chief among them fidelity and family loyalty. What Isabel allows Pierre, then, is not so much to conceive of (male) virility as to conceive of (female) conception, to become aware that a conceptual energy not necessarily gendered as male or dependent on masculinity can exist outside the order of things as he has known it. Simply put, some stories conflict.

Isabel Banford, the dark-eyed, dark-haired, mysterious woman is on the surface the perfect conventional Dark Lady antithesis to Lucy's blue-eyed, blond Light Lady. Further, Isabel's portrayal echoes Melville's other intratextual representations of the feminine—she is as dark and as strange as the Lima intriguante: "With a single toss of her hand [she] tumbled her unrestrained locks all over her, so that they tent-wise invested her whole kneeling form close to the floor, and yet swept the floor with their wild redundancy. Never Saya or Limeean girl, at dim mass in St. Dominic's cathedral, so completely muffled the human figure" (P, 167). She is as silent as the "silent cascades" of the Typean valley but as full of promise, as pregnant— "the pregnant fact of Isabel" (P, 117)—as the Leviathan mothers of *Moby-Dick*.

This is a femininity different from that of either Mary Glendinning or Lucy Tartan. Yet Isabel Banford is also, as Lydia Maria Child might have written, a violent spirit that has been bottled up: "Her unadorned and modest dress is black; fitting close up to her neck, and clasping it with a plain, velvet border. To a nice perception that velvet shows elastically; contracting and expanding as though some choked, violent thing were risen up here within the teeming region of her heart. But her dark, olive cheek is without a blush or sign of any disquietude" (P, 52). This description is given before Pierre has a name to put on the mournful olive girl. And although the only sound she makes at the Miss Pennies' sewing bee is a shriek, Isabel transfixes

Pierre with it. She enchants him as the Marquesan women enchant sailors in *Typee* when Tommo, sailing into the island bay, sights a startling picture: "At first I imagined it to be a shoal of fish sporting on the surface, but our savage friends assured us that it was caused by a shoal of 'whihenies' (young girls), who in this manner were coming off from the shore to welcome us. As they drew nearer . . . and I watched the rising and sinking of their forms . . . and their long dark hair trailing beside them as they swam. I almost fancied they could be nothing else than so many mermaids:—and very like mermaids they behaved too" (*T*, 14).

Their mermaidlike behavior consists of climbing aboard Tommo's ship, the *Dolly*, and capturing it with their wild grace. They in fact supersede the restrained, conventional, nineteenth-century doll-woman, displacing her as an object of desire. In this way Isabel is very like a mermaid; as dark as the "whihenie" Fayaway, she is so much a creature of the sea that when she encounters ocean tides, she wants to fling herself into them and rise and sink with the waves. And, just as the Marquesan women in *Typee* point up the artificial restraints of such women as the British missionary's wife, so too does Isabel Banford supersede both Mary Glendinning and Lucy Tartan. For his half-sister, Pierre will abandon both.

While this mystic mermaid (herself something of a parody of mermaid figures) appears to unmask the constraints of Saddle Meadows, however, she is at the same time an emblem of danger. She is the shrieking siren whose wordless cry lures Pierre to his eventual doom. Through her watery associations, as well as her "sisterly" link through Pierre to Mary Glendinning ("sister Mary," "sister Isabel"), Isabel is a representative of maternal power, as potent as Mary Glendinning's port but lacking the older woman's patriarchal restraints. The elastic velvet she wears is not the same as a cut-glass bottle-stopper. Thus her song, just as incestuous as Mary Glendinning's call to her "brother" Pierre, is wholly illicit within the gender-polarized social, moral and political order and will be, within that order, a death knell.

In pursuing Isabel, Pierre attempts to reach beyond the gendered order of his society and to break down its oppositions—vice/virtue, good/evil, and ultimately, behind all other oppositions, male/female—thus yielding to the seduction of the mother's womb-song without patriarchial ropes, realizing, within himself, conceptual vitality: both to accede to the mermaid's captivity and to end it. In *Amer-*

ican Hieroglyphics John T. Irwin reads Pierre's dilemma according to a strict Freudian model in which Isabel becomes the "Medusa, the sight of whose face turned men to stone." She is "a petrifying image of the primal scene, of the 'original' merging of opposites represented by the conjunction of the Gorgon's phallic snaky hair and vagina dentata mouth. . . . the Gorgon's fate—its decapitation by Perseus—as clearly links petrification and castration as does the tale of Enceladus, where the two are associated as punishments for incest (the substitutive reenactment of the primal scene)."[15] In Irwin's framework, if Pierre responds to Isabel's seduction, and if she is truly his half-sister, he may be committing incest, "a kind of parricidal displacement of the father's authority . . . punishable by castration."[16] Thus Pierre's dream of Enceladus, in which he is reduced to an armless torso battering vainly at the wall of Isabel's impenetrability, prefigures his "actual" castration in the novel's conclusion.

As Irwin states, in recognizing Isabel's ultimately unreadable mystery (is she his sister? is she his wife? is she his mother?) in recognizing that the sign of the legitimate father cannot be located on her body, Pierre also recognizes that the "bipolar norm vice/virtue is precisely that the poles have no separate external existence in themselves, that they are a mutually constitutive opposition, a function of the bipolar structure of self-consciousness." The self, as defined in a patriarchal bipolarity, is then ultimately unstable, "unable to become anything, precisely because in itself it is nothing."[17] Pierre cries out "I am a nothing!" (*P*, 304), and gendered oppositions collapse in the vortex of an unstable identity. In the final moments of the novel Pierre, clasping "both hands to his two breasts . . . [tears] out both pistols" (*P*, 400)—loaded with the empty, genteel authority/words of his patriarchally defined cousin Glendinning Stanley—and murders Stanley with them. Pierre then seizes Isabel and cries, "In thy breasts, life for infants lodgeth not, but death-milk for thee and me!" (*P*, 401) In other words, breasts both male and female become the same in their lethalness. All boundaries have been crossed; all polarities collapse to cancel each other out: entropy.

Indeed, within the phantasmal context of a Freudian framework, the illusion of selfhood vanishes without the Name of the Father to produce and protect heterosexual differentiation. Death can be the

15. Irwin, *American Hieroglyphics*, 311.
16. Ibid., 319.
17. Ibid., 311.

only result. But by the same (Freudian) token, Pierre's death should act as a transmission point; it should produce meaning for the narrative. Much of the critical debate about *Pierre* stems from the fact that Pierre's death appears to resolve nothing and produce no meaning, that his journey becomes a futile descent into hell, a failed Odyssean attempt to steer between the Scylla-Lucy and the Charybdis-Isabel of the feminized. Yet to interpret Pierre's story as a failure to revitalize a patriarchally defined self is to limit *Pierre*'s project. Though Isabel is certainly a Medusan figure, Melville also emphatically claims that for Pierre the "terrors of [her] face were not those of the Gorgon; not by repelling hideousness, did it smite him so, but bewitchingly allured him by its nameless beauty and its long suffering hopeless anguish" (*P*, 55). And when Isabel asks the question that Irwin cites as proof that she is Medusa—"Tell me, do I blast where I look? Is my face Gorgon's?"—Pierre's answer, is a compelling contradiction to a reading of her as monstrous: "Nay, sweet Isabel; but it hath a more sovereign power; that turned to stone; thine might turn white marble into mother's milk" (*P*, 211). Though by the end of the novel Pierre can no longer find mother's milk in Isabel, he did once did find it there. But now, instead of continuing to read her as a woman whose breasts produce nourishment—whose look makes stone into food— he insists on naming her a girl ("Girl! wife or sister, saint or fiend!") with only "death-milk" to offer (*P*, 401). Although he is aware that the bipolarity of his social norm is unstable, he assents to it by restating traditional oppositions and essentially differentiating himself from Isabel.

By assenting to the bipolarity and insisting upon the danger of its collapse, Pierre accedes not only to his "castration" but also to his inability to incorporate and redefine the feminine as self in a world whose meaning is organized so that the sexual female cannot be voiced but must remain "dead." To be able to name Isabel as a figure for self or, in other words, to see the Medusa as an emblem of a fierce, uncontained, and vital regenerativity which is unmarked by paternal control, would be to destroy the patriarchy without destroying a concept of selfhood—to accept Lucy without her Tartan genealogy and so institute a radical change in the social pattern of the relation called marriage. In Homans's terminology, Pierre would then be able to hear the literal voice of the sexualized female as surviving not behind or beyond the symbolic but beside it: "The daughter therefore speaks two languages at once."[18] Isabel Banford's aphasia would vanish, and her story would become legible alongside of, if different from, Pierre's.

But instead, Pierre casts out the feminine, consigning the women to a traditionally constructed, hybridized, gendered monstrosity: "Ye two pale ghosts, were this the other world, ye were not welcome. Away—Good Angel and Bad Angel both—For Pierre is neuter now!" (P, 401). In essence, he accedes to his castration out of panic over the sexualized, antipatriarchal mother. He cannot tolerate the possibility that there might be more than one way to tell Medusa's story and so he accepts the position of traditional eunuch in order to keep her story in line with past models. Unlike Tommo, who simply flees the mermaid's song, Pierre enters into what his world has defined as the mermaid's captivity. But he is unable to free either himself or her from the traditional drive of the narrative to death. In death he wears upon his lips a "scornful innocence" (P, 403), a phrase that echoes an earlier description of Isabel's "long scornful hair" (P, 179). The dying Isabel, whose speech has been punctuated throughout the text by silence, and whose most potent aphasic communication has been through the semiotic music of her own dead mother's guitar, in dying speaks the last uttered words of the whole novel: "All's o'er, and ye know him not!" she cries about Pierre (P, 403), implying, of course, but only in a negative sense, that she does. Like his character Pierre, Melville, in attempting to construct a living voice for the semiotic in a social context demanding that such a voice necessarily remain unintelligible, generates a narrative whose ability to communicate has been called as vexed as Isabel's ability to speak. Curiously, though, just like that of Stowe's maternal hymns, the power of a woman's song in *Pierre* is the power of negation and death. Nevertheless, Isabel's speech is what *Pierre* is consistently and urgently attempting to hear.

The Fruit of a Heart's Desire

If sexually potent Woman was an unstable paradox for the antebellum imaginary—as both *Uncle Tom's Cabin* and *Pierre*, indicate—the "fruits" of female potency could also prove dangerous. As Lydia Maria Child's shifting policy on disciplinary whipping makes clear,

---

18. Homans, *Bearing the Word*, 7–13. Homans works through both Kristeva and Lacan.

and as sentimental discourse in general often hints, children, though pictured as angelic redeemers, were also often cast as the possible agents of misrule who must be brought under violent control.[19] The rhetoric out of which the figure of the child was created displays the same sort of metaphoric strategies as the rhetoric employed to represent women, workers, and slaves. The child was described as an animal, a wild, helpless, formless, or uncontrolled thing that must be directed, formed, and whipped into shape. Despite the growing ideology of the child as innocence incarnate, despite a shift in child-care practices that questioned the effectiveness of corporal punishment as a means of instilling obedience, there remained a strong Calvinist belief that to "spare the rod was to spoil the child."

Moreover, the idea that children *belonged* to their parents, most specifically their father, was deeply ingrained in the language of the culture. It was literalized not only in the slavocracy, where some of a white man's children became his disposable property, but also in the national court system, which recognized paternal rights as primary in child custody cases. That the parents owned their children, and had sovereign rights over those children, was considered, indeed, a natural and sacred law. In her *Treatise on Domestic Economy* Catharine Beecher states that children are socially placed in the household like servants, artisans, or laborers in that they are subject to a divinely ordained hierarchy of domestic control. The Father-Creator, says Beecher, "has given children to the control of parents, as their superiors, and to them they remain subordinates, to a certain age, or so long as they are members of their household. And parents can delegate such a portion of their authority to teachers and employers, as the interests of their children require."[20] Thus Catharine Beecher situates the child in the naturalized, subordinate position that slaveholders appealed to when justifying slavery as a benevolent patriarchal institution resembling the sanctified family.

Not only were the roles of slave and child similar in the nineteenth-century American imagination, but a rhetorical uneasiness about the status of a child haunts twentieth-century grammar. When Eric Sundquist writes of Little Eva, he chooses to denote this "child" as a thing, as an "it": "Mediating between master and slave is the figure of the

19. Richard Brodhead, "Sparing the Rod: Discipline and Fiction in Antebellum America," *Representations* (Winter 1988), 67–96.
20. Catharine Beecher, *Treatise on Domestic Economy* (New York: Harper, 1847), 25–27.

child . . . a 'slave' itself, but morally superior to its parents and masters."[21] Such rhetorical confusion has political consequence. How can
anyone not designated by a pronoun indicating personhood claim
civil rights? The 1992 debate over whether or not children below the
age of consent should be legally able to "divorce" their (abusive) parents reveals how much the designation "child" has identified a being
that belongs like a piece of property to others, those who occupy the
role of "parents."[22]

Harriet Beecher Stowe took up an oppositional stance to her sister
Catharine in the writing of *Uncle Tom's Cabin*. By describing the child
as an innocent stripling and the very embodiment of "human" beauty,
over which the business of buying and selling should have no control,
Stowe seems to question whether a child should occupy the same
position as a servant just as much as she was attempting to question
the validity of slavery. Stowe's quadroon boy, Harry, is "remarkably
beautiful and engaging. His black hair, fine as floss silk, hung in
glossy curls about his round, dimpled face, while a pair of large, dark
eyes, full of fire and softness, looked out from beneath the rich, long
lashes" (*UTC*, 43). The description asks a reader to fall in love with
young Harry and become horrified at his probable fate. Such beatific
representation, however, (which makes Harry sound very much like
an infant Isabel Banford), acts as a smoke screen for the metaphorical
objectification at work. After all, Harry is a slave; his genealogy makes
him a literal commodity.

Although Stowe's representation is designed to deflect and criticize
this commodification, her portrayal serves to reinforce the idea of
child as (sex) object, making Harry metaphorically into a rag dolly
with silk hair that can be activated by the controlling words of its
owner: " 'Now Jim [Crow],' says Mr. Shelby, 'show this gentlemen
how you can dance and sing.' The boy commenced one of those wild,
grotesque songs common among the negroes, in a rich, clear voice,
accompanying his singing with many comic evolutions of the hands,
feet, and whole body all in perfect time to the music" (*UTC*, 44).

Further, within Harry's "charming" performance—a performance

---

21. Sundquist, introduction to *New Essays on "Uncle Tom's Cabin,"* 26.
22. Arguments pertaining to child custody and child-parent "divorce" came to the
fore in 1992 around the Florida cases of Gregory K. (see "Boy Divorcing Parents Can
Speak, Judge Rules," *Gainesville Sun*, August 9, 1992) and Kimberly Mays, who was
switched at birth with another child and, at fourteen, claimed to have no desire to be
returned to parents whose only claim to her was genetic.

prompted by fatherly words that have alienated the boy both from both his given name and from his mother—lies the threat that Stowe's sentimental rhetoric tries to hide but Catharine Beecher's rhetoric of subordination points to: that is, the protean, changeable, and potentially chaotic ability of a "child" to grow up into anyone—or, to use the terminology of fear, any*thing*—at all. Harry's song is wild and grotesque; he is "flexible" (*UTC*, 44) and can physically metamorphose into old Uncle Cudjoe and Elder Robbins. In other words, Harry has the terrifying capability to reproduce mimetically the patriarch (or anyone for that matter) and thus usurp patriarchal roles, to take "his master's stick in his hand" (*UTC*, 44), and become the master. And so, while Shelby would prefer to protect the child and not sell him, the master's fear of losing control prevails: Shelby explains his sale of Harry on the grounds that he must sacrifice the boy in order to preserve the farm on which the boy's *mother* will continue to live—and reproduce?—under the paternal benevolence Shelby represents.

Stowe's view of Harry makes the child into both a precious, purchasable object and an uncontainable, unknown quantity. Thus, like his narrative stepsister Isabel Banford, he is an emblem of potentiality uncertainly controlled. Stowe's rhetoric both tames and yet consistently reinstates him as untamable, since even as she attempts to "free" him, she "contains" his potential. His existence remains an emblem of indecipherability, for he calls into question the very Christian stabilities Stowe wished to uphold and instate. For instance, by denominating him a quadroon, she both represents and yet also defuses the underlying truth of the slavocracy's rape economy. Most people marketed as mulatto or quadroon were the children of rape or of forced liaisons between slaves, but Harry, whose parents are both mulatto and "married" to each other, has a peculiarly unique and legitimized interracial heritage. Stowe's creation of such legitimacy upholds the paradigm of antebellum marriage while Harry's existence marks off the hypocrisy of that paradigm.

And if "emancipated," who would the Harrys of the antebellum world become? Stowe's description not only confuses the racial identification of this "boy" and forces the violence of his heritage into view by denying it but also confuses both his class and gender placement. After all, Stowe has given this slave boy a prince's name; though a "common" enough American boy's name, "Harry" echoes both historical and "literary" (Shakespeare's Prince Hal) Anglo royalty. Stowe also makes this boy beautiful in the manner of his mother, giving him glossy curls, long lashes, and drowning-pool eyes and dressing him in "a gay robe of scarlet and yellow plaid . . . [which] set off to advantage the dark and rich style of his beauty" (*UTC*, 46). Still, Harry is also named a "young gentleman" and "a little devil"; like Little Eva's cousin, the cruel Henrique, Harry is comparable to any antebellum, white middle-class family's pride and joy and heart's desire: a "first-born son" (*UTC*, 547,46,91). Akin to both Eva (indeed nearly "passing" as a version of her aboard a steamboat where his "dark" beauty draws as "many flattering comments from the passengers" [*UTC* 548] as had Eva's "light" beauty) and to Henrique, Harry is his newly legitimated (middle-class) family's heart as much is Eva is hers. Yet he is also a gay and "fancy article" (*UTC*, 46) as the slave trader calls him—a little prince, as beautiful as the "pretty young fellow" (*UTC*, 545) that his own mother Eliza (in disguise) is later called (see Figs.6 and 7). To whose desire does Harry appeal?

Whoever else Harry might be, in antebellum terms he is rhetorically and preemptively both "emasculated" and "whitened," for empathy's sake, long before he is dressed up as a "white" girl in order to secure his passage to freedom. In many ways, Stowe's description of him marks off just how unreadable, uncomfortable, and yet utterly familiar she hoped to make him by depicting him as such; after all, Harry, when he is metamorphosed into a white girl, becomes Harriet.

But again, who is this "child"? In *Moby-Dick* Melville creates a similarly heterogeneous and charged image: "Black Little Pip," the "poor Alabama boy" who, "when sent for to the great quarterdeck on high . . . was bid strike in with angels and beat his tambourine in glory" (*MD*, 217). Pip bears the burden of becoming a "living and ever-accompanying prophecy" (*MD*, 521) of the *Pequod*'s fate, much as Harry is the "prophecy" of freedom in *Uncle Tom's Cabin*. Pip's misfortune not only prefigures both Ishmael's and Ahab's destiny; his doomed history is an embryonic version of the novel.

When Pip first appears in chapter 27, "Knights and Squires," he is already an anomaly. Neither a knight nor a squire in the hierarchy of the whaler's court but more properly a jester, supplied with bells in the form of a tambourine, the boy appears out of nowhere, tacked on almost as an afterthought (as Isabel is the afterthought of her father's mysterious liaison?) to Melville's detailed description of the crew. Thus an outcast in the chapter wherein he is born, he is an outcast too among the *Isolatoes*. Unlike his shipmates, he is assigned no specific function with regard to whaling. Melville further constructs for

Figure 6. A slumbering Harry—or Harriet? (George Thomas, 1852).

the boy the mysterious fate of preceding the rest of the crew into the unknown—"oh no!—he went before" (*MD*, 217). And so, from his first appearance, Pip is the lowliest, "the most insignificant of the Pequod's crew" (*MD*, 521), utterly dispossessed, without work, poor, black, a slave-child and impotent in a place where only men have power. He is, as well, one who "loved life and all its peaceable securities" (*MD*, 522) and is thus essentially a girl and "feminine" (at least to his adventure-seeking shipmates), a poltroon, as small and as dormant as his name suggests—poor little Pip, a seedling.

Yet dormancy also implies potentiality: seeds grow. Pip may be a seed, but his full nickname, Pippin, is the name of a king and a king's son (as are those of both Stowe's Harry and Melville's Ahab). And though Pip is designated lowly—a "thing" as Stowe (or Sundquist) might have said—he is also described by Melville as bright and as

Figure 7. Harry, imitating Uncle Cudjoe (George Thomas, 1852).

brilliant as the "lustrous ebony, paneled in king's cabinets" (*MD*, 522). Not content with that duality, Melville flips the two-sided coin yet again: in chapter 93, "The Castaway," he makes the boy a symbol of paradox by turning his black brightness into hellfire. As pure as a diamond (coal), the boy becomes "a crown jewel stolen from the king of Hell" (*MD*, 523), sea-changed by his encounter with a whale.

Pressed into unskilled service aboard second mate Stubb's boat, Pip faces a whale chase three times, a trilogy of trial that prefigures Ahab's three-day pursuit of Moby-Dick once they find him. The first of Pip's encounters is a warning, as is the *Pequod*'s first encounter with the white whale. The second causes Pip to leap overboard, carrying with him the harpoon (umbilical) line in which he becomes entangled, as Ahab's shadow-prophet Fedallah will be during the second day of the quest for Moby-Dick. Pip is also nearly hanged, as Ahab will be ultimately. But Stubb saves the boy and loses the whale, a chance for salvation that Ahab refuses when his own shadow-prophet is lost. Pip's third encounter results in his abandonment. He clears the whale line and is left behind—"Out of the center of the sea, poor Pip turned his crisp, curling black head to the sun, another lonely castaway, though the loftiest and the brightest" (*MD*, 524–25)—just as Ishmael will be at the end of the book, an orphan whose weeping mother (significantly, the biblical Rachel, who was used as an anti-slavery figure by both white and black authors, particularly women) finds him at last.

To Pip, the abandonment of himself to himself is a journey from which he returns mad: "The sea had jeeringly kept his finite body up, but drowned the infinite of his soul" (*MD*, 525). The sea, however, is not the malevolent causes of the boy's madness. Rather, it is the indifference of God-the-Father from whom Pip had asked salvation, and the boy's abysmal loneliness with only himself (his self-reliance) to fill the whole horizon. The encounter with himself leaves him incapable of coherence. Afterward he voices only prophecy, as a Cassandra (and an Isabel Banford) must—incoherently, in riddles. He is now and forever an object; having been abandoned "like a hurried traveler's trunk," he is swallowed "like a head of cloves" (*MD*, 524). A hell-jewel of fiery brilliance, he is as insensate as the indifferent, heartless sun that shone beautifully as the boy went mad. Granted visions through this death, he has no way to speak them comprehensibly. A damned and alienated angel, he is silenced by incoherence as the *Pequod* itself will be silenced, swallowed by the sea with an angel-eagle crucified on a mast, completing a journey to hell where Pip has gone before. But until Pip is silenced forever, he babbles to the reader, just as like-abandoned Ishmael returns home with the riddle of Moby-Dick.

Children, denominated "angelic" or "magical," served not only as a ciphers for prophecy, then, but also as harbingers of potentially disrupting and wholesale cultural change. Harry and Pip are the seeds of the future. So too are the infantile Dark Lady/Light Lady pair of Topsy and Little Eva, who, despite being designated as iconographic opposites or "representatives of two extremes of society," share supernatural qualities: Eva may be "fair and noble," but Stowe also calls her a "shadow" and a "fairy," Topsy, who is "black and subtle," is also described as more than "mortal," a "conjurer" (*UTC*, 361, 231). In children, where the mark of sexual "depravity" cannot come into play as a marker dividing good from bad, the descriptive divisions

Figure 8. "The representatives of their races." George Thomas's Eva and Topsy, as supposedly definitive opposites in 1852.

between "black" and "white" or "boy" and "girl" get extremely muddled. Small wonder that on stage and in illustrations well into the twentieth century (Figs. 8 and 9), much energy was expended to nail down the idea that Stowe's Eva and Topsy were, indeed, absolute opposites. Children, being in the popular antebellum imagination sexually null, were, in many ways yet to be defined. Potentials, they bodied forth questions about gender and racial identities, and particularly about the composition of the future national body: who will be a legitimate American? How can one tell?

And because the icon of Mother was tied inextricably to the image of her child, her own agency in the production of that child became, in a patriarchal system dependent upon paternal genealogy for its underlying legality, frighteningly suspect. Whose child is that baby at

Figure 9. James Daugherty's 1929 version shows a continuing emphasis on the supposed opposition between Eva and Topsy expressed in appearance and manner. Here, however, Topsy is the speaker or story-teller, while Eva appears static, if not transfixed.

the breast? And who might that child become? Will he be black or white—or both and neither? Will she be good or bad, Hawthorne's unfathered Pearl or the titled lady his fathered Pearl becomes? And in either case, what will happen to paternal ownership rights if mothers should become citizens with property rights and suffrage? The reinstatement of a "benign" patriarchy at the end of *Uncle Tom's Cabin*, where the spirit of good Father Tom inspires his white "son" George Shelby, suggests that the spectre of a maternity and a maternal "fruit," unmarked by the Name of the Father, was too far outside the "legit-imate" for Stowe to endorse.

The Drive to Youth-anasia

Long after the Civil War and Reconstruction, when the political question of who was an American citizen had become as deeply trou-bling as *Uncle Tom's Cabin*'s denouement seemed to forecast, Herman Melville wrote *Billy Budd*. This book might seem to have little to do with either slavery, Reconstruction, or, indeed, maternity. It has been read, like *Pierre*, as focused on the priorities and necessity of patriar-chal authority for cultural stability. Yet in this story the rhetorical tropes that constitute mother and child in both *Pierre* and *Uncle Tom's Cabin* reappear, and in imagery and resolution *Billy Budd* illustrates the murderous logic that all patriarchal authority—whether slavoc-racy or democracy—depends upon for systemic survival.

Melville begins his "inside narrative" by introducing "that signal object," the Handsome Sailor, who first appears in the guise of a "common sailor so intensely black that he must needs have been a native African," a "black pagod" who is worshipped almost as Quee-queg's totemic statue was.[23] Immediately, the black man's role as the Handsome Sailor is transferred to welkin-eyed Billy Budd—"or Baby Budd, as more familiarly, under circumstances hereafter to be given, he at last came to be called"—a young white sailor impressed into service aboard a British warship like a "goldfinch popped into a cage" (*BB*, 44–45). These descriptions signal the young man's close identifi-cation with the "children" of *Uncle Tom's Cabin* and with animals, women, workers, slaves. Not only is Budd instantly linked to the Af-rican and named Baby, but his physical presence earns him also the nickname Beauty, and his "position aboard the seventy-four was something analogous to that of a rustic beauty transplanted from the provinces and brought into competition with the highborn dames of the court" (*BB*, 46). Thus Melville identifies Billy as the child/slave/woman/worker. A bud like Pip or like Topsy and Little Eva, he is both a seed and a jewel, both a potentially generative and a valuable,

23. Herman Melville, *Billy Budd, Sailor (An Inside Narrative)*, ed. Harrison Hayford and Merton H. Sealts, Jr. (Chicago: University of Chicago Press, 1962), 43 (hereafter cited as *BB*).

objectified commodity, to be used or abused by the system that so characterizes him.

Also, like Stowe's Harry, Melville's Billy threatens the patriarchal order with his flexibility. The quality that makes him so valuable, his ability to get on in any situation, deeply threatens (like Harry's or Topsy's mimetic powers) the authority that maintains order and keeps a tight seventy-four ticking. When Billy is first transferred from the English ship the *Rights-of-Man* to the *Bellipotent*, he stands up and waves goodbye to his Rights, "a terrible breach of naval decorum" (*BB*, 49) even if done in innocence and out of a "gay" heart.[24] Although Billy, like Stowe's Harry, is the embodiment of innocence, his actions and manner are a (homosocial) threat. And, just as Harry's quadroon heritage signals the threat of various illegitimacies, is Billy's foundling status is a sign of his menace. A child without legitimate origin, a motherless child who like Topsy, motherless may have "just growed," a manchild who lacks evidence of sufficient paternal control, Billy must be identified and made submissive.

One of the most curious parts of this disciplinary scenario is that Billy does not protest or resist his capture. His passivity inevitably recalls Christ's silence in the face of condemnation, and Budd accedes to the military death sentence as Christ agrees to crucifixion, or Uncle Tom to his own martyrdom. Melville's use of Christian imagery makes this connection impossible to ignore. Budd's passivity has generally been read as his acceptance of the Father's divinity and power, His sacred right to rule or, as Catharine Beecher put it, the Father-Creator's right to control his creation. Indeed, until the end of his short life Billy expects, like a child aboard a sinking ship, that the (still operative) cultural promise of "women and children first" will be met; like Christ or Isaac of the Old Testament, he trusts that the Father/God/Captain will rule wisely, benignly, and protectively. Under that rule, Billy cannot fear or comprehend a punishment such as death by execution when he has done no wrong. According to the definitions created by the social order that created him, killing Claggart was tantamount to killing off Evil. Budd expects Captain Vere to have his— the child's—best interests at heart, no matter if this means that Billy will die. As Hoffert remarked, nineteenth-century narratives featuring infant death scenes suggested that children were often better off dead,

---

24. For an excellent reading of Billy as an emblem for gay culture, see Sedgwick's argument in *Epistemology of the Closet*, 91–130.

since an early death would preserve their spiritual innocence. And so Billy feels no sense of betrayal or guilt when condemned. To the chaplain who visits him while he is chained to the gun deck awaiting execution, he seems a "slumbering child in the cradle when the warm hearth-glow of the still chambers at night plays on the dimples that at whiles mysteriously form in the cheek" (*BB*, 119).

Chained into the society and the representational order that have made him a (permanent) child in the first place, Billy Budd has no place else to go but into death, if he is to preserve what he, as the child, most desperately needs: the love of the father, authority Captain Vere. Yet to perform fully the parental role Billy expects of him, not to be simply "old enough to have been Billy's father" (*BB*, 115) but to choose "the father in him, manifested towards Billy" over the "disciplinarian" alone (*BB*, 100), Vere would have to choose social (political) suicide; the captain would have to "go down with the ship," so to speak. Vere cannot make that choice in this crisis, not because of his self-interest, but because he has identified for himself the role of the captain-patriarch, whose self-concern has been hidden or submerged within his concern for the ship's—or the ship of state's—welfare. He is Starry Vere, whose light of leadership must guide that ship. Thus, when he announces Budd's impending death to the crew, he does not even whisper the word mutiny, as if the rumored mutiny had nothing to do with the execution. Indeed, as far as Vere is concerned at this point in the situation, the mutiny Claggart hinted at has been silenced: military discipline and the need for imposed social order "should be made to speak for itself" (*BB*, 117) inside the heads of the sailors.

As captain, then, Vere maintains order not to please himself but for the sake of the other sailors, the sons who have not disrupted the ship as Billy has. The sailors, as good sons, will know this. Unlike the emotion-ruled Ahab—who discards the restricting, tight-reined role of protector and patriarch, who casts off his responsibility as Father in order to give himself up to his passions, who will indeed go down with the ship of his (American) sons—Vere sees himself as the good father, unencumbered by passion or the vicissitudes of the heart. As Melville puts it, Vere does not acknowledge the "feminine in man" (*BB*, 111).

Moreover, Vere's exhortation to the drumhead court not only reveals his commitment to the image he has of himself as benevolent (asexual) guardian but also shows his self-identification as a son of

the law. When Vere says to the court, "I feel as you do for this unfortunate boy. But did he know our hearts, I take him to be of that
generous nature that he would feel even for us on whom in this military necessity so heavy a compulsion is laid" (BB, 113), he speaks not
as Billy's father but for himself-as-Billy. They are, after all, sons of the
same system. This eulogy of forgiving acceptance of a murderous-
suicidal rule must apply to both Vere and Billy. Both will die serving
it. Jesus Christ, in the beatitudes of the New Testament says, "Blessed
are the peacemakers, for they shall be called the sons of God." Billy,
the social peacemaker aboard the *Rights-of-Man,* will achieve crucifixion. Vere, the military peacemaker aboard the *Bellipotent* will eventually be killed by a musketball from a French warship significantly
named the *Athée* (atheist). Vere and Billy both die not resisting (moral)
evil, as they are led to believe, but as sacrifices to the maintenance of
a murderous order. Billy is compared to "a condemned vestal priest-
ess in the moment of being buried alive, and in the first struggle
against suffocation" (BB, 99). His death is a stay against the collapse
of the system that engendered him.

In this light, the question asked of the surgeon by the accountant,
Mr. Purser, after Billy's death—that is, whether Billy died by the rope
or through his own willpower—becomes the central question posed
by the text as a whole. While the surgeon, a man of science allied to
Vere in his adherence to the facts, discredits the notion of euthanasia,
the accountant continues to believe that Budd's death was not "ef-
fected by the halter" (BB, 125) but was rather caused by Billy's will
to die. The surgeon, by quitting the conversation, has the final word,
but the question "hangs" in the air: did the vestal-child Budd stifle
himself out of a need for the love promised by the God-Father Vere?
The charge of euthanasia is obviously warranted: Melville never states
that Billy was hanged but only that like Christ and his Mother, who
both bless the Father who has required their sacrifice in order to ensure social and spiritual integrity, he ascends.

What Billy's death records, then, is the way in which a patriarchal
order that represents itself as removed from, and not responsible to,
the requirements of the heart, is suspicious of the very children it has
created and has promised to protect. Like mules (and mulattoes) they
wear a (cultural) halter and die in service to it. Such an order will not
only suffocate those children but will also, in killing its own sons, fail
to survive. What has gotten lost and is being punished is potency,
along with desires that do not fit the traditional script—in other

words, the unknowable and yet to be scripted potentiality of living altogether. After all, Claggart isn't "just" a snake, although he is represented as one. Nor is Budd a baby. Both have the potential to tell their own desires, their own stories; indeed, both try to make Captain Vere "see" their side of the story. But like a child on a sinking ship, Billy's trust that a supposedly benign patriarchal love will favor him is grimly misplaced. He will be sacrificed in order to keep masked the Father's desires, even as Vere, in an attempt to be the patriarch, will, like Pierre, stifle the Budd within himself, convinced that the suffocation is necessary for social survival.

In Melville's *Confidence Man*, all social interaction is shown to be a con game: "Confidence is the indispensable basis of all sorts of business transactions. Without it, commerce between man and man, as between country and country, would, like a watch, run down and stop."[25] That is, without the con, entropy would result. By the time Melville writes *Billy Budd*, however, the watch does not just run down; overwrought by the ever increasing restraints of a newly invigorated father-oriented order that could not even abide its own heart's desire, it snaps: "Budd's heart, intensified by extraordinary emotion at its climax, abruptly stopped—much like a watch when in carelessly winding it up, you strain at the finish, thus snapping the chain" (*BB*, 125). *Billy Budd* was Melville's last narrative (he died from an enlargement of the heart in 1891).[26] It was written from inside a "restored" American "democratic" patriarchy that had denied women citizenship and severely restricted a newly freed, African-American population.

25. Herman Melville, *The Confidence Man* (New York: Holt, Rinehart & Winston, 1964), 138.
26. Leon Howard, *Herman Melville: A Biography* (Berkeley: University of California Press, 1951), 337.

7

The Delicate Organisms and
Theoretic Tricks of Henry James

He is intoxicated with the fragrance of the tenderest blossom of
maternity that ever bloomed among men.
—Henry James, "The Madonna of the Future"

In *The Portrait of a Lady*, as the incarcerative reality of her marriage
becomes palpable, Isabel Archer Osmond ponders her husband's idealized description of his daughter: "His tone . . . however, was that of
a man not so much offering an explanation as putting a thing into
words—almost into pictures—to see, himself, how it would look. . . .
Isabel gave an extreme attention to this little sketch. . . . It seemed to
show her how far her husband's desire to be effective was capable of
going—to the point of playing *theoretic tricks on the delicate organism*
of his daughter."[1] Isabel finds Gilbert Osmond's "sketch" of Pansy, a
"striking example of her husband's genius" (*PL*, 443). Despite having
earlier dismissed Osmond's talent as "a genius for upholstery" (*PL*,
324), Isabel sees in this sketch a "heroine of a tragedy" (*PL*, 443), even
though Pansy is elsewhere belittled, called a "Dresden-china shep-
herdess" (*PL*, 301). She is, in fact, a Gothic heroine in a nunnery/
prison, with a determined if fumbling suitor and a threatening if benevolent papa.
　　James displays yet mocks a Gothic formula with regard to Pansy's
story, as is noted by the peevish figure of her suitor, Edward "Ned"
Rosier. Rosier is "haunted by the conviction that at picturesque per-
iods young girls had been shut up . . . to keep them from their true
loves, and then, under the threat of being thrown into convents, had
been forced into unholy marriages" (*PL*, 308). James's seems to invoke
and deflect Gothicism in much the same way that Melville attempts

---

1. Henry James, *The Portrait of a Lady*, ed. Robert D. Bamberg (New York: Norton,
1975), 442 (emphasis added). This edition is hereafter cited as *PL*.

to mock the sentimental by overuse. Pansy's nunnery is no ghoulish hole but a quiet home, but she is confined to it. The "mothers" there are hardly sadistic, yet they do discipline Pansy. And although Pansy's lover is a pathetic specimen whom James calls "poor Rosier" (*PL*, 312), he is also a "melancholy youth" (*PL*, 371). James's deflation of Gothic images may keep us from taking Pansy's tragedy too seriously, but he does draw a specifically Gothic veil around her, and her eventual "sequestration" (*PL*, 462) causes Isabel to view the convent as "a well-appointed prison . . . which affronted and almost frightened her" (*PL*, 456).

The Prisonhouse of (Gothic) Fiction

Isabel's story (which the reader is expected—even commanded by James—to take seriously) has a trajectory that eerily parallels her stepdaughter's. For one thing, Isabel is the subject of James's portrait in the same way that Pansy is the subject of Osmond's sketch. For another, she and Pansy are both described as "frail vessels."[2] Further, both live inside Osmond's suffocating atmosphere (like *Billy Budd*, perhaps this is an "inside" narrative?). Finally, Isabel, too, according to James and his critics, is a tragic heroine.[3] Indeed, Isabel's fate is repeatedly linked to Pansy's tale, and thus the Gothic trappings of the child's life begin to shroud her stepmother's.

Pointing to Pansy as a figure for Isabel Archer's fate may appear, at the outset, as extreme as the Gothic itself is lurid James did often write in a Gothic strain (in, for example, such ghost stories as *The Turn of the Screw*, "The Altar of the Dead," and "The Jolly Corner", but traces of Gothicism can be found in most of his works, even in those which, like *The Portrait of a Lady*, have been read as concerned primarily with social manners. Leslie Fiedler has noted that James was "deeply influenced by Gothic modes" so that even in the society piece *Daisy Miller* he uses a Gothic device, the "malaria, the *miasma* which arises from decaying ruins."[4]

---

2. James refers to Isabel as slight or frail in his preface to the 1907 edition of *The Portrait of a Lady* and in his notebooks; see *The Complete Notebooks*, ed. Leon Edel and Lyall H. Powers (New York: Oxford University Press, 1987), 13.

3. Various critics have termed Isabel's story "tragic"; see Charles Feidelson, "The Moment of *The Portrait of a Lady*," in *PL*, 749.

4. Fiedler, *Love and Death*, 131.

James is clear, however, that the lady, Isabel Archer, and the mock-Gothic maiden, Pansy Osmond, are not wholly congruent. Isabel is not a watercolor sketch but a rich masterpiece, no diminutive "pansy" but the full-blown rose, no mere popular Gothic heroine but a tragic woman, a complex "Subject" (*PL*, 8). In her story there is no corpse in a wall, skeleton in the closet, or nun bearing the devil's whelp—or is there? What *does* constitute Isabel's tragedy? Might not the hidden truth behind *The Portrait of a Lady* be, after all, the sad, murderous, and decidedly Gothic story of a woman who has borne a fiend's illegitimate child?

Leslie Fiedler has described the Gothic novel as one in which, "through a dream landscape, usually called by the name of some actual Italian place, a girl flees in terror and alone amid crumbling castles, antique dungeons and ghosts who are never really ghosts." In his view, terror has resulted from an incestual perversion of Freud's Oedipal drama: the girl, or the son's *anima*, flees the horror of incest. For Fiedler, the paradigmatic Gothic plot tracks the way a son's taboo love for a lost mother makes him a sadistic, erotic anti-hero who is fascinating because of his Oedipal "breach of the primal taboo," his "offense against the father." The Gothic thus reveals Western cultural anxieties about a "crumbling" of paternal authority, beneath which "lies the maternal blackness, imagined by the gothic writer as a prison, a torture chamber." For Fiedler, "the guilt which underlies the gothic and motivates its plots is the guilt of the revolutionary haunted by the (paternal) past which he has been striving to destroy."[5]

As Claire Kahane points out in "The Gothic Mirror," however, Fiedler's focus on the villain-hero's psyche fails to account for the fascination that Gothicism has exerted on women authors, nor does it adequately explain the path many female protagonists take in Gothic novels. Kahane alters Fiedler's synopsis to provide a slightly different psychodynamic basis for Gothic agony: "Within an imprisoning structure . . . a young woman whose mother has died is compelled to seek out the center of a mystery, while vague and usually sexual threats to her person from some powerful male figure hover on the periphery of her consciousness. Following clues that pull her onward and inward—blood-stains and mysterious sounds—she

5. Ibid., 127, 132–33, 129.

penetrates the obscure recesses of a vast labyrinthine space and discovers a secret room sealed off by its association with death."[6]

Kahane assumes here Nancy Chodorow's revision of Freud, in which the girl who flees is more than *anima*, more than a mere shadow-half of a male psyche.[7] For Kahane, what lies "locked into the forbidden center of the Gothic" is "the spectral presence of a dead-undead mother, archaic and all-encompassing, a ghost signifying the problematics of femininity which the heroine must confront."[8] Positing a female psyche as the center of Gothic gravity, Kahane shifts away from a strict Freudian reading. She suggests that when the girl goes prowling about what Fiedler has described as maternal darkness, what she discovers is that the mother, who is a mirror to her self, is not simply missing, she has been murdered. Or, as Margaret Homans argues in *Bearing the Word*, the fantasy of Freud's Oedipal drama, as a metaphor for Western cultural aesthetics, depends "not merely on the regrettable loss of the mother, but rather on her active and overt murder."[9]

Still, despite Kahane's revision of Fiedler, both critics see a version of the maternal as intrinsic to Gothicism. Fiedler's mother may be a "tomb," but access to this sexuality is what is behind the horror. For Kahane, Gothic terror lies in an ambivalent search for the mother. Indeed, both Fiedler and Kahane not only focus on a version of the mother to explain Gothicism but also see a ghost when they look for her. Fiedler's ghost-mother is she who took part in an original disregard of the father's primary reproductive claim upon her. Kahane's ghost is that of an archaic, repressed, murdered, pre-Oedipal maternity. And if, as many Gothic stories themselves suggest, this maternal murder is actually a precondition to the plot of the continuing (strict or post-) Freudian fantasy Western culture tells itself, it is no wonder both Fiedler and Kahane see ghosts. As Homans argues, within a Freudian economy the mother must be dead in order for the son to create; otherwise, she will lure him to his death. Yet a female poet, being identified with the mother if not *as* a mother, obviously cannot

6. Kahane, "Gothic Mirror," 334.

7. See Nancy Chodorow, *The Reproduction of Mothering: Psychoanalysis and the Sociology of Gender* (Berkeley: University of California Press, 1978), 111–29.

8. Kahane, "Gothic Mirror," 336.

9. Homans, *Bearing the Word*, 12. Homans revises Oedipal dynamics dually, using Chodorow to reexamine both Freud and Jacques Lacan's use of the Oedipus complex with regard to language.

abide such a murder. Thus it is hardly surprising that Fiedler, being focused on the male psyche, should see the maternal as a prison or coffin, whereas Kahane, looking for a female psyche, sees a spectral dead-undead mother.[10]

Now even though castles, bloodstains, mysterious sounds, and Oedipal or pre-Oedipal ghostly mothers do not seem, on the surface, to be integral to *The Portrait of a Lady*, Fiedler and Kahane are still revealing guides. Pansy and Isabel are both versions of Kahane's young woman whose mother has died. Isabel's very name recalls other Gothically dark heroines, such as the mysterious orphaned Isabel of Herman Melville's *Pierre*, and Isabella in Hugh Walpole's *Castle of Otranto*. Further, James's Isabel is trapped in the imprisoning structure of an Italian castle called Roccanera, Osmond's crumbling "pile . . . which smelt of historic deeds, of crime and craft and violence" (*PL*, 307). In fact, this paradigmatic architectural imprisoning of a heroine, so basic to almost any description of the Gothic,[11] finds a curious echo in James's 1907 preface to his revised *Portrait*. There he describes Isabel herself as a "plot of ground" over which he will build a "neat and careful proportioned pile of bricks. . . . I would build large—in fine, embossed vaults and painted arches . . . and yet never let it appear that the chequered pavement, the ground under the reader's feet, fails to stretch, at every point, to the base of the walls" (*PL*, 11). This "literary monument" (*PL*, 11) that James builds in the preface bears an eerie resemblance to Osmond's own "pile." Indeed, James's references to his novel as "a square and spacious house . . . put up round [a] slim shade" of a girl (*PL*, 8), although specific to Isabel, nevertheless blur later distinctions between houses and girls, as the pattern of massive house and frail, slight girl is replicated in Pansy.

One might say that Isabel is doubly immured, first by her husband and then by her author's description of her. Yet unlike Pansy, Isabel is also compelled by her author to seek out what has happened to her, as Kahane suggests a Gothic heroine must. And it is Isabel Archer's intelligence that distinguishes her from her mock-Gothic step-

10. Ibid., 7–13.
11. For this argument, I am most concerned with the nineteenth-century Gothic. See Kahane, "Gothic Mirror"; Fiedler, *Love and Death*; Eve Kosofsky Sedgwick, "The Beast in the Closet: James and the Writing of Homosocial Panic," in *Papers for the English Institute* (Baltimore: Johns Hopkins University Press, 1987); and Sedgwick, *Between Men: English Literature and Male Homosocial Desire* (New York: Columbia University Press, 1985), 83–96.

daughter. In the course of wandering about her "prison-house" of fiction,[12] Isabel pushes at the limitations of self-consciousness. She not only wonders why she has been trapped in a gloomy, Gothic marriage but also attempts to see beyond the boundaries of her knowledge. By so doing, Isabel transforms or, to use a favored Jamesian description, "expands" herself. It is this expansion that makes her an original of conscious individuality.

Striving, then, to puzzle her way through her own memoir, Isabel sits by the fire, contemplating her life's story. James himself, and many critics such as Charles Feidelson, focus on the scene of chapter 42 as the central moment, the pivot of the novelistic *"tragedy* of consciousness" (*PL,* 749) that is the *Portrait.* Isabel begins her self-examination by groping her way around not her own dilemma but Pansy's. She asks herself, does her former suitor, Lord Warburton, seek Pansy's hand simply to be nearer the "rose"? If so, doesn't that make him rather base? "Isabel wandered among these ugly possibilities until she had completely lost her way. . . . Then she broke out of the labyrinth" (*PL,* 355). Traipsing through the labyrinth of Pansy's Gothic entrapment leads Isabel to a disturbing discovery: she sees that her own life is as encompassed by vague terrors as is poor Pansy's. Osmond's mind has "become her habitation" (*PL,* 358) and it grows dark, soon "impenetrably black" (*PL,* 356). At last her wandering leads to a memory that seems to hold an eerie secret. She recalls seeing "her husband and Madame Merle unconsciously and familiarly associated" (*PL,* 364).

When Isabel finally opens the door to that dark association, what she discovers may not be literally a ghost or a secret room of death. Yet she does find a secret that has been silenced by a death and haunted by a ghost who isn't (as Fiedler has written of Gothic specters) *really* a ghost. This is the secret of Serena Merle's maternity. Madame Merle's motherhood has been covered up by the actions she and Osmond took to hide Pansy's birth, which being the result of infidelity, had to be hidden for the sake of propriety. Using the death of Gilbert Osmond's first wife as a cover, Osmond claims that Pansy's mother is dead. But the secret of Pansy's origin is haunted by the

12. See Fredric Jameson, *The Prison-House of Language* (Princeton: Princeton University Press, 1972). Isabel Archer's story aptly illustrates Jameson's head quote from Nietzsche: "The Prison-House of Language / We have to cease to think if we refuse to do it in the prison-house of language; for we cannot reach further than the doubt which asks whether the limit we see is really a limit."

ghost of the motherly solicitude Madame Merle maintains toward her denied child. And most it is Serena Merle's maternity that has caused Isabel's own ill-fated, deathlike, Gothic incarceration of a marriage—for, as she tells herself, Madame Merle, in desiring the Osmond marriage, had a "conception of gain" (*PL*, 432), a gain that the Countess Gemini lays bare when she says to Isabel, "Osmond's marriage has given his daughter a great lift. . . . And do you know what the mother thought? That you might take such a fancy to the child that you'd do something for her" (*PL*, 454).

Isabel discovers, in fact, that—as she herself puts it—a mother has "married her" (*PL*, 430) and so is at the heart of her mysterious fate, just as Fiedler and Kahane have put the maternal (differently emphasized) at the heart of Gothicism. Moreover, since the nineteenth-century United States of James's upbringing, says Kahane, "define[d] the true woman in predominantly biological terms, locating feminine identity within the straits of passive sexuality and selfless maternity,"[13] the traditional Gothic heroine is a particularly revealing figure for Isabel as American abroad. That is, given that the prevailing construction of ideal femininity was the maternal, for a nineteenth-century American heroine engaged in a search for self, the mother is the primary emblem of that selfhood. Upon opening the door to the cultural mandate of a selfless maternity, seeking a pattern for her own being, the Gothic heroine of nineteenth-century fiction quite often finds, as in Louisa May Alcott's "A Whisper in the Dark,"[14] that the secret of her own horror story is bound to the secret of her murdered, missing, or ghostly mother. Finally, although Fiedler's mother-ghost and Kahane's spectral mother may seem theoretical opposites (since Fiedler is on the trail of masculine authority, and Kahane is tracking female selfhood), yet in Isabel Archer's tragedy and in Pansy's mock-Gothic mirror of it, it is precisely the intersection of these two ghost stories—that is, the dialectic between a strict Freudian fantasy of proprietal possession of the mother and the post-Freudian fantasy of the pre-Oedipal mother's murder—that fuels the deepest horror in *The Portrait of a Lady*. In other words, what James maps out in this novel is the horror of a culturally mandated matricide.

13. Kahane, "Gothic Mirror," 350.
14. Louisa May Alcott, "A Whisper in the Dark," *Frank Leslie's Illustrated Newspaper*, June 1863; rpt. in *The Hidden Louisa May Alcott*, ed. Madeline Stern (New York: Avenel Books, 1984), 537–89.

The Spectral Mother

Isabel, in tracing out the Gothic labyrinth of her life and supposedly expanding her "self" consciousness in the process, eventually finds what Kahane has described as the dead/undead mother. She discovers Serena Merle, who, as Pansy's mother, is both alive and yet has been represented to Isabel, in the guise of Osmond's first wife, as deceased. Isabel also finds out that this dead/undead mother is the ghost in the machine of her marriage. Serena Merle says of herself that she is "everything" (PL, 430) to Isabel, just as a mother is at the hidden center of a Freudian female identity.

Although Madame Merle is not Isabel's mother (who, like most Gothic mothers, is dead before the story begins), James makes it clear that Merle's importance to Isabel is suggestive of a mother-daughter bond. When Madame Merle first appears, she exerts an immediate and inexplicable pull on Isabel, which grows as Isabel discovers a cluster of facts that draw her to this woman. She finds that they are compatriots—both Americans—and that her cousin Ralph, of whom she is inordinately fond, was once in love with Serena: "the cleverest woman I know,"he tells Isabel, "not excepting yourself" (PL, 154). Ralph remarks, too, that his own mother "would like to be Madame Merle" (PL, 155), while Ralph's father, Daniel Touchett, has noted that Isabel reminds him of his wife. Madame Merle is thus tied into the family by association and linked to Isabel by national and maternal reference.

In fact, Serena and Isabel develop what amounts to an "eternal friendship": "The gates of the girl's confidence were opened wider than they had ever been; she said things to this amiable auditress that she had not yet said to any one" (PL, 163). Surely this a description of how a daughter, at least ideally, relates to her mother. Madame Merle, then, is both a role model for Isabel and something a little more; as she says, "I should like awfully to be so!" This "so" refers to the "great lady" (PL, 165–66) Isabel sees in Madame Merle, who looks "as if she were a Bust, Isabel judged—a Juno or a Niobe" (PL, 154). This Niobe has, in fact, said of herself that she "will never be anything but abject with the young; they touch me and appeal to me too much" (PL, 170). Her one fault might be that "she existed only in her relations, direct or indirect, with her fellow mortals" (PL, 167) although Isabel is undecided as to whether that is a fault or a virtue. All these attributes indicate that Isabel finds in Serena Merle a classic mother figure to adopt as her own pattern. After all, both Juno and Niobe were classical goddess-mothers. And it is a mother, a person known primarily by her relational status within the familial/social circle, who is supposed to be particularly "abject"[15] with the young. Finally, Ralph has assured Isabel that Serena Merle would "be sure to spoil" a child, should she have one. (*PL*, 155). So, when Madame Merle tells Isabel, "I give you *carte blanche* . . . I shall . . . horribly spoil you" (*PL*, 170), the string of descriptive associations drawn between this symbolic mother and daughter becomes tighter.

Madame Merle is, in fact, a Kahanian ghost signifying the problematics of femininity for Isabel. Isabel's desire to be Serena Merle, "in a word a woman of strong impulses kept in admirable order" (*PL*, 154), is a sign of her attempt to recreate what Homans calls "her symbiotic closeness with her mother."[16] Indeed, throughout what Feidelson has denominated the "social comedy" (*PL*, 747) part of this novel—that is, before Isabel sees her husband and Madame Merle as closer than old friends need be—she is passionately, almost libidinally, tied to Madame Merle. She has qualms, but they resolve into a wish "to imitate her" (*PL*, 338).

That connection retains its pull, if not its strength, until the actualized crisis of selecting Pansy's husband. It is then that Isabel begins to comprehend how a longing for the mother can be both psychically and socially dangerous. As the novel modulates into Feidelson's "comedy of triumphant consciousness" (*PL*, 748) after Isabel's interior journey of chapter 42, Madame Merle's influence, specifically with regard to Pansy's marital prospects, becomes suspect. In psychic terms, the daughter (Isabel or Pansy), despite her connection to the mother (Serena), must also resist that tie if she is going to avoid engulfment. Even as Isabel desires to be like Serena, she sees in that woman something to be resisted, something Gothically horrific: "It was a worse horror than that [of insolence]. 'Who are you—what are you?' Isabel murmured. 'What have you to do with my husband?'" (*PL*, 430). Madame Merle herself has earlier hinted at her own problematic status: "I've been shockingly chipped and cracked. . . . I've been cleverly mended . . . but when I've to come out and into strong light—then, my dear, I'm a horror!" (*PL*, 168). Finally, when the novel turns into Feidelson's "tale of an evil fate" (*PL*, 748) and flowers into

15. See Julia Kristeva, "Stabat Mater," in *The Kristeva Reader*, ed. Toril Moi (New York: Columbia University Press, 1986), 160–87; and Kristeva, *Powers of Horror*.
16. Homans, *Bearing the Word*, 25.

the tragedy of Isabel's consciousness, what she uncovers is that the unnamed horror hanging over her is Madame Merle's illicit maternity.

Once Isabel has pulled the veil from Madame Merle's hidden self, "the truth of things, their mutual relations, their meaning, and for the most part their horror, [rise] before her with a kind of architectural vastness" (PL, 465). Motherhood is the hidden biological fact that allows Isabel to see the house of fiction built upon her. Her dawning consciousness, then, rises from the Gothic discovery of her "mother's" (and her own) sexuality, the reproductive power marking all women with the ability to be mothers.

It is not simply a daughter's psychodynamic fear of maternal engulfment, however, that explains Isabel's reaction of chill despair toward Madame Merle. Rather, it is Isabel's realization that no matter what form of resistance she forges, she will not forget Madame Merle or separate from her entirely. It does not matter that Isabel's "eyes were absent from her companion's face," because "there were phrases and gradations in her speech, not one of which was lost upon Isabel's ear" (PL, 458). Serena Merle will remain mysterious and forever something of a painful loss; as Isabel mourns, "the only thing to regret was that Madame Merle had been so unimaginable" (PL, 465). Isabel finds herself caught in the paradoxical fastness of a Western cultural (Gothic) fantasy wherein the daughter, having taken up the attractive image of the pre-Oedipal mother/self, is then coerced into a denigration of that image in exchange for a legitimized place in her society. In Isabel's case, although she has loved Madame Merle, she must forget her in exchange for the social power of a limited but nevertheless legal wifehood. To leave Osmond would be to leave social legitimacy and become as outcast and as "unimaginable" as Madame Merle, a fate she has learned to fear.

But Isabel's turning away from Serena results not in adjustment, as strict Freudians might say, but in despair, or in what Kaja Silverman identifies in *The Acoustic Mirror* as the definitive melancholia of female subjectivity. According to Silverman, melancholia is fundamental to female subjectivity because the daughter, having first accepted a positive mother *imago*, is then coerced, in order to function in society, into despising "her."[17] In this curiously evocative way, Feidelson's structural mapping of *The Portrait of a Lady* dovetails with Silverman's re-

---

17. Kaja Silverman, *The Acoustic Mirror: The Female Voice in Psychoanalysis and Cinema* (Bloomington: Indiana University Press, 1988), 152–59.

mapping of Oedipal dynamics: this novel is a "social" comedy that turns out to be, after all, a tragedy about female self-consciousness or, as Feidelson so eloquently suggests, the tale of an evil fate.

Indeed, to look at *The Portrait of a Lady* from Madame Merle's point of view (as it were) is to see a strong relational web of mother-daughter bonding between Serena Merle, Isabel Archer, and Pansy Osmond, a web whose importance Claire Kahane's analysis of Goth-icism helps to illuminate. That is, since these relations have seldom been examined for their similarities rather than for their differences, much of the significance of the *Portrait*'s trajectory has gone unre-marked, leaving critics grasping at straws in order to explain Isabel's fate. For instance, although it has been noted that Isabel and Pansy resemble each other, the resemblance is seen as triumphantly com-parative: Pansy is Isabel's little foil, the empty vessel Isabel is not. More important, the connection between these women has not been well integrated into any discussion of the novel's ending. Having un-covered Serena Merle's manipulation of her marriage and conse-quently the hollowness of that bond, having seen that Pansy will never disobey her father, why should Isabel return to Osmond? Pan-sy's part in Isabel's retreat to Osmond's horror show does not go unnoticed but most critics speak of Pansy as a weak plot device.[18] Dorothy Van Ghent's summary is representative: "The quaint figure of Pansy, always only on the edge of scenes, is of great structural importance in the latter half of the book; for she shows the full meas-ure of the abuse Isabel resists and it is to nourish in her [Pansy] what-ever small germ of creative volition may remain—to salvage really, a life—that Isabel returns to Rome and to Osmond's paralyzing ambi-ance" (*PL*, 699).

Pansy is both a marginalized foil and the *raison d'être* for the novel's odd ending. Critics tend to claim that Isabel's choice to return to Os-mond, like her choice to marry him, is made "freely" and done altru-istically for Pansy's sake.[19] Furthermore, in various discussions that focus on Isabel's flight from Caspar Goodwood (most often read as

18. See Dorothy Van Ghent, "On *The Portrait of a Lady*," in *PL*, 689–704; and William Veeder, *Henry James: The Lessons of the Master* (Chicago: University of Chicago Press, 1975).

19. On Isabel's limited consciousness as her freedom, see also Feidelson, "Moment" (in *PL*); Veeder, *Henry James*; and Dorothea Krook, *The Ordeal of Consciousness in Henry James* (New York: Cambridge University Press, 1962). James himself saw Isabel as pri-marily a consciousness in the process of becoming unique.

her flight from heterosexuality),[20] it is Isabel's limited freedom of a heightened consciousness, purchased at the expense of sexual expression, that makes her so much more valuable than either poor Pansy or the "horror" of Serena Merle. Indeed, Isabel's consciousness, "deprived of every reference point except its own intrinsic freedom," as Feidelson argues (*PL*, 750-1), makes her the stunning original that she is to him and, I might add, to James himself.

Yet what remains unaccounted for is Isabel's clear knowledge that she cannot save Pansy. Nor is it for Pansy's sake that she will return to Osmond, as she admits to her friend Henrietta Stackpole:

> "Well," said Miss Stackpole at last, "I've only one criticism to make. I don't see why you promised little Miss Osmond to go back."
> "I'm not sure I myself see now," Isabel replied. "But I did then."
> "If you've forgotten your reason perhaps you won't return."
> Isabel waited a moment. "Perhaps I shall find another." (*PL*, 469)

It also remains obscure that Isabel's creative volition is purchased at the rather violent expense of her connection to Madame Merle. James offers Isabel no choice. She must trade in her view of Serena as a powerful Juno, after whom she had patterned herself, for a view of Merle as one who lacks morality.

In fact, Isabel's tragedy, if viewed as a daughter's search for her self, is the tragedy of a female subjectivity in the process of the melancholic discovery that in order to achieve a social self, she must both become like her mother and learn to hate her. She must pattern herself on the Juno and yet aid in covering up the shameful secret of a culturally inscribed maternal diminishment. If, like Pansy, Isabel plays a daughter's role to Madame Merle's motherhood, then Pansy's veiled mock-Gothic operetta becomes a vividly congruent parallel to Isabel's opera. In this context, Pansy's last conversation with Isabel takes on a powerfully suggestive resonance: "I don't like Madame Merle!" she says. Isabel replies, "You must never say that—that you don't like Madame Merle" (*PL*, 463). It is as if Isabel, in echoing and yet altering her stepdaughter's statement, acknowledges both that Pansy has spoken for her and that in order for a daughter to survive she must help to hide the mother's (social and by extension moral) diminishment

20. See Veeder, *Henry James*, 86; and Alfred Habegger, *Gender, Fantasy and Realism in American Literature* (New York: Columbia University Press, 1982), 76.

and her own (self) hatred. This congruence leads me to question whether the expansion of Isabel's consciousness is a triumph at all— for do not Pansy's fate and Isabel's acknowledgment of it indicate a darker future for the heroine than most criticism allows? Isabel herself recognizes that "she should never escape" (*PL*, 466). How much creative volition does she have? And ultimately the darkness of these daughters' twin fates leads me to reexamine whose tragedy the *Portrait* describes—especially when Madame Merle herself claims that "the tragedy's for me!" (*PL*, 436).

In the Father's House

To treat the *Portrait* as a Gothic novel still begs a question: does a ghost of Oedipal paternal anxiety also haunt Roccanera? I have been at pains to outline how Isabel's consciousness is linked to her discovery of Madame Merle's maternity. Is paternity not implicated as well? If Pansy and Isabel share a Gothic heritage, and if they both bear a daughterly relation to Serena Merle, then they should also be related to Osmond as father. This relation is suggested in the dark association between Osmond and Merle, especially since Isabel's discovery of it bears an uncanny resemblance to Freud's narrative of how a child might unknowingly witness the parental sexual relation. More compelling, though, is James's description of Osmond's desire toward Isabel in terms congruent to Osmond's relation with Pansy. Pansy is Osmond's figurine, a part of his castle's decor. When Isabel is introduced to him, she tells her Aunt Lydia that she is to go and "see his view, his pictures, his daughter" (*PL*, 215), as if all three were in some fashion equal—and all at Osmond's disposal. James then shows that Osmond believes Isabel should belong to him in the same way Pansy does. Finding that Isabel has rejected Lord Warburton's proposal, Osmond thinks she has "qualified herself to figure in his collection of choice objects by declining so noble a hand" (*PL*, 258) and Isabel finds that her mind is to be "attached to his own like a small garden-plot to a deer-park . . . a pretty piece of property for a proprietor" (*PL*, 362).

Of course, it is undeniable that Isabel, unlike Pansy, feels the full horror of becoming a (daughterly) piece of property. As James tells us, Isabel knows that Roccanera is "the house of darkness, the house of dumbness, the house of suffocation" (*PL*, 360), and she ultimately learns that "the real offense" to Osmond is "her having a mind of her own at all" (*PL*, 362). Having made his daughter "a blank page, a pure white surface successfully kept so" (*PL*, 268), upon which he is at liberty to paint, Osmond believes that Isabel as well will be "richly receptive. He ... expect[s] his wife to feel with him and for him, to enter into his opinions" (*PL*, 362). But Isabel has ideas of her own. Osmond cannot paint over her because she is not a blank page. At least, not for Osmond.

She *is* a blank page to somebody else, however, that somebody being her author.[21] In his preface to the *Portrait*, Henry James names Isabel his "unattached character" and "the mere slim shade of an intelligent but presumptuous girl" (*PL*, 5, 8), images that are seemingly better suited to Pansy. More telling, though, is the congruence between Osmond's paternal view of Pansy as his own "precious work of art" (*PL*, 442), which he wishes to place in advantageous social niches and James's attitude toward Isabel. He sees her as "an acquisition I had made ... after a fashion not here to be retraced. Enough that I was, as it seemed to me, in complete possession of it" (*PL*, 7), a property he wishes to place in the world as a masterpiece. He goes on to speak of Isabel in terms that could apply equally to Osmond's view of his daughter: "The value I here speak of is the image of the young feminine nature that I had had for so considerable a time all curiously at my disposal" and for which the creator harbors "a pious desire but to place [his] treasure right" (*PL*, 8). Although Henry James distances himself from Osmond by expressing the darkness of Isabel's condition, he echoes Osmond when he prefaces his novel with such proprietary descriptions.

Nor is it simply the preface that links James to Osmond. During Isabel's famed interior journey, she is suddenly not by the fire alone; James's "I" intrudes: "When she saw this rigid system [of Osmond's mind] close about her, draped though it was in pictured tapestries, that sense of darkness and suffocation of which I have spoken took possession of her" (*PL*, 361). It is as if Isabel had a doubled consciousness, her own and this overseeing "I" who speaks for her just as Osmond claims an unquestioned right to speak for his daughter. What Pansy desires "doesn't matter" (*PL*, 315), says Osmond, because she is his "winged fairy in the pantomime" who only "soars by the aid of the dissimulated wire ... prettily ... directed and fashioned" (*PL*,

21. For a discussion of the woman as art object, see Gubar, "The Blank Page," 73–95.

267). James aligns himself with Osmond's paternal right to create a world for his "daughter": he both speaks for Isabel and allows Osmond to claim, "I'm talking for my wife as well as for myself" (*PL*, 420); further, he makes of Isabel, if not a fairy, another winged creature—"the angel of disdain" (*PL*, 402). When Theodora Bosanquet, James's last secretary, remarks that the author felt "paternally responsible" (*PL*, 494) for his literary progeny, her estimation is a shade more than acute.

James's attitude toward Isabel is thus analogous to Osmond's relation to Pansy as daughter, since both exhibit a possessive paternalism that equates feminine nature with precious objects. Desire is then figured as a pious wish to place the daughter/artwork well within the realm of the social, to put her where she won't, as Osmond says of Pansy, get "knocked about too much" (*PL*, 442). Perhaps "knocked up" would be the more modern way to describe Osmond's anxiety? Certainly it is the disposition of Pansy's sexuality that is at stake in the heated contest over her marriage, and that contest makes clear that if money and sexuality are bound together, they are linked as well to the father's financial status. As Pansy candidly laments to Isabel, her father is not wealthy, and "it costs so much to marry!" (*PL*, 268). Just as Isabel's relation to Madame Merle is that of daughter to mother, so does Isabel's status as James's possession mirror Pansy's relation to Osmond. The *jeune fille*, in fact, is the material upon which creativity will be inscribed. Insofar as the pure Pansy is as virginal as that blank page to which Osmond has "transferred . . . the delicate, finely-tinted disk" (*PL*, 444) of an antique coin, insofar as Pansy and her *belle-mère* "are like two sisters" (*PL*, 462–63), Pansy is a figure for the metaphorical prize Isabel becomes—a prize that the American artist/father must possess in order to create. In this psychic economy, the father who lacks a daughter is a failure. Without a masterpiece, there can be no master. Owning the daughter allows the father to own creative potential, or, as Isabel notes, Osmond's genius is evident in the delicate organism of Pansy.

Paternal possession of the daughter is clearly sexual as well as proprietal. The incestual nature of a father-daughter relation is suggested symbolically by Isabel, if she stands in a daughter's position as Osmond's property, but Pansy herself makes a bald reference to it: "I don't care for any gentleman; I mean any but him. If he were not my papa I should like to marry him" (*PL*, 268). Several important analyses have shown that the Freudian Oedipal crisis, while forbidding

mother-son incest, encourages or even institutes, father-daughter incest as a constitutive part of a successful partriarchal economy.[22] Such
an incestual economy has a particular resonance for nineteenth-
century American culture, as Martha Banta and Carolyn Porter have
pointed out in focusing on the daughter as a figure for value. Indeed,
Banta, in *Imaging American Women*, uses Isabel Archer as the prototype
of the white American Girl whom white, Protestant, bourgeois American cultural iconography privileged as the "visual emblem of the
greatness of a nation which 'had nothing left to be desired.' "[23] Porter
traces out the implications of this national desire when she argues
that James, in attempting to rescue the cultural value accorded to feminine nature from the commodification of an expanding marketplace
economy, enacts "the behavior of a patriarchal father who uses his
authority both to protect and to control his daughter."[24]

Paradoxically, protective paternalism is still based on the idea that
female = money = commodity = value. James may attempt to rescue
Isabel/daughter/value from a commodity status, but what he creates
is yet another version of an exchangeable object, an American "portrait." The father is caught in a double bind. In order to increase his
status, he ought to marry off his daughter, but in order to claim creativity and avoid losing capital, he ought to retain her—just as Osmond retains Pansy by putting her in the convent while claiming that
this action will make her more marriagable. As Porter argues, like
Claire of James's *The American*, "Isabel herself must return behind the
stone walls of Osmond's dark prison, but her value remains enshrined
in the portrait" so that James can retain "possession of . . . an 'original'
which the preface serves to place in his own personal Louvre—the
New York Edition."[25] The daughter, as precious as an antique gold
coin, must be saved, since she is wealth, she must be capitalized upon.

Indeed, the successful patriarchal social contract is one that operates
not only on a "traffic in women"[26] but also, and with increasing pres-

22. See, e.g., Judith Herman, *Father-Daughter Incest* (Cambridge, Mass.: Harvard University Press, 1981).
23. Banta, *Imaging American Women*, xxviii.
24. Carolyn Porter, "Gender and Value in *The American*," in *New Essays on "The
American*," ed. Martha Banta (New York: Oxford University Press, 1987), 126.
25. Ibid., 126.
26. See Lynda E. Boose, "The Father's House and the Daughter in It: The Structures
of Western Culture's Daughter-Father Relationships," in *Daughters and Fathers*, ed.
Lynda E. Boose and Betty S. Flowers (Baltimore: Johns Hopkins University Press, 1989),
25–32. See also Gayle Rubin, "The Traffic in Women: Notes on the Political Economy

sure under capitalism, on the conflicting incestuous demand that the father save his daughter for himself. Further, for this economy to run smoothly, the capital in question, while emanating from the daughter, must never remain in her hands. In *The Portrait of a Lady* capital does not remain in Isabel's control; she seems to be only a source of value, merely facilitating a transfer of one father's wealth into another father's house and thus keeping value under masculine direction. As James says, "At bottom her money had been a burden, had been on her mind, which was filled with the desire to transfer the weight of it ... to some more prepared receptacle" (*PL*, 358). Isabel is left as bankrupt of value as I believe she is bankrupt of that independent volition so often ascribed to her. All belongs to the "father"—no matter whether friend or fiend.

To expand: it is known from the outset that Ralph Touchett's paternal legacy—an American banker's legacy—is Isabel's treasure. This monetary capital forms her chief source of desirability for Osmond; as Madame Merle tells her, the Touchetts "imparted to you that extra lustre which was required to make you a brilliant match" (*PL*, 464). Reading this lustre from a more sexualized angle, one should recall with Kahane that the erotic threat in the Gothic, being incestual, can come from either a father or a brother. In Isabel's case, her "father" is on one level Osmond, on another level Uncle Daniel Touchett, and on a third level Henry James. But her "brother" is certainly her cousin Ralph Touchett, who has inadvertently threatened her by making of her an object of social as well as sexual desire. The erotic threat Isabel tries to flee is not only a combination of fatherly and brotherly love but also part of the constitutively incestual nature of a nineteenth-century patriarchal masculinity. Just as a nineteenth-century ideal wedded femininity to maternity, so it tied masculinity to paternity. All the men in the book want to own Isabel; as James says, "They all had Isabel for subject" (*PL*, 271). This desire is frequently expressed through a paternal medium of precious objects and is considered benign:after all, the Touchetts do not mean Isabel harm; she herself comes to name Daniel Touchett "the beneficent author of her infinite woe" (*PL*, 358). Isabel believes this benevolence is safer to her liberty than heterosexual desire. She refuses both Goodwood and Warburton because they are active men who have a social importance. Isabel fears

of Sex," in *Toward an Anthropology of Women*, ed. Rayna R. Reiter (New York: Monthly Review Press, 1975), 157–210.

that Goodwood's sexualized activity would erase her, that Warburton's aristocratic wealth would make her a dependent. When Aunt Lydia says of Osmond, "There's nothing of him," Isabel replies, "Then he can't hurt me" (*PL*, 282), implying that her former lovers might have. What she has not understood is that the aggressive Goodwood, the aristocratic Warburton, and the benign Osmond all belong to the same paternal order.

In this sense, I would agree with those critics who feel that Isabel tries to flee sexuality, because the homosocial, heterosexual imperative of a nineteenth-century psychic economy requires her to be a mirror for the father and a possession who, in learning to loath her (m)other (self), must acquiesce to being a ghost within a Western cultural patriarchy that binds men together by making her into that ghost. Eve Kosofsky Sedgwick has argued in her essay on Henry James's "The Beast in the Jungle" that "the normal condition of the male heterosexual entitlement" in the nineteenth century was a panicky, paranoid state of both homophobia and homosociality; for Sedgwick, evidence of this unstable entitlement is most evident in a nineteenth-century Gothicism that showed a marked "preference of atomized male individuality"[27] or for what she calls a sarcastic bachelor figure.

Interestingly, both Ralph Touchett and Gilbert Osmond fit Sedgwick's "bachelor taxonomy."[28] Both have acute powers of sarcastic observation and Isabel herself believes that Ralph and Osmond share the "appearance of thinking that life [is] a matter of connoisseurship" (*PL*, 225). They are also said to hate each other. Isabel's portrait seems, in fact, to have been painted first by Touchett's money and then by Osmond's use of that fortune. Despite their supposed hatred of one another, Touchett and Osmond are bound together by their concern with Isabel; she is "between" these "men."[29] Touchett is nearly Osmond's halo. To Isabel, he personifies the generosity her husband lacks, he is "a lamp in the darkness" (*PL*, 363), whose brightness, however, gains its most illuminating shine only against Osmond's perfidy. In effect, Isabel separates and connects the two men. There is a wedge of hatred between Gilbert Osmond and Ralph Touchett, yet their opposition, projected onto Isabel, glues them together, Janus-faced. She is their common desire; they both want possession of her (her own desire seems to weigh very little in this contest). So too, the

27. Sedgwick, "The Beast in the Closet," 159.
28. Ibid., 155.
29. Sedgwick, *Between Men*.

difference between Henry James and Gilbert Osmond shrinks when seen in light of Ralph Touchett's bonded relation to Osmond. Bluntly, because James sympathizes with Ralph Touchett, the psychic economy of all three American men—Osmond, Touchett, James—if viewed as interlocking parts of a paternal, homosocial entitlement, seem weirdly congruent. For aren't Osmond and Touchett two sides of the same psychic coin, that coin being the paternal consciousness of Henry James?

Ghosts in the Paternal Machine

This paternalistic scenario, as well as Isabel's relation to Madame Merle, leaves Isabel standing primarily in a daughter's position. So if, in the father's Freudian/Gothic fantasy, the mother is the locus of paternal desire, what is the daughter doing here? But if, according to the paternal economy I've just sketched out, the daughter represents value, does the father need the mother? After these familial positions have been shuffled around the psychic chessboard, where *does* Isabel stand?

First, her discovery of Madame Merle's maternity puts Serena Merle into a maternal role toward both Pansy and Isabel. Then, if one follows out the metaphorics in the fatherly plot of possession, again, symbolically, Madame Merle plays mother to Isabel. But in the course of the novel Isabel takes over maternity, changing from Pansy's sister into Pansy's stepmother—becoming, in effect, a daughter who is, as well, a mother. Alternatively, by examining how the bonds of homosocial entitlement operate, one can detect a drift-line of "fatherhood" that leads irrevocably back through Osmond as proprietor, Ralph Touchett as procurer, Daniel Touchett as patron, to Henry James as painter. Here, Isabel is a daughter who represents the virginal value of "a quick fanciful mind which saved one repetitions and reflected one's thought on a polished, elegant surface" (*PL*, 296); she plays the role of value-*cum*-daughter.

Given these two daughterly roles, what becomes clear is that Isabel stands at a crossroad: she is both virginal property and potentially sexual mother. Still, Isabel is not maternal in the way that her "mother" is; she will never be wholly tainted with a threatening re-productivity. Her physical maternity is missing: her child dies, and her pregnancy is unrepresented. And, as the Lady is inscribed upon the blank *jeune fille* in the *Portrait,* both are recoded as masculine conceptions. The maternal (Serena) from which both maiden and lady (Pansy and Isabel) come, at least in part, is diminished and disposed of (exiled to America), leaving the father (Osmond) in possession of the field. The daughter role is a blind for the fact that the father, in order to ensure his position in this economy, must show potency and yet obliterate any reproductive creativity besides his own. He must demonstrate "fatherhood" without revealing his dependency on the maternal. The daughter is a perfect blind for this: being ideally virginal and also ideally the father's creation or possession alone, she is safe from the taint of an alien reproductivity. Isabel's power as a character comes from the fact that she appears to remain virginal while stepping blindly into Serena Merle's dispossessed maternity. She occupies the mother's place while remaining daughterly. Isabel replaces Serena Merle as Pansy Osmond's mother and adopts Serena Merle's personal style—and yet, as her affect grows to resemble the serenity invoked by Serena's name, she becomes a static work of daughterly art without an independent erotic desire. She becomes, in fact, what James calls her: an exquisite Madonna (*PL,* 392), Western culture's most developed icon of maternal daughterhood.

In this light, motherless Pansy is the figure who most sharply reveals Henry James's relation not only to Isabel but more broadly to the *Portrait* as an art object of the highest valuation upon which its author, retrospectively in his 1907 New York edition, founded a new family of American literature. That is, what Pansy's (and Isabel's) daughterly Gothic fates reveals is that the Jamesian "house of fiction" (*PL,* 7) is dependent on but also ruthlessly compelled to deface, or at least diminish, a conceptual energy defined or represented as maternal—a position that Serena Merle inhabits and Isabel inherits from her. In other words, as Isabel—the pure and valued creation—expands, Serena Merle, the alien mother, contracts and is at last swept out of the picture. She leaves behind a daughter who has acquired her attributes but who is marked as a male-generated possession, a representation of the father's art.

Still, in coming to be as serene as Serena and in discovering the dead/undead mother, Isabel has actually begun to discover what will become of her "self." What happens to Isabel's consciousness, her valuable, original selfhood. By figuratively transferring a conceptual power designated as an implicitly sexual, biological maternity from the mother Serena Merle to the patriarchally created, sexually inert daughter Isabel; by essentially transferring the notion of "conception" from mother to daughter and then incarcerating the daughter in a perpetual patriarchal daughterhood, James can, through the ownership of Isabel's virginal (daughterly) consciousness, appropriate for himself the power of "conception"—and, I would argue, self-conception. The supposedly invisible (male) artist with a (female) consciousness can then gestate and bring to term a perfect portrait without risking either a threatening involvement with the taboo mother or a homosexually tainted brush with the feminized—without himself risking the gender confusion that marks all the artistic male characters in the novel. For who owns the consciousness that is Isabel's sensitivity? What *The Portrait of a Lady* reveals is that aesthetic value derives from the acquisition and regendering of the power to *conceive*, a power that had been culturally defined as maternal.

The extrusion of the mother upon which mastery rests, however—a mastery which James does not entirely arrogate to himself, but which has been "bestowed" upon him by later critics—is a painful process that leaves traces of agony. When Isabel hears Countess Gemini's account of how Serena Merle lost her daughter, she weeps, nor is it surprising to find Madame Merle herself described as a Niobe. In weeping for the children, in weeping for each other, these women are weeping for themselves. Another painful trace of erasure remains in James's notebooks and, like a Gothic ghost, haunts the hallways of the *Portrait*'s architecture; it is a scene that James described as "the great scene" but did not include in the final versions of the novel: "Isabel resents Madame Merle's interference and demands of her what she has to do with Pansy; whereupon, Madame Merle, in whose breast the suppressed feeling of maternity has long been rankling, and who is passionately jealous of Isabel's influence over Pansy, breaks out with the cry, 'she alone has the right'—that Pansy is her daughter."[30] I suggest that James found himself almost forced to omit this

---

30. James, *Complete Notebooks*, 14. See also *Ten Short Stories of Henry James*, ed. Michael Swan (London: John Lehmann, 1948). This sort of agony appears repeatedly in James's work. In "The Last of the Valerii" (1868), a young Italian count who has married an American falls in hopeless, possessive love with an unearthed and unearthly statue of the mother goddess, Juno. He nearly dies of his love but is saved when his daughterly wife has the mother reburied. The reburial agonizes everyone in the tale, but as the count's wife exclaims, "She's beautiful, she's noble, she's precious, but she must go back! . . . We must smother her beauty in the dreadful earth" in order to survive. Since James "resurrects" Juno to play the part of Serena, this early parable tells us something,

scene because it would have revealed too sharply and too painfully what *The Portrait of a Lady* enacts. This novel sets out to establish who has the cultural right to both create a girl and endow her with value. That "who" is the painter of *The Portrait of a Lady*, the master left standing in the most prominent paternal position in relation to her— for it certainly can no longer be, as Isabel's sadness, fear, and ultimate incarceration reveal, the child (or the mother) herself.

I think, about who Madame Merle is and for what fate such a mother is destined.

In "The Madonna of the Future" (1873) a male artist seeking to paint the ultimate representation of the Madonna ends up with "a canvas that [is] a mere dead blank cracked and discolored by time." He fails because he cannot sufficiently possess the woman/mother who has inspired him. His inability imaginatively to overcome the taboo of mother-son incest kills him.

In "The Author of Beltraffio" (1884), the successful literary creations of a male author cause the death of both his son and his wife. The books—tainted by an unnamable sexuality that critics have often allied with Oscar Wilde, James Swinburne, and the emerging homosexual consciousness of the late nineteenth century—so horrify the (demonized) mother that she allows her son to die of diphtheria rather than live to be corrupted by them, and she too sinks "into a consumption and fade[s] away." A book and a son and a mother seem to be displaced by one another, suggesting once again that a male authorship and a female maternity cannot exist in the same space. The survival of the one (gendered as masculine and homosocial) depends upon the appropriation (as male artists take on traditionally female attributes) and subsequent erasure of the (m)other.

Afterword:
Shadows of the National Banner

> Republicans understand the bondage between mother and child.
> —J. Danforth Quayle

"I was born," says Madame Merle to Isabel Archer, "under the shadow of the national banner." Unlike Mrs. Touchett, who claims that Merle is "too full of mystery," I find these particular words, and the description that follows them, very clear. Madame Merle "came into the world," she says, "in the Brooklyn navy-yard. My father was a high officer in the United States Navy, and had a post—a post of responsibility—in that establishment" (*PL*, 153). This description of flag and father records a maternal absence. Yet Merle's anxiety about her father's post also seems to lengthen the shadow under which she was born, since, as James says, "it would never have been supposed that she had come into the world in Brooklyn though one could doubtless not have carried through any argument that the air of distinction marking her in so eminent a degree was inconsistent with such a birth" (*PL*, 154).

In the first edition of *The Portrait of a Lady*, the awkward phrase "it would never have been supposed" reads "Isabel would never have supposed that [Madame Merle] had been born in Brooklyn" (*PL*, 514). According to James's first version of this moment, then, Madame Merle's geographical origin is an issue for Isabel (and for the narrator) by *not* being at issue. Brooklyn, which by 1881 had become home to a diverse, immigrant laboring population, appears as a sign of denied social division.[1]

Indeed, the "white blackbird," to use the term Joseph McCullough coined for Serena Merle in 1975,[2] casts other historical and cultural

---

1. See Ryan, *Womanhood in America*.
2. Joseph B. McCullough, "Madame Merle: Henry James's 'White Blackbird,' " *Papers*

shadows. Madame Blackbird's duplicitous French sobriquet is histor-ically resonant. It may not only signify the ethnic, racial, and moral dubiety that "French" denoted within predominant antebellum con-ventions in the United States; it may also recall the immense and in-ternational popularity of such postbellum entertainment as Haverly's Minstrels, featuring "white men [and women] in burnt cork . . . imi-tation niggers."[3] "White" actresses—from San Francisco's Charlotte Crabtree to Hollywood's Judy Garland—have used blackface imita-tions (originally of Stowe's Topsy) to launch and sustain careers.[4] In-deed, the continued stage life of Jarrett and Palmer's *Uncle Tom* (the company ran five London productions simultaneously in 1878) se-cured a place for minstrelsy's "Jim Crow" in popular culture even as Jim Crow laws rent the reconstituted Union and Judge Lynch ran riot.[5] Clearly, "white blackbird" can be read as more than a mere descrip-tion. Commenting on Gertrude Stein's "Melanctha" of her *Three Lives* (1909), Martha Banta even points to the possibility of reading Madame Merle as a figure for covert racial coding in the *Portrait*: "Stein be-lieved . . . blacks are static and fixed; they are complete as Madame Merle is complete."[6]

James's first edition of the novel describes Serena Merle as having a "world-wide smile, a thing that over-reached frontiers" (*PL*, 517). In the later New York edition James revised this appropriative, colon.iz-ing smile. It became simply fine and frank, but the trace of its poten-tially imperial excess remains: "She had a liberal, full-rimmed mouth which when she smiled drew itself upward to the left side" (*PL*, 154). The left side is, of course, the *sinister* (Latin, "left") side.

Black or white? Appropriated or appropriator? Graceful or affected? Sinister or frank? In light of Merle's later and infamously "vile" be-havior, the narrator's early description of her provides a tellingly con-fused opposition: "It was true that the national banner had floated immediately over her cradle, and the breezy freedom of the stars and stripes might have shed an influence upon the attitude she there took

on Language and Literature 11 (1975): 312–16. See also William T. Stafford, "The Enigma of Serena Merle," *Henry James Review* 7 (Winter–Spring 1986).

3. Birdoff, *World's Greatest Hit*, 247. The racist rhetoric of Birdoff's "history" is also worth examination.

4. Ibid., 220–21, 406–7.

5. See also Chapter 3, n. 49, above; and Birdoff, *World's Greatest Hit*, 241–47. On minstrelsy in popular culture, see Eric Lott, "Love and Theft: The Racial Unconscious of Blackface Minstrelsy," *Representations* 39 (Summer 1992): 23–50.

6. Banta, *Imaging American Women*, 331.

towards life. And yet she had evidently nothing of the fluttered, flapping quality of a morsel of bunting in the wind; her manner expressed the repose and confidence which come from a large experience" (*PL*, 154). The narrator denies that fluttering and flapping are apt descriptions of Madame Merle, yet suggests she takes an attitude of breezy freedom toward life from the morsel of bunting that bears the stars and stripes. Liberality and a kind of unseemly, flapping looseness are presented together in the passage. So the question seems to hang in the air: is Merle a figure for Liberty, or is she just a loose woman?

According to Lauren Berlant, "the regularity with which Miss Liberty becomes an object of sexual speculation and erotic fantasy evokes the way citizens formulate the nation as an object of idealized love"[7] The claim is pertinent here. A "common symbolic denominator" in a national fantasy, Lady Liberty, "the Mother of Exiles," was often imagined as common or, to use a favored Jamesian word, vulgar. Madame Merle is likewise described as a figure for amplitude and completeness. She is quick, free, engaging, replete, liberal. She is utterly American, yet utterly foreign. The narrator speaks of her as if she could be of any nation or class, French (Lady Liberty was, after all, a gift from France to the United States), German, Austrian; a princess, baroness, countess. Or, to be vulgar, she could be a Navy brat from Brooklyn. At her final appearance in the novel, we are told, seeing her "was like suddenly, and rather awfully, seeing a painted picture move. Isabel had been thinking all day of her falsity, her audacity, her ability, her probable suffering; and these dark things seemed to flash with a sudden light as she entered the room. Her being there at all had the character of ugly evidence, of handwritings, of profaned relics, of grim things produced in court" (*PL*, 456).

In other words, Madame Merle's serene, dark ability and grim, Gothic audacity may mark the boundary at which Isabel's "intelligence must drop"—and yet this "unimaginable" profanation, this Madame Merle who is a moving picture, has generated a clarifying flash of sudden light (*PL*, 456). Resplendently dark, yet as perfectly shaped and as flawlessly white as her own hands, she is also a horror of old, "born before the French Revolution" (*PL*, 170). Madame Merle's white hand bears no ring, no proprietary sign, and yet it is she above all who has the greatest respect, as she puts it, for properties such as wedding rings, things that carry social and, indeed, political signifi-

7. Berlant, *The Anatomy of National Fantasy*, 26–27.

cance. It is as if she were herself a profaned but revered relic masking the bloody scars and hideous republican evidence of inappropriate liberalities or Enlightenment revolutions (*PL*, 170). As a white black-bird, she almost seems to hark back to Ishmael's famous musings on whiteness.

> The Albino is as well made as other men—has no substantive defor-mity—and yet this mere aspect of all-pervading whiteness makes him more strangely hideous than the ugliest abortion. Why . . . is [whiteness] at once the most meaning symbol of spiritual things, nay, the very veil of the Christian's Deity; and yet . . . the intensifying agent in things the most appalling to mankind[?] . . . all other earthly hues . . . are but subtle deceits, not actually inherent in substances, but only laid on from with-out; so that all deified Nature absolutely paints like the harlot, whose allurements cover nothing but the charnel-house within. (*MD*, 291–96)

Complete and multiple, liberal and a libertine, the white blackbird dons a smiling, even-tempered mask. And at the end of the novel, the text locates—and exiles—such horrific liberality in the United States.

In a gesture of closure for the project I have pursued here, I am tempted to rename Madame Merle Lady Liberty, even at the risk of reductiveness. Merle's description of her birth and her own situation as a hidden mother are reminiscent of the issue of maternal absence which I have traced throughout this book. In addition, however, the descriptions of Serena Merle that follow her mysterious natal procla-mation allow her to be read as a late nineteenth-century personifica-tion of a prior, static, sentimental, maternal America that will, in James's narrative, give way to a New Woman.

Yet as *The Portrait of a Lady* shows, although this New Woman sig-nified a certain freedom, it served in its own manner to install an icon of nationality. In different ways but with fully as much force as its paradigmatic predecessor, this icon worked to recontain the revela-tions of revolutions, even as it appeared to represent them. Thus, as Martha Banta points out, by 1893 an "official American image began to compose itself from the fluid elements of the times. 'America' was female, young, pretty, Protestant, and northern European. She was the heiress of America's history as edited by the American Whigs. Her features were 'regular' and Caucasian. Her bloodline was pure and vigorous. That she might have 'nerves' and that her will was at times inconveniently strong, was, after all, to be expected."[8] Banta then uses Isabel Archer as her literary prototype for the New Woman.[9]

Yet what interests me is how Serena Merle stands behind Isabel Archer like a ransacked prototype out of which a new paradigm is generated. Postbellum Madame Merle has inherited that antebellum trope of Woman as Angel/Demon with which I began this book—a trope that abolitionist Angelina Grimké experienced as a form of public castigation when she was repeatedly renamed Devilina by the conservative and pro-slavery press.[10] The figure of Madame Merle is offered as a model out of which certain useful elements are extracted and attached to Isabel Archer. James's text thus recasts the shape of a fractured maternal iconography in order to resituate, and revalue, those elements necessary to the status quo, elements that had become part of a maternal liberality that was far too liberal and far too loose to reproduce the status quo faithfully.

For example, the idea of nurture as unquestionably, instinctually maternal is a predominant one in midcentury constructions of sentimental maternal iconography: think of Eliza Harris. Nurture is still seen as maternal at the end of the century: think of the way the portrait of Lydia Touchett emphasizes just how nonnurturing and therefore nonmaternal her behavior is. Earlier texts, such as Harriet Beecher Stowe's and Harriet Jacobs's, identify nurture as a quintessence of the maternal that crosses race and class boundaries. But James revalues nurturance as that which might once have properly belonged to the biological maternal, to Serena Merle, but has perforce migrated elsewhere—to Isabel Archer. This resituation of nurture produced its own set of contradictions and alters the way maternal iconography operates in twentieth-century representations. Yet nurture remains a determining factor in the maternal iconography of liberty. Lady Liberty is still imagined as a caring and nurturing mother.

If, as I have claimed, those attributes once read as maternal were regendered and revalued, then we might agree with Henry Adams's claim that by the turn of the century "an American virgin would never dare command; an American venus would never dare exist."[11] In his

8. Banta, *Imaging American Women*, 91.

9. Henrietta Stackpole is, of course, another version of the New Woman, as William Veeder (*Henry James*), among others, has noted (see Chapter 7 above). I have wondered why Henry James named Stackpole after himself—made her his own *ficelle*, a diminutive Henry.

10. Lerner, *The Grimké Sisters from South Carolina*, 8.

11. *The Education of Henry Adams*, 385.

representation, "Woman" as a nationalized figure has been cleansed of contact with either messy, sentimental origins or the mortality of maternity. In other words, an American "Woman" is neither sentimental devil nor sanctified angel here. Adams uses instead the terms "venus" and "virgin." Both these images, unlike the angel/devil of sentimental Christianity, are neoclassical icons of "high"—European—art. But further, Adams's claim suggests that the immured and passive virgin has won out over what the venus signified: the passive virgin may not dare wield authority, but the venus doesn't even exist.[12] By ensuring that a representative economy in virgin figures such as Isabel Archer, James's work and the "value" it consolidates helped to structure interpretive practices that still place a sloppy sentimentality in opposition to more restrained (and valued) literary practices. That is why both domestic and abolitionist literatures in the United States—burdened, as some might say, with the sentimental—have so often been designated as material more suited to cultural or historical than to literary appreciation.

More generally, I have been chasing the shadows cast by the fluttering national banner across nineteenth-century representational strategies, trying to see who and what has been hidden there, and seeking to ask questions about how those shadows condition contemporary thought. The mother can still be mobilized in contemporary narrative both as a symbol of the shared, liberal democratic bond of natural and genetic or hereditary affections and also as a sign of rankling violence, a historical sign of horrific dependencies or the bondage of the flesh.

In current debates about "the" maternal instinct, many people still ask whether mothering is a social role and thus historically conditioned, or an inherent drive replete with a natural wisdom that sets the mother apart from other people as a separate breed. For instance, we can see the representational economy that still persists when the essayist Katha Pollitt, on being urged to join an antiwar group called Mothers For Peace in 1992, asked, "Were mothers the natural leaders of the peace movement, to whose judgment non-mothers, male and female, must defer? I was indeed a woman. Was motherhood with its special wisdom somehow deep inside me, to be called upon when needed, like my uterus?"[13]

12. See also Fiedler, *Love and Death*, 293–94.
13. Katha Pollit, "Are Women Morally Superior to Men?" *The Nation*, December 28, 1992, 799–807.

So I must ponder how nineteenth-century arguments remain pertinent to my own history. Such ruminations chillingly force former Vice-President Dan Quayle's hilariously garbled diction, in the epigraph above, to conjure up another image of bondage, this one reported to Lydia Maria Child from North Carolina in the winter of 1828: "Mr. Hedding, of Chatham County, held a slave woman. In order to prevent her running away, a child about seven years of age was connected with her by a long chain fastened to her neck."[14] In 1860, when Child compiled *The Patriarchal Institution, as Described by Members of Its Own Family* for the American Anti-Slavery Society, what the pro-slavery press called "Black Republicanism" claimed to understand and to reject the moral, social, and political wrong of the slavocratic, legal bondage between a slave mother and child: the infamous law that "the child shall follow the condition of its mother." By 1865 the Emancipation Proclamation had rendered that law null and void. Yet the issue of bondage did not disapear with the dissolution of legal slavery. The language of bondage, upon which the logic of legal enslavement rested, still shadows later Republican—and other—claims to an understanding of how to regulate the condition of mother and child.

In 1831 middle-class mothers from Boston to Savannah bought Lydia Maria Child's *The Mother's Book* for ethical and practical use. Many parents of a much later and supposedly much freer generation bought Dr. Benjamin Spock's *Baby and Child Care* for the same sort of regulatory guidance. Despite the legal rhetoric of individual freedom and civil rights, both popular wisdom and the U.S. system of jurisprudence still maintain that a mother and a child are in fact bound together, often in a sort of psychological and physiological bondage that inhibits or, at the very least confuses, the concept of individuality. At the "right" end of our contemporary political spectrum, the "individual" threatened is the fetus or, as Operation Rescue sees it, the "little astronaut" marooned in the vastness of a possibly threatening maternal "space." Such a representation, as Peggy Phelan argues in *Unmarked: The Politics of Performance*, makes "the fetus the focus of the visible spectacle" and "erases the pregnant woman"; it thus "limits sympathy for her situation and represses ethical uncertainty about her liberty."[15]

14. Child, *Patriarchal Institution*, 23.
15. Peggy Phelan, *Unmarked: The Politics of Performance* (New York: Routledge, 1993), 133.

One of the central concerns of this book has been to show that *to conceive, to become great, to labor,* and *to bear* are viscerally charged, specifically gendered images. Yet in our own time such gendered images have been overlooked or indeed effaced, not only in the arena of specifically political representations and performances such as those orchestrated by Operation Rescue, but also in what is still imagined ideally as a sphere separate from politics: that is, the labor of the arts. Steadfast self-reliance, individual authority, and moral certitude—virtues the National Endowment for the Arts of the 1980s maintained were vital to funding—are not generally recognized as terms related to a pregnancy. In other words, to become great with a child of the mind, to dream "art," is generally taken to demonstrate an autonomous individuality, whereas to become great with a child is to fall either into a state of uncomfortable dependency or into some form of wordless, dyadic ecstacy.[16]

To "conceive," then, conjures up a different image of "generation" if the person doing the conceiving has the physical ability to gestate a child. As Nina Baym frequently notes, Hester Prynne cannot deny the deed, and Daniel Cottom says that "Pearl symbolizes Hester's inability to transcend physicality."[17] That is, to represent pregnancy as a trap rhetorically grants to "envisioning" (abstractly imagining) the future more value than is granted to "bearing" the future—in the form of a living child. This logic can be seen in present-day arguments about the shape and condition of an appropriate family, adoption within nontraditional households, abortion rights, the legalities of reproductive technologies, surrogate mothers, and the problems of childhood poverty and teenage pregnancy. All are symptomatic of how reproductive management, particularly of a state called "maternity," remains centrally important to American culture at large.

Indeed, pregnancy and maternity are still represented as altered states; for some, pregnancy is both a form of disability (perhaps even a permanently debilitating illness) and a liability. A student at the University of Florida recently told me with complete assurance that women's bodies, as a result of childbearing, wear out faster than men's; therefore, women as employees should be paid less because they will wear out first—as if bodies came with warranties for prospective employers. That is to say, although I am primarily concerned

16. See esp. Kristeva, "Stabat Mater."
17. Cottom, "Hawthorne versus Hester," 58.

in this book with the nineteenth century's heated public debate about the mechanics of proper maternity—a debate that gave rise to a spate of tracts, articles, books, and folklore on the proper maintenance of all phases of the maternal condition, from conception to the marriage of full-grown children—I am also curious as to how this concern has both flourished and changed. Anxiety about the maternal condition has a terribly familiar, twentieth-century ring.

In 1989 such concern surfaced in legal arguments over maternal surrogacy, arguments made highly visible in the now infamous Baby M case. Interestingly, Mary Beth Whitehead-Gould defended her right to a breach of surrogacy contract by saying, "Mother and child—that is what America is built on."[18] These words neatly encapsulate a tension between the supposed primacy of the mother-and-child dyad and the status of that dyad as an object upon which the abstract political unity "America" is built. Whitehead-Gould's appeal was meant to invoke the urgency of her claim to Baby M; ironically, however, it points to just why her claim was such a cultural earthquake and so legally contestable. If a "ground" (such as Isabel Archer) should get up and start making demands, what will happen to the American (literary) house built upon it? Indeed, Whitehead-Gould's statement also suggests a striking restructuring of the nuclear family, leaving the role of the "father" rhetorically assignable only to the entity named "America." This reassignment begs the question, what will happen to the validity or shape of fatherhood? In fact, Whitehead-Gould's words begged the very question that the "genetic" father posed: was he or the "state" the appropriate father? Sarah Conner, a character in the popular 1991 film *Terminator 2*, offered something of an answer in noting grimly that a nation-state's killing machine is the best father a son could have.[19]

In the mid-1990s, surrogacy remains a practice of legal and ethical dubiety. In the Whitehead-Gould case, the surrogate was denied outright custody of her child for complex reasons. However, because Whitehead-Gould was not merely a "gestational" surrogate, having provided genetic material (her eggs) to the process, she was granted visitation rights. This ruling, however, depends on excluding the rest of a woman's reproductive system—womb, placenta, and umbilical cord—not to mention her body as a whole organism, from the legal

18. Quoted in the *San Francisco Chronicle*, June 25, 1989.
19. *Terminator 2: Judgment Day* (James Cameron, dir., Tri-Star, 1991).

definition of motherhood. A gestational surrogate who provides only the "donor womb" is generally regarded as having less right to the child she carries.

France has outlawed gestational surrogacy as an industry entirely, but surrogacy is still legal in much of America—although the growing variety of surrogacy practices is challenging that legality. In August 1991, for example, Arlette Schweitzer of Aberdeen, South Dakota, was reported as having agreed to carry her own daughter's twins to term "as an act of love for her daughter, Christa Uchytil . . . who was born without a uterus." Many worry over what such visceral confusions will do to the legal definition of personhood (and, it might be added, citizenship) as it is currently written into law. What will the children's birth certificate read? "Is the grandmother the grandmother or the mother?"inquired the press.[20] The redefinitions involved in such cases may very well tear apart the traditional notions of family cultivated during the nineteenth century.

The technologies that have made "gestational" surrogacy possible will also change previously unalterable biological "laws." Since cultural and social codes have been based, in part, on many of the so-called natural laws of biology, changes are radically unsettling. In Michigan in 1988, for example, Kim Hardy was arrested and charged with felony drug-dealing—for delivering cocaine to her child through her umbilical cord. "To avoid becoming embroiled in debates over when the fetus becomes a person," reported Ian Hoffman, "the prosecutor contended that Hardy delivered crack to her son through her umbilical cord during the 90 seconds or so after the child had left the birth canal but before the cord was cut."[21] The conceptual consequence is staggering when a legal system can name one mother a criminal "drug dealer" on the basis of an umbilical cord, and the same legal system can, in another case, define that cord as irrelevant to parentage. And Hardy's situation is instructive. Although her other children were healthy and although she was voluntarily seeking help for her addiction at the point when her son was born, all three of her children were separated from her and placed in foster homes designated by the state as more appropriate. Economic, psychological, and cultural questions about why a young, divorced, blue-collar African-American mother

20. Gina Kolata, "When Grandmother Is Mother, until Birth," *New York Times*, August 11, 1991.

21. Jan Hoffman, "Pregnant, Addicted—and Guilty?" *New York Times Magazine*, August 19, 1990, 34.

of three children might have gotten addicted to crack in the first place were not factored into the decision. Her fight to provide for and to raise these children was not made visible in court. Hardy was criminalized, and the logic of the ruling situated her as her son's drug supplier rather than as his mother.[22]

Might it not be claimed, then, that America as a legal, political, cultural, and economic network is still built in large measure, as Mary Beth Whitehead-Gould claimed, upon the sanctity of an ideal, passive, primarily white, private unity called the mother-and-child? The cases cited above, at any rate, suggest that the nation-state seems extraordinarily concerned with defining and regulating—legally, socially, and morally—the person who takes on the role of mother. Yet curiously, in the most "advanced" definition of legal maternity (or paternity, in paternity suits based on DNA matching), maternity has been reduced to an abstract genetic relation. To gestate, feed, clothe, house, and raise a child does not appear to grant a legally definitive basis upon which to claim parentage. And though it is often sentimentally remarked that "the children" represent "our" future, children collectively are at present the most materially impoverished, most frequently abused group in the country—if not in the world.[23]

Indeed, the child as an icon in and of itself, an icon representing the future, is the abstract descendant of those future Americans who climbed off Emerson's mind-ark and peopled the new world. Child-as-icon is the figure termed the "mind child" in Hans Moravec's 1988 book *Mind Children: The Future of Robot and Human Intelligence*. The mind child, like the image of the unborn fetus as doughty spaceman, is a powerful and abstract token of the creative potentiality of humanity. Moravec, however, as the director of the Mobile Robot Unit at Carnegie Mellon University, has drawn up a map for the future that is slightly different from the one Emerson imagined. To Moravec, the future America will be an entirely mechanistic Eden, "a postbiological world dominated by self-improving, thinking machines, . . . a population consisting of unfettered mind children."[24] The mind will

22. Ibid., 55.
23. See Ruth Sidel, *Women and Children Last: The Plight of Poor Women in Affluent America* (New York: Viking, 1986); Sidel, *Urban Survival: The World of Working-Class Women* (Boston: Beacon Press, 1978); and T. Berry Brazelton, "Why Is America Failing Its Children?" *New York Times Magazine*, September 9, 1990, 40.
24. Hans Moravec, *Mind Children: The Future of Robot and Human Intelligence* (Cambridge, Mass.: Harvard University Press, 1988), 5.

do away with biology, the fettering body, the inconvenience of a living child or an umbilical cord.

Mind children, not of woman born and indeed unborn, do not wear diapers. An actual child might. An actual child might need food, support, medicine, clothes; he or she might be sickly, be a dependent or a burden. An actual child might even become, like Emerson's son Waldo, the source of a grief that forbids, perhaps confounds, so-called creative articulations: faced with his son's sudden illness and unexpected death, Emerson left a blank page in his journal to mark the day his son died. Such an absolute silence is clearly also a sign, but how does one read the sign? How does the "blank page" generate meaning?[25]

In the late 1980s and early 1990s, debates among feminists over whether and how such potentially procreative blank pages should signify have illustrated the difficulty of theoretical questions concerning biology, and in particular that function deemed biological called "maternity." Domna C. Stanton writes: "The overdetermination of the maternal militates against . . . overcoming the conceptual impasse it represents."[26] Jacqueline Rose suggests as well that "the object becomes the very structure of representation through which it fails to be thought, the impasse of conceptual thinking itself."[27] Recent investigations within new historical, feminist, cultural, African-American, and queer theory have often focused on representations of the body and the relation of such representations to desire. Particularly urgent have been questions about nonreproductive practices and the sexualities to which they became attached. But often across these debates, "reproduction" as an issue has been seen, disturbingly, as merely an essentialist concern, one that needs to be gotten around. Reproduction is a heterosexual norm, compulsory, middle-class, nostalgic, even simplistic.[28]

Yet when the issue of reproduction and representation is ignored,

25. Porte, *Emerson in His Journals*, January 27, 1842.

26. Domna C. Stanton, "Difference on Trial: A Critique of the Maternal Metaphor in Cixous, Irigaray, and Kristeva," in *The Poetics of Gender*, ed. Nancy K. Miller (New York: Columbia University Press, 1986), 176.

27. Jacqueline Rose, "Where Does the Misery Come From? Psychoanalysis, Feminism, and the Event," in *Feminism and Psychoanalysis*, ed. Richard Feldstein and Judith Roof (Ithaca: Cornell University Press, 1989), 34.

28. I am thinking particularly of the way Teresa de Lauretis, in a 1989 seminar at the University of California, Berkeley, dismissed questions about the representation of maternity as irrelevant to the construction of a lesbian identity. When asked whether maternity should be left to the patriarchy, she responded in the affirmative. For a brief

the historical and critical denigration of the maternal and thus by association in American culture the sentimental, is substantiated and extended. Jane Tompkins's troubling question about the aesthetic value of sentimental culture in the United States, so definitively and historically tied to how the "maternal" is read both past and present, will become truly a rhetorical one: "But is it any *good?*" will continue to answer itself with a "No."

I have addressed myself to this persistent "no" primarily because I so frequently confront the surprising fact that to invoke the term "sentimental" remains a sure means to damage a reputation, trash a work, or bewail the carnivalesque degradation of taste in the twentieth-century American cultural wasteland.[29] As an example, novelist George Garrett (*Death of a Fox, The Finished Man, Magic Striptease*) says in his 1992 review of Dorothy Allison's first novel, *Bastard Out of Carolina*, that "sentimentality, with all its inherent denigration of intelligence and the human spirit, has become an acceptable mode in this sentimental age of ours."[30] Garrett's assessment in the late twentieth century so closely echoes reviews written a hundred yearsago that one might be tempted to think the nineteenth century never properly came to an end. Yet his statement gestures toward the enduring power of the sentimental, despite the aspersions so obsessively cast at it.

Heavily overdetermined, subject to underexamined outbursts of critical disgust, a site of many dismissals as well as many avowals, the sentimental remains a potent cultural phenomenon, particularly when represented by the mother-and-child icon. From the Children's Defense Fund poster of decapitated Mama Liberty to the transfixing, politically explosive photographs of American mother/soldiers leaving their children to serve their country during the Gulf War; from recent prosecution procedures designed to criminalize so-called "crack mothers"[31] to "pro-life" and "pro-choice" advocacy, maternal

---

index to questions of essentialism in feminist theories, see also Diana Fuss, *Essentially Speaking: Feminism, Nature, and Difference* (New York: Routledge, 1989); and Fuss, ed., *Inside/Out: Lesbian Theories, Gay Theories* (New York: Routledge, 1991).

29. The use of "sentimentality" as an unexamined, underexplained, and depoliticized term for "bad" taste or "trivial pursuits," particularly with regard to American culture, has gained a revitalized popularity through such works as Paglia's *Sexual Personae*; James Twitchell's *Carnival Culture: The Trashing of Taste in America* (New York: Columbia University Press, 1992).

30. George Garrett, "No Wonder People Got Crazy as They Grew Up," *New York Times Book Review*, July 5, 1992.

31. It should be noted that according to recent medical research, the term "crack

ideologies and the images they evoke and the narratives that arise from them still raise pertinent, vexed questions about how freedom, individuality, civil rights, and the nature of legal citizenship in a republican democracy can be interpreted.

_____

baby" may be inaccurate; a link between the mothers' cocaine use and the health problems from which most of these children suffer has not been proved. Malnutrition, the lack of readily available prenatal care, premature birth, and other factors may account for the baby's symptoms.

Selected Bibliography

Adams, Henry. *Democracy: An American Novel.* London: Macmillan, 1882.
——. *The Education of Henry Adams.* Ed. Ernest Samuels. Boston: Houghton Mifflin, 1973.
Abbott, Rev. John S. *The Mother at Home; or, The Principles of Maternal Duty.* New York: American Tract, 1833.
Alcott, Louisa May. "A Whisper in the Dark." *Frank Leslie's Illustrated Newspaper.* June 1863. Rpt. in *The Hidden Louisa May Alcott,* ed. Madeline Stern. New York: Avenel Books, 1984.
Ammons, Elizabeth. *Critical Essays on Harriet Beecher Stowe.* Boston: G. K. Hall, 1980.
——. "Heroines in *Uncle Tom's Cabin.*" *American Literature* 49 (May 1977). Rpt. in Ammons, *Critical Essays on Harriet Beecher Stowe.* Boston: G. K. Hall, 1980.
——. "Stowe's Dream of the Mother-Savior: *Uncle Tom's Cabin* and American Women Writers before the 1920s." In *New Essays on "Uncle Tom's Cabin,"* ed. Eric J. Sundquist. New York: Cambridge University Press, 1990.
Andrews, William. *To Tell a Free Story.* Urbana: University of Illinois Press, 1986.
Arac, Jonathan. "The Politics of *The Scarlet Letter.*" In *Ideology and Classic American Literature,* ed. Sacvan Bercovitch and Myra Jehlen. London: Cambridge University Press, 1987.
Arms, Suzanne. *Immaculate Deception: A New Look at Women and Childbirth in America.* Boston: Houghton Mifflin, 1975.
Baer, Helene G. *The Heart Is Like Heaven: The Life of Lydia Maria Child.* Philadelphia: University of Pennsylvania Press, 1964.
Baker, Houston, Jr. *Blues, Ideology, and Afro-American Literature.* Chicago: University of Chicago Press, 1984.
——. *The Journey Back: Issues in Black Literature and Criticism.* Chicago: University of Chicago Press, 1980.

Banta, Martha. *Imaging American Women: Idea and Ideals in Cultural History.* New York: Columbia University Press, 1987.

Barker-Benfield, G. J. *The Horrors of the Half-Known Life: Male Attitudes toward Women and Sex in Nineteenth-Century America.* Boston: Harper & Row, 1976.

Baym, Nina. "Hawthorne's Women: The Tyranny of Social Myths." *Centennial Review* 15 (1971).

——. "Melodramas of Beset Manhood: How Theories of American Fiction Exclude Women Authors." In *The New Feminist Criticism,* ed. Elaine Showalter. New York: Pantheon, 1985.

——. *Novels, Readers, and Reviewers: Responses to Fiction in Antebellum America.* Ithaca: Cornell University Press, 1984.

——. "The Romantic *Malgré Lui*: Hawthorne in 'The Custom House.' " In *The Scarlet Letter,* by Nathaniel Hawthorne. New York: Norton, 1988.

——. *Women's Fiction: A Guide to Novels by and about Women in America, 1820–1870.* Ithaca: Cornell University Press, 1978.

Beecher, Catharine. *Treatise on Domestic Economy.* New York: Harper, 1847.

Bercovitch, Sacvan. *The Office of the Scarlet Letter.* Baltimore: Johns Hopkins University Press, 1991.

Bercovitch, Sacvan, and Myra Jehlen. *Ideology and Classic American Literature.* New York: Cambridge University Press, 1987.

Berlant, Lauren. *The Anatomy of National Fantasy: Hawthorne, Utopia, and Everyday Life.* Chicago: University of Chicago Press, 1991.

Berner, Robert L. "A Key to the 'Custom House.' " In *The Scarlet Letter.* New York: Norton, 1988.

Berzon, Judith R. *Neither White Nor Black: The Mulatto Character in American Fiction.* New York: New York University Press, 1978.

Birdoff, Harry. *The World's Greatest Hit: "Uncle Tom's Cabin."* New York: S. F. Vanni, 1947.

Blassingame, John. *Slave Testimony: Two Centuries of Letters, Speeches, Interviews, and Autobiographies.* Baton Rouge: Louisiana State University Press, 1977.

Blight, David W. *Frederick Douglass' Civil War: Keeping Faith in Jubilee.* Baton Rouge: Louisiana State University Press, 1989.

Bogden, Janet. "Care or Cure? Childbirth Practices in Nineteenth-Century America." *Feminist Studies* 4 (June 1978).

Boose, Lynda E. "The Father's House and the Daughter in It: The Structures of Western Culture's Daughter-Father Relationships." In *Daughters and Fathers,* ed. Lynda E. Boose and Betty S. Flowers. Baltimore: Johns Hopkins University Press, 1989.

Boydston, Jeanne, Mary Kelley, and Anne Margolis. *The Limits of Sisterhood: The Beecher Sisters on Women's Rights and Women's Sphere.* Chapel Hill: University of North Carolina Press, 1988.

Bradford, William. *Of Plymouth Plantation,* ed. Samuel Eliot Morison. New York: Knopf, 1952.

Brazelton, T. Berry. "Why Is America Failing Its Children?" *New York Times Magazine,* September 9, 1990, 40.

Brodhead, Richard. *Hawthorne, Melville, and the Novel*. Chicago: University of Chicago Press, 1976.

——. "Sparing the Rod: Discipline and Fiction in Antebellum America." *Representations* 21 (Winter 1988).

Brown, Gillian. "Getting in the Kitchen with Dinah: Domestic Policies in *Uncle Tom's Cabin*." *American Quarterly* 36 (Fall 1984).

Butler, Judith. *Gender Trouble*. New York: Routledge, 1990.

Carby, Hazel. *Reconstructing Womanhood: The Emergence of the Afro-American Woman Novelist*. New York: Oxford University Press, 1987.

Cargill, Oscar. "Nemesis and Nathaniel Hawthorne." In *Critical Essays on Ralph Waldo Emerson*, ed. Robert E. Burkholder and Joel Myerson. Boston: G. K. Hall, 1983.

Charvat, William. Introduction. *The Scarlet Letter*. Columbus: Ohio State University Press, 1962.

Chevigny, Bell Gale. *The Woman and the Myth: Margaret Fuller's Life and Writings*. Old Westbury, N.Y.: Feminist Press, 1976.

Child, Lydia Maria. *An Appeal in Favor of That Class of Americans Called Africans*. Boston: Allen and Tichnor, 1833.

——. *Flowers for Children*. Vols. 1 and 2. New York: C. S. Francis, 1845; Boston: J. H. Francis, 1845.

——. *Hobomok, and Other Writings on Indians*. Ed. Carolyn L. Karcher. New Brunswick, N.J.: Rutgers University Press, 1986.

——. *The Mother's Book*. Boston: Carter, Hendee & Babcock, 1831. Rpt. New York: Arno Press, 1972.

——. *Over the River and through the Wood*. Illustrated by Brinton Turkle. New York: Coward, McCann & Geoghegan, 1974.

——. *The Patriarchal Institution, as Described by Members of Its Own Family*. New York: American Anti-Slavery Society, 1860.

——. *Philothea, a Romance*. Boston: Otis Broaders, 1836.

——. "The Quadroons." In *The Other Woman*, ed. Susan Koppelman. Old Westbury, N.Y.: Feminist Press, 1984.

——. *A Romance of the Republic*. Boston: Ticknor & Fields, 1867.

——. *Selected Letters, 1817–1880*. Ed. Milton Meltzer and Patricia G. Holland. Amherst: University of Massachusetts Press, 1982.

Chodorow, Nancy. *The Reproduction of Mothering: Psychoanalysis and the Sociology of Gender*. Berkeley: University of California Press, 1978.

Cixous, Hélène, and Catherine Clément. *La jeune née*. Paris: Union Générale d'Editions, 1975.

Cooper, James Fenimore. *The Last of the Mohicans*. New York: New American Library, 1963.

Cott, Nancy. *The Bonds of Womanhood: "Woman's Sphere" in New England*. New Haven: Yale University Press, 1977.

Cottom, Daniel. "Hawthorne versus Hester: The Ghostly Dialectic of Romance in *The Scarlet Letter*." *Texas Studies in Literature and Language* 24 (Spring 1982).

Crews, Frederick. *The Sins of the Fathers*. New York: Oxford University Press, 1966.

Cunningham, George P. " 'Called into Existence': Race, Gender, and Voice in Frederick Douglass's *Narrative* of 1845." *Differences: A Journal of Feminist Cultural Studies* 1.5 (1989).

Davidson, Cathy N. *Revolution and the Word: The Rise of the Novel in America*. New York: Oxford University Press, 1986.

Davis, Angela Y. *Women, Race, and Class*. New York: Random House, 1981.

de Lauretis, Teresa. "Feminist Studies/Critical Studies: Issues, Terms, and Contexts." In *Feminist Studies/Critical Studies*. Bloomington: Indiana University Press, 1986.

"Deserter Regrets War Protest Failed." *Gainesville Sun*. April 12, 1992.

Dinnerstein, Dorothy. *The Mermaid and the Minotaur*. New York: Harper Colophon Books, 1977.

Doriani, Beth Maclay. "Black Womanhood in Nineteenth-Century America: Subversion and Self-Construction in Two Women's Autobiographies." *American Quarterly* 43 (June 1991).

Douglas, Ann. *The Feminization of American Culture*. New York: Avon, 1978.

Douglass, Frederick. *The Life and Times of Frederick Douglass*. London: Collier Books, 1962.

——. *The Life and Writings of Frederick Douglass*. Vol. 3. New York: International Publishers, 1953.

——. *My Bondage and My Freedom*. Ed. William L. Andrews. Urbana: University of Illinois Press, 1987.

——. *The Narrative of the Life of Frederick Douglass, an American Slave, Written by Himself*, ed. Houston A. Baker, Jr. New York: Penguin American Library, 1982.

DuBois, Ellen Carol. *Feminism and Suffrage: The Emergence of an Independent Women's Movement in America, 1848–1869*. Ithaca: Cornell University Press, 1978.

Du Bois, W. E. B. *The Souls of Black Folk*. 1903. New York: Signet, 1969.

Emerson, Ralph Waldo. *Selections*. In *The Harper American Literature*. Vol. 1, ed. Donald McQuade. New York: Harper & Row, 1987.

——. *Selections from Ralph Waldo Emerson*. Ed. Stephen E. Whicher. Boston: Houghton Mifflin, 1960.

Erlich, Gloria C. *Family Themes and Hawthorne's Fiction: The Tenacious Web*. New Brunswick, N.J.: Rutgers University Press, 1984.

Feidelson, Charles. "The Moment of *The Portrait of a Lady*." In *The Portrait of a Lady*, by Henry James. New York: Norton, 1975.

Fetterley, Judith. *Provisions: A Reader from 19th-Century American Women*. Bloomington: Indiana University Press, 1985.

Fiedler, Leslie A. *Love and Death in the American Novel*. New York: Dell, 1966.

Fields, Annie. *Life and Letters of Harriet Beecher Stowe*. Boston: Houghton Mifflin, 1898.

Fineman, Joel, Catherine Gallagher, and Neil Hertz. "More about 'Medusa's Head.' " *Representations* 4 (Fall 1983).

Fitzhugh, George. *Cannibals All! or Slaves without Masters*. Richmond, Va.: A. Morris, 1857.

——. *Sociology for the South; or, The Failure of Free Society*. Richmond, Va.: A. Morris, 1854.

Foner, Philip S., ed. *Frederick Douglass on Women's Rights*. Westport, Conn.: Greenwood Press, 1976.

Foreman, P. Gabrielle. "The Spoken and the Silenced in *Incidents in the Life of a Slave Girl* and *Our Nig.*" *Callaloo* 13 (Spring 1990).

Foster, Francis Smith. *Witnessing Slavery: The Development of the Ante-Bellum Slave Narrative*. Westport, Conn.: Greenwood Press, 1979.

Foucault, Michel. *The History of Sexuality*. Vol. 1, *An Introduction*. Trans. Robert Hurley. New York: Vintage, 1980.

Fox-Genovese, Elizabeth. *Within the Plantation Household*. Chapel Hill: University of North Carolina Press, 1988.

Franchot, Jenny. "The Punishment of Esther: Frederick Douglass and the Construction of the Feminine." In *Frederick Douglass: New Literary and Historical Essays*, ed. Eric J. Sundquist. New York: Cambridge University Press, 1990.

Frederickson, George M. *The Inner Civil War: Northern Intellectuals and the Crisis of the Union*. New York: Harper Torchbooks, 1965.

Freeman, Mary Wilkins. "Old Woman Magoun." In *Short Fiction of Sarah Orne Jewett and Mary Wilkins Freeman*, ed. Barbara H. Solomon. New York: New American Library, 1979.

Fryer, Judith. *The Faces of Eve: Women in the Nineteenth-Century American Novel*. New York: Oxford University Press, 1976.

Fuller, Margaret. "American Literature: Its Position in the Present Time, and Prospects for the Future," from *Papers on Literature and Art*. In *The Harper American Literature*, vol. 1, ed. Donald McQuade. New York: Harper & Row, 1987.

——. *Woman in the Nineteenth Century*. 1845. New York: Norton, 1977.

Fuss, Diana. *Essentially Speaking: Feminism, Nature, and Difference*. New York: Routledge, 1989.

——, ed. *Inside/Out: Lesbian Theories, Gay Theories*. New York: Routledge, 1991.

Gallagher, Catherine. "More about 'Medusa's Head.'" *Representations* 4 (Fall 1983).

Garrett, George. "No Wonder People Got Crazy as They Grew Up." *New York Times Book Review*. July 5, 1992.

Gates, Henry Louis, Jr. "Binary Opposition in Chapter One of *The Narrative of the Life of Frederick Douglass, an American Slave, Written by Himself.*" In *Afro-American Literature: The Reconstruction of Instruction*, ed. Robert B. Stepto and Dexter Fisher. New York: Modern Language Association, 1978.

Gibson, Donald B. "Reconciling Public and Private in Frederick Douglass' Narrative." *American Literature* 57 (December 1985).

Gilbert, Sandra, and Susan Gubar. *Madwoman in the Attic*. New Haven: Yale University Press, 1979.

Gillman, Susan. "The Mulatto, Tragic or Triumphant? The Nineteenth-Century American Race Melodrama." In *The Culture of Sentiment: Race, Gender, and Sentimentality in Nineteenth-Century American Culture*, ed. Shirley Samuels. New York: Oxford University Press, 1992.

Girard, René. *Deceit, Desire, and the Novel: Self and Other in Literary Structure.* Baltimore: Johns Hopkins University Press, 1965.

Goldberg, Jonathan. "Bradford's 'Ancient Members' and a 'Case of Buggery amongst Them.' " In *Nationalisms and Sexualities*, ed. Andrew Parker, Mary Russo, Doris Sommer, and Patricia Yaeger. New York: Routledge, 1992.

Grimké, Charlotte Forten. *The Journals of Charlotte Forten Grimké*, ed. Brenda Stevenson. New York: Oxford University Press, 1988.

Grossberg, Michael. "Who Gets the Child? Custody, Guardianship, and the Rise of a Judicial Patriarchy in Nineteenth-Century America." *Feminist Studies* 9 (Summer 1983).

Gubar, Susan. "The Birth of the Artist as Heroine: (Re)production, the *Kunstlerroman* Tradition, and the Fiction of Katherine Mansfield." In *The Representation of Women in Fiction*, ed. Carolyn Heilbrun and Margaret Higonnet. Baltimore: Johns Hopkins University Press, 1981.

——. " 'The Blank Page' and the Issues of Female Creativity." In *Writing and Sexual Difference*, ed. Elizabeth Abel. Chicago: University of Chicago Press, 1982.

Gunning, Sandra. "Facing 'A Red Record': Racial Violence, Class, and Gender in Turn of the Century American Literature." Ph.D. diss. University of California, Berkeley, 1991.

Habegger, Alfred. *Gender, Fantasy, and Realism in American Literature.* New York: Columbia University Press, 1982.

Halttunen, Karen. "Gothic Imagery and Social Reform: The Haunted Houses of Lyman Beecher, Henry Ward Beecher, and Harriet Beecher Stowe." In *New Essays on "Uncle Tom's Cabin,"* ed. Eric J. Sundquist. New York: Cambridge University Press, 1986.

Harris, Susan K. " 'But Is It Any *Good*?': Evaluating Nineteenth-Century American Women's Fiction." *American Literature* 63 (March 1991).

Hartouni, Valerie. "Containing Women: Reproductive Discourse in the 1980s." In *Technoculture*, ed. Constance Penley and Andrew Ross. Minneapolis: University of Minnesota Press, 1991.

Hawthorne, Julian. *Nathaniel Hawthorne and His Wife.* Boston: Houghton Mifflin, 1884.

Hawthorne, Nathaniel. *The American Notebooks.* New Haven: Yale University Press, 1932.

——. "Chiefly about War Matters." *Atlantic Monthly* 10 (July 1862).

——. *The Scarlet Letter.* New York: Norton, 1988.

——. *A Wonder-Book.* Pt. 1. New York: Houghton Mifflin, 1898.

Herbert, T. Walter, Jr. *Dearest Beloved: The Hawthornes and the Making of the Middle-Class Family.* Berkeley: University of California Press, 1993.

Herman, Judith. *Father-Daughter Incest.* Cambridge, Mass.: Harvard University Press, 1981.

Hertz, Neil. "Medusa's Head: Male Hysteria under Political Pressure." *Representations* 4 (Fall 1983).

Herzog, Kristin. *Women, Ethnics, and Exotics: Images of Power in Mid-Nineteenth-Century American Fiction.* Knoxville: University of Tennessee Press, 1983.

Hoffert, Sylvia D. *Private Matters: American Attitudes toward Childbearing and Infant Nurture in the Urban North, 1800–1860.* Chicago: University of Illinois Press, 1989.

Hoffman, Jan. "Pregnant, Addicted—and Guilty?" *New York Times Magazine.* August 19, 1991, 34.

Homans, Margaret. *Bearing the Word: Language and Female Experience in Nineteenth-Century Women's Writing.* Chicago: University of Chicago Press, 1986.

hooks, bell. "Is Paris Burning?" In *Black Looks.* Boston: South End Press, 1992.

Howard, Leon. *Herman Melville: A Biography.* Berkeley: University of California Press, 1951.

Irigaray, Luce. *Ce sexe qui n'en est pas un.* Paris: Minuit, 1977.

Irwin, John. *American Hieroglyphics: The Symbol of the Egyptian Hieroglyphics in the American Renaissance.* Baltimore: Johns Hopkins University Press, 1983.

Jacobs, Harriet. *Incidents in the Life of a Slave Girl.* Ed. Jean Fagan Yellin. Cambridge, Mass.: Harvard University Press, 1987.

Jacobus, Mary. "*Dora* and the Pregnant Madonna." In *Reading Woman: Essays in Feminist Criticism.* New York: Columbia University Press, 1984.

James, Henry. *The Complete Notebooks.* Ed. Leon Edel and Lyall H. Powers. New York: Oxford University Press, 1987.

——. *Hawthorne.* Ithaca: Cornell University Press, 1956.

——. *The Portrait of a Lady.* Ed. Robert D. Bamberg. New York: Norton, 1975.

——. *Stories of Writers and Artists.* Ed. F. O. Matthiessen. New York: New Directions, n.d.

——. *William Wetmore Story and His Friends.* Boston: Houghton Mifflin, 1903.

Jameson, Fredric. *The Prison-House of Language.* Princeton: Princeton University Press, 1972.

Jay, Gregory S. *America the Scrivener: Deconstruction and the Subject of Literary History.* Ithaca: Cornell University Press, 1990.

Jehlen, Myra. *American Incarnation: The Individual, the Nation, and the Continent.* Cambridge, Mass.: Harvard University Press, 1986.

——. "Archimedes and the Paradox of Feminist Criticism." In *Feminist Theory: A Critique of Ideology,* ed. Nannerl O. Keohane, Michelle Z. Rosaldo, and Barbara C. Gelpi. Chicago: University of Chicago Press, 1982.

Jordan, June. "Problems of Language in a Democratic State." In *On Call: Political Essays.* Boston: South End Press, 1985.

Kahane, Claire. "The Gothic Mirror." In *The (M)Other Tongue: Essays in Feminist Psychoanalytic Interpretation*, ed. Shirley Nelson Garner, Claire Kahane, and Madelon Sprengnether. Ithaca: Cornell University Press, 1985.

Kahn, Coppélia. "The Hand That Rocks the Cradle: Recent Gender Theories and Their Implications." In *The (M)Other Tongue: Essays in Feminist Psychoanalytic Interpretation*, ed. Shirley Nelson Garner, Claire Kahane, and Madelon Sprengnether. Ithaca: Cornell University Press, 1985.

Kaplan, E. Ann. *The Representation of Motherhood*. New York: Routledge, 1992.

Karcher, Carolyn L. "Censorship, American Style: The Case of Lydia Maria Child." In *Studies in the American Renaissance 1986*, ed. Joel Myerson. Boston: Twayne, 1986.

——. "Lydia Maria Child's *Romance of the Republic*: An Abolitionist View of America's Racial Destiny." In *Slavery in the Literary Imagination*, ed. Deborah E. McDowell and Arnold Rampersad. Baltimore: Johns Hopkins University Press, 1989.

——. "Rape, Murder, and Revenge in 'Slavery's Pleasant Homes': Lydia Maria Child's Antislavery Fiction and the Limits of Genre." *Women's Studies International Forum* 9.4 (1986). Rpt. in *The Culture of Sentiment: Race, Gender, and Sentimentality in Nineteenth-Century American Culture*, ed. Shirley Samuels, New York: Oxford University Press, 1992.

Kelley, Mary. *Private Woman, Public Stage: Literary Domesticity in Nineteenth-Century America*. New York: Oxford University Press, 1984.

Kerber, Linda. *Women of the Republic: Intellect and Ideology in Revolutionary America*. Chapel Hill: University of North Carolina, 1980.

——. *Women's America: Refocusing the Past*. New York: Oxford University Press, 1982.

Kolata, Gina. "When Grandmother Is Mother, until Birth." *New York Times*. August 11, 1991.

Kolodny, Annette. *The Lay of the Land: Metaphor as Experience and History in American Life and Letters*. Chapel Hill: University of North Carolina Press, 1975.

Kristeva, Julia. *Powers of Horror: An Essay on Abjection*. New York: Columbia University Press, 1982.

——. "Stabat Mater." In *The Kristeva Reader*, ed. Toril Moi. New York: Columbia University Press, 1986.

Krook, Dorothea. *The Ordeal of Consciousness in Henry James*. New York: Cambridge University Press, 1962.

Lauter, Paul. "Race and Gender in the Shaping of the American Literary Canon." In *Feminist Criticism and Social Change*, ed. Judith Newton and Deborah Rosenfelt. London: Methuen, 1985.

Leitch, Vincent B. *American Literary Criticism*. New York: Columbia University Press, 1988.

Lerner, Gerda. *The Grimké Sisters from South Carolina*. New York: Schocken, 1971.

Leverenz, David. *Manhood and the American Renaissance*. Ithaca: Cornell University Press, 1989.

——. "Mrs. Hawthorne's Headache: Reading *The Scarlet Letter*." *Nineteenth-Century Fiction* 37 (March 1983).

Levine, George, and U. C. Knoepflmacher, eds. *The Endurance of Frankenstein*. New York: Methuen, 1983.

Lincoln, Abraham. *Abraham Lincoln's Speeches*. Ed. L. E. Chittenden. New York: Dodd, Mead, 1895.

Lorde, Audre. "The master's tools will never dismantle the master's house." In *Sister Outsider*. Trumansburg, N.Y.: Crossing Press, 1984.

Luker, Kristin. *Abortion and the Politics of Motherhood*. Berkeley: University of California Press, 1984.

McDowell, Deborah E., and Arnold Rampersad, eds. *Slavery and the Literary Imagination*. Baltimore: Johns Hopkins University Press, 1989.

McFarland, Joanne. "Those Scribbling Women: A Cultural Study of Mid-Nineteenth-Century Popular American Romances by Women." *Journal of Communication Inquiry* 9 (Summer 1985).

McFeely, William. *Frederick Douglass*. New York: Norton, 1991.

Martin, Waldo E. *The Mind of Frederick Douglass*. Chapel Hill: University of North Carolina Press, 1984.

Marx, Leo. *The Machine in the Garden: Technology and the Pastoral Ideal in America*. New York: Oxford University Press, 1964.

Matthiessen, F. O. *The American Renaissance*. New York: Oxford University Press, 1941.

Meese, Elizabeth, and Alice Parker. *The Difference Within: Feminism and Critical Theory*. Philadelphia: John Benjamins, 1989.

Mellor, Anne K. *Mary Shelley: Her Life, Her Fiction, Her Monsters*. New York: Routledge, 1987.

Meltzer, Milton. *Tongue of Flame: The Life of Lydia Maria Child*. New York: Dell, 1965.

Melville, Herman. "Benito Cereno." In *Selected Tales and Poems*. New York: Holt, Rinehart & Winston, 1963.

——. *Billy Budd, Sailor (An Inside Narrative)*. Ed. Harrison Hayford and Merton H. Sealts, Jr. Chicago: University of Chicago Press, 1962.

——. *The Confidence Man*. New York: Holt, Rinehart & Winston, 1964.

——. *Moby-Dick*. New York: Penguin Books, 1978.

——. "The Paradise of Bachelors and The Tartarus of Maids." In *Selected Tales and Poems*. New York: Holt, Rinehart & Winston, 1963.

——. *Pierre*. Ed. Harrison Hayford, Hershel Parker, and G. Thomas Tanselle. Chicago: Northwestern University Press and the Newberry Library, 1971.

——. *Selected Tales and Poems*. New York: Holt, Rinehart & Winston, 1963.

——. *Typee*. Evanston, Ill.: Northwestern University Press and the Newberry Library, 1978.

Miller, Perry. *Margaret Fuller: An American Romantic*. New York: Doubleday, 1969.

Mills, Bruce. "Lydia Maria Child and the Endings to Harriet Jacobs's *Incidents in the Life of a Slave Girl*." *American Literature* 64 (June 1992).

Minh-ha, Trinh T., ed. "She, the Inappropriate/d Other." Special Issue, *Discourse* 8 (Fall–Winter 1986–87).

——. *Woman, Native, Other: Writing Postcoloniality and Feminism.* Bloomington: Indiana University Press, 1989.

Moers, Ellen. "Female Gothic." In *The Endurance of Frankenstein,* ed. George Levine and U. C. Knoepflmacher. New York: Methuen, 1983.

Moi, Toril. *Sexual/Textual Politics: Feminist Literary Theory.* New York: Methuen, 1985.

Moravec, Hans. *Mind Children: The Future of Robot and Human Intelligence.* Cambridge, Mass.: Harvard University Press, 1988.

Morrison, Toni. *Beloved.* New York: Knopf, 1987.

Moses, Wilson J. *The Golden Age of Black Nationalism, 1850–1925.* New York: Oxford University Press, 1978.

Nelson, Dana D. *The Word in Black and White: Reading "Race" in American Literature, 1638–1867.* New York: Oxford University Press, 1992.

Nudelman, Franny. "Harriet Jacobs and the Sentimental Politics of Female Suffering." *ELH* 59 (1992).

O'Brien, Mary. *The Politics of Reproduction.* Boston: Routledge & Kegan Paul, 1981.

Osborne, William S. *Lydia Maria Child.* Boston: Twayne, 1980.

Paglia, Camille. *Sexual Personae.* New Haven: Yale University Press, 1990.

Parker, Andrew, Mary Russo, Dorris Sommer, and Patricia Yaeger, eds. *Nationalisms and Sexualities.* New York: Routledge, 1992.

Parker, Hershel. *The Recognition of Herman Melville: Selected Criticism since 1846.* Ann Arbor: University of Michigan Press, 1967.

Patmore, Coventry. *The Angel in the House,* 2 vols. London: Macmillan, 1863.

Patterson, Mark. "Redefining Motherhood: Surrogacy and Race in American Reconstruction." Talk delivered at the American Studies Association's annual conference. November 2, 1991.

Phelan, Peggy. *Unmarked: The Politics of Performance.* New York: Routledge, 1993.

Phillips, Anne. *Engendering Democracy.* University Park: Pennsylvania State University Press, 1991.

Pollit, Katha. "Are Women Morally Superior to Men?" *The Nation.* December 28, 1992.

Porte, Joel, ed. *Emerson in His Journals.* Cambridge, Mass.: Harvard University Press, 1982.

Porter, Carolyn. "Gender and Value in *The American.*" In *New Essays on "The American,"* ed. Martha Banta. New York: Oxford University Press, 1987.

——. *Seeing and Being: The Plight of the Participant Observer in Emerson, James, Adams, and Faulkner.* Middletown, Conn.: Wesleyan University Press, 1981.

Prichard, James Cowles. *The Natural History of Man: Comprising Inquiries of Physical and Moral Agencies on the Different Tribes of the Human Family.* London: N. Bailliere, 1845.

Reynolds, Larry J. *"The Scarlet Letter* and Revolutions Abroad." *American Literature* 77 (1985).

Reynolds, Moira Davison. *"Uncle Tom's Cabin" and the Mid-Nineteenth-Century United States.* Jefferson, N.C.: McFarland, 1985.

Rich, Adrienne. *Of Woman Born: Motherhood as Experience and Institution.* New York: Norton, 1976.

Rogin, Michael. *Subversive Genealogy: The Politics and Art of Herman Melville.* New York: Knopf, 1983.

Romero, Lora. "Vanishing Americans: Gender, Empire, and New Historicism." *American Literature* 63 (1991). Rpt. in *The Culture of Sentiment: Race, Gender, and Sentimentality in Nineteenth-Century American Culture,* ed. Shirley Samuels, New York: Oxford University Press, 1992.

Rose, Jacqueline. "Where Does the Misery Come From? Psychoanalysis, Feminism, and the Event." In *Feminism and Psychoanalysis,* ed. Richard Feldstein and Judith Roof. Ithaca: Cornell University Press, 1989.

Rubin, Gayle. "The Traffic in Women: Notes on the Political Economy of Sex." In *Toward an Anthropology of Women,* ed. Rayna R. Reiter. New York: Monthly Review Press, 1975.

Ruddick, Sara. "Maternal Thinking." *Feminist Studies* 6.2 (1976).

Ryan, Mary. *Womanhood in America.* New York: New Viewpoints, 1975.

Samuel, Herbert, ed. *Maternity: Letters from Working Women.* London: G. Bell, 1915.

Samuels, Shirley, ed. *The Culture of Sentiment: Race, Gender, and Sentimentality in Nineteenth-Century American Culture.* New York: Oxford University Press, 1992.

Sánchez-Eppler, Karen. "Bodily Bonds: The Intersecting Rhetorics of Feminism and Abolition." In *The Culture of Sentiment: Race, Gender, and Sentimentality in Nineteenth-Century American Culture,* ed. Shirley Samuels, New York: Oxford University Press, 1992.

Scott, Joan. "Gender as a Useful Category of Historical Analysis." In *Gender and the Politics of History.* New York: Columbia University Press, 1988.

Sedgwick, Eve Kosofsky. "The Beast in the Closet: James and the Writing of Homosocial Panic." In *Papers for the English Institute.* Baltimore: Johns Hopkins University Press, 1987.

——. *Between Men: English Literature and Male Homosocial Desire.* New York: Columbia University Press, 1985.

——. *Epistemology of the Closet.* Berkeley: University of California Press, 1990.

Sidel, Ruth. *Urban Survival: The World of Working-Class Women.* Boston: Beacon Press, 1978.

——. *Women and Children Last: The Plight of Poor Women in Affluent America.* New York: Viking, 1986.

Silverman, Kaja. *The Acoustic Mirror: The Female Voice in Psychoanalysis and Cinema.* Bloomington: Indiana University Press, 1988.

——. *The Subject of Semiotics.* New York: Oxford University Press, 1983.

Smith, Sidonie. *Where I'm Bound: Patterns of Slavery and Freedom in Black American Autobiography*. Westport, Conn.: Greenwood Press, 1974.

Smith, Valerie. *Self-Discovery and Authority in Afro-American Narrative*. Cambridge, Mass.: Harvard University Press, 1987.

Smith-Rosenberg, Carroll. *Disorderly Conduct: Visions of Gender in Victorian America*. New York: Oxford University Press, 1985.

Solomon, Barbara H., ed. *Short Fiction of Sarah Orne Jewett and Mary Wilkins Freeman*. New York: New American Library, 1979.

Spillers, Hortense. "Changing the Letter: The Yokes, the Jokes of Discourse, or Mrs. Stowe, Mr. Reed." In *Slavery in the Literary Imagination*, ed. Deborah E. McDowell and Arnold Rampersad. Baltimore: Johns Hopkins University Press, 1989.

——. "Mama's Baby, Papa's Maybe: An American Grammar Book." *Diacritics* 17 (Summer 1987).

——. "Notes on an Alternative Model—Neither/Nor." In *The Difference Within: Feminism and Critical Theory*, ed. Elizabeth Meese and Alice Parker. Philadelphia: John Benjamins, 1989.

Stafford, William T. "The Enigma of Serena Merle." *Henry James Review* 7 (Winter–Spring 1986).

Stallybrass, Peter, and Allon White. *The Politics and Poetics of Transgression*. Ithaca: Cornell University Press, 1986.

Stanton, Domna C. "Difference on Trial: A Critique of the Maternal Metaphor in Cixous, Irigaray, and Kristeva." In *The Poetics of Gender*, ed. Nancy K. Miller. New York: Columbia University Press, 1986.

Stepto, Robert B. *From Behind the Veil: A Study of Afro-American Narration*. Chicago: University of Illinois Press, 1976.

Stern, Madeleine B. "A Biographer's View of Margaret Fuller." In *Critical Essays on Ralph Waldo Emerson*, ed. Robert E. Burkholder and Joel Myerson. Boston: G. K. Hall, 1983.

Stowe, Charles Edward. *The Life of Harriet Beecher Stowe*. Boston: Houghton Mifflin, 1889.

Stowe, Harriet Beecher. *A Key to Uncle Tom's Cabin, Presenting the Original Facts and Documents upon Which the Story Is Founded, Together with Corroborative Statements Verifying the Truth of the Work*. Cleveland, Ohio: John P. Jewett; London: Low, 1853.

——. *Uncle Tom's Cabin*. New York: Penguin American Library, 1985.

Stuckey, Sterling. *Slave Culture: Nationalist Theory and the Foundations of Black America*. New York: Oxford University Press, 1987.

Suleiman, Susan Rubin. "Writing and Motherhood." In *The (M)Other Tongue: Essays in Feminist Psychoanalytic Interpretation*, ed. Shirley Nelson Garner, Claire Kahane, and Madelon Sprengnether. Ithaca: Cornell University Press, 1985.

Sundquist, Eric J. "Frederick Douglass: Literacy and Paternalism." *Raritan* 6 (Fall 1986).

——. *Home as Found*. Baltimore: Johns Hopkins University Press, 1979.

———, ed. *Frederick Douglass: New Literary and Historical Essays*. New York: Cambridge University Press, 1990.

———, ed. *New Essays on "Uncle Tom's Cabin."* New York: Cambridge University Press, 1986.

Thoreau, Henry David. *Collected Poems*, ed. Carl Bode. Baltimore: John Hopkins University Press, 1970.

———. *Journal*. Excerpts in *The Harper American Literature*, ed. Donald McQuade. New York: Harper & Row, 1987.

———. *The Writings of Henry David Thoreau*, ed. Bradford Torrey. Boston: Houghton Mifflin, 1906.

Tompkins, Jane. *Sensational Designs: The Cultural Work of American Fiction, 1790–1860*. New York: Oxford University Press, 1985.

Twain, Mark. *The Tragedy of Pudd'nhead Wilson*. New York: Penguin, 1987.

Twitchell, James. *Carnival Culture: The Trashing of Taste in America*. New York: Columbia University Press, 1992.

Van Ghent, Dorothy. "On *The Portrait of a Lady*." In *The Portrait of a Lady*, by Henry James. New York: Norton, 1975.

Veeder, William. *Henry James: The Lessons of the Master*. Chicago: University of Chicago Press, 1975.

Walker, Peter F. *Moral Choices: Memory, Desire, and Imagination in Nineteenth-Century American Abolition*. Baton Rouge: Louisiana State University Press, 1978.

Walters, Ronald G. "The Erotic South: Civilization and Sexuality in American Abolition." *American Quarterly* 25 (May 1973): 179–80.

Watson, David. *Margaret Fuller: An American Romantic*. New York: St. Martin's Press, 1988.

Wells, Ida B. *Crusade for Justice: The Autobiography of Ida B. Wells*, ed. John Hope Franklin. Chicago: University of Chicago Press, 1970.

Wertz, Dorothy C., and Richard W. Wertz. *Lying-In: A History of Childbirth in America*. New York: Schocken, 1979.

Wilson, Forrest. *Crusader in Crinoline: The Life of Harriet Beecher Stowe*. Philadelphia: Lippincott, 1941.

Yarborough, Richard. "Race, Violence, and Manhood: The Masculine Ideal in Frederick Douglass's 'The Heroic Slave.' " In *Frederick Douglass: New Literary and Historical Essays*, ed. Eric J. Sundquist. New York: Cambridge University Press, 1990.

———. "Strategies of Black Characterization in *Uncle Tom's Cabin* and the Early Afro-American Novel." In *New Essays on "Uncle Tom's Cabin,"* ed. Eric J. Sundquist. New York: Cambridge University Press, 1986.

Yellin, Jean Fagan. *Women and Sisters: The Antislavery Feminists in American Culture*. New Haven: Yale University Press, 1989.

Zelizer, Viviana A. *Pricing the Priceless Child: The Changing Social Value of Children*. New York: Basic Books, 1985.

Žižek, Slavoj. *The Sublime Object of Ideology*. London: Verso, 1989.

Index

Abjection, 7–8, 118–21, 141, 196–97
Abolition, 22–68, 73, 89–106, 112–59, 215;
  and anti–slavery movement, 6, 11, 34,
  44, 48, 56, 59, 62, 91, 93, 122, 137,
  181
Abortion, 24, 44, 59, 70, 214, 217–18
Acoustic Mirror, The (Silverman), 198
Adam/Adamic, 6, 163–64
Adams, Henry, 23, 25, 75–76, 215–16
Aesthetics, 4–9, 18, 20–21, 26–27, 39, 86,
  116–18, 128, 131–88, 192–210
Africa/African, 14, 24, 34–68, 80, 95–159,
  177–88, 217, 220–22; African-American,
  14, 24, 34–68, 95–159, 188, 220–22;
  Liberia, 95, 99, 102
Afro-American Literature (Stepto and
  Fisher), 113
Alcohol/Alcoholism, 49, 167–68, 170
Amalgamation, 18, 48, 57–59, 73
America and the American People (Von
  Raumer), 73
American Equal Rights Association
  Convention. *See Equal Rights
  Convention*
American Hieroglyphics (Irwin), 165, 172–
  74
American Literary Criticism (Leitch), 6, 8
American Revolution, the, 136–37
America the Scrivener (Jay), 125
Ammons, Elizabeth, 90–91, 95, 98, 108–9,
  112, 142
Anatomy of National Fantasy, The
  (Berlant), 11, 13–14, 213
Andrews, William L., 111–12, 116, 125,
  139–44
Angel, 9, 11, 14, 20, 66, 96–97, 102,

104(illus.), 107, 109, 111, 115–16, 174–
  75, 178, 181, 203, 215–16
Anglo-American, 1, 18–19, 37–38, 63, 91,
  139, 166
Anglo-Saxon, 98, 130, 132
Animal/Animalism, 45, 59, 99, 184, 188
Arac, Jonathan, 20–23, 25
Aristocracy, 48, 74, 125, 128, 137, 177–81,
  195, 201, 206, 213

Bailey: Betsy, 124–27; family (*see also*
  Douglass, Frederick), 115–27; Frederick
  Augustus Washington, 124; Harriet,
  115, 133; Hester, 119–24
Baker, Houston, Jr., 112–13, 117, 134–35,
  155
Bakhtin, M. M, 140–41
Banta, Martha, 11, 111, 204, 212–15
Bastard. *See* Illegitimacy
Baym, Nina, 6, 11, 20–21, 218
Bearing the Word (Homans), 14–15, 94,
  174–75, 192–97
Bedlamite. *See* Madness
Beecher: Catharine, 43, 175–77, 185;
  family (*see also* Stowe, Harriet Beecher)
  34, 90, 98, 175–77, 185; Harriet (*see*
  Stowe, Harriet Beecher); Henry Ward,
  98; Lyman, 98
Beloved (Morrison), 111, 146
Bercovitch, Sacvan, 16–19, 23
Berlant, Lauren, 11, 13–14, 21, 23
Between Men (Sedgwick), 193, 206
Bible, the, 94, 109, 114, 135, 163–64, 181
Birth, 5, 14–17, 77, 83, 95, 106, 138, 211–
  24; childbearing, 14, 77, 83, 106, 138; as
  class designation, 211–15; as

Birth (*cont.*)
  monstrous, 16–17; as trope, 16, 77, 95,
  211–24. *See also* Maternity; Mother
Black/Blackness, 11–17, 34–68, 90–110,
  119–59, 171–88, 212–24
Black Looks (hooks), 101
Blood, 56, 72, 75, 111, 116, 120, 132, 191,
  193, 214
*Blues, Ideology, and Afro-American
  Literature* (Baker), 112–13, 134–35
Bondage. *See* Slavery
Bonds of Womanhood, The (Cott), 42,
  113
Boston (Massachusetts), 23, 63–64, 151,
  153, 217
Bourgeois, 38, 65, 204
Bradford, William, 32, 52
Britain. *See* Great Britain
Butler, Judith, 41, 156

Calvinism. *See* Religion
Cannibals All! (Fitzhugh), 44
Captivity, 32, 109–10, 171. *See also*
  Slavery
Carby, Hazel, 14, 18, 41–42, 111–12, 114–
  15, 118, 121, 124, 132, 138, 142–43, 145–
  48
Caucasian. *See* White/Whiteness
Ce sexe qui n'en est pas un (Irigaray), 156
Chase, Salmon (abolitionist), 44, 47
Child, Lydia Maria Francis, 5–6, 15, 18,
  25, 31–68, 93, 107, 118, 159, 170, 174,
  217; and brother (Convers Francis), 48;
  and husband (David), 47
—Fiction: *Flowers for Children,* 31, 40–41;
  Hobomok, 5, 18, 32, 36, 52–53; *Juvenile
  Miscellany,* 31; "New England Boy's
  Song, A," 31, 33 (illus.), 40; *Philothea,*
  32, 43; "Quadroons, The," 32, 65;
  Romance of the Republic, A, 6, 34, 37–38,
  63–68
—Nonfiction: *Appeal in Favor of That
  Class of Americans Called Africans,* 35–
  36, 41–42, 45; *Authentic Anecdotes of
  American Slavery,* 64; *Mother's Book,
  The,* 15, 38, 41–52, 60–62, 107, 118, 217;
  *Patriarchal Institution, as Described by
  Members of Its Own Family, The,* 44, 46–
  48, 50, 217; *Selected Letters,* 35, 48–49,
  55, 66
Childhood, 31, 40, 41–52, 73, 92–94
Children's books, 31, 40, 45
Children's Defense Fund, the, 13, 223
Christ. *See* Jesus Christ
Christianity. *See* Religion

Citizenship, 44, 50, 52, 93, 141–59, 184–
  88, 211–24
Civil Rights. *See* Politics
Civil War, 16, 23, 26, 36, 58–60, 65, 73,
  106, 136, 184. *See also* War
Cixous, Hélène, 156, 222
Class, 4–5, 15–22, 34–68, 76–78, 92–95,
  100–105, 129–39, 169, 211–24; as critical
  issue, 22, 76, 129–39, 169, 211–24; in
  economics, 15, 38, 78, 139; middle/
  middling, 4, 15, 34–35, 38, 41–52, 59,
  65–68, 92–95, 100–105, 175–184, 217,
  222; propriety of, 5, 41–52, 194; as
  "race," 5, 66–68, 129–31, 139, 218–24
Collected Poems of Henry David Thoreau
  (Bode), 69, 73
Colonial/Colonization, 32, 65, 80–81, 212
Columbia, 11, 69
Complete Notebooks, The (Edel and
  Powers), 190
Confederacy, 58, 136
Cooper, James Fenimore, 5–6; *Deerslayer,
  The,* 5; *Last of the Mohicans,* 5
Corporal punishment. *See* Slavery
Cottom, Daniel, 2, 21, 218
Crews, Frederick, 22–23, 94
Crime, 49–58, 98–115, 123–24, 137, 154,
  165, 172–74, 186–88, 191–193;
  euthanasia, 187; felony drug–dealing,
  220–21; genocide, 5, 32, 123–24;
  infanticide, 24, 98–107; matricide, 195;
  murder, 58, 98–100, 107–10, 113, 115,
  191–92; mutiny, 186–87; parricide, 165,
  172–74; suicide, 106, 137, 154, 186–88;
  treason, 46
Critical Essays on Harriet Beecher Stowe
  (Ammons), 98
Critical Essays on Ralph Waldo Emerson
  (Burkholder and Myerson), 73, 85
Crucifixion, 91, 108, 181, 185–87
Crusader in Crinoline (Wilson), 90
Culture, 1–8, 15–25, 41–52, 70–86, 89–105,
  146–59, 233–24; heritage, 70, 86, 146–
  59, 163–88, 191; popular, 15, 25, 41–52,
  72, 89–105, 128, 136–39, 163–88, 211–24.
  See also Sentimentalism/Sentimentality
Culture of Sentiment, The (Samuels), 34–37

Dark Lady/Light Lady, 11, 101, 170,
  181–83
Daugherty, James (illustrator), 101–2, 104
  (illus.), 183 (illus.)
Daughters and Fathers (Boose and
  Flowers), 204
Dearest Beloved (Herbert), 23

Death, 5, 9, 78, 91–96, 98–106, 110, 115, 137–38, 142, 144, 146, 148–59, 166–69, 171–74, 185–88, 192–201; of a child, 91–96, 98–106, 185–86; in fiction, 5, 78, 91–96, 98–100, 110, 169, 171–74, 185–88, 192–201; as gendered, 9, 145, 166, 172–74, 192–201

de Lauretis, Teresa, 222–23

Democracy (Adams), 25

Democracy. *See* Politics

Demon, 4–16, 44, 98–105, 111–18, 124, 126, 178–88, 192–210, 215; child as, 4, 178–88; as female, 8, 10–12, 16, 44, 98–105, 111–12, 115, 118, 126, 192–210, 215; mother as, 8, 10, 12, 14, 98–106, 111–18, 126, 192–210

Desire. *See* Psychoanalysis

Devil, 97, 102, 178, 191, 215–16

Difference Within, The (Meese and Parker), 34

Disorderly Conduct (Smith–Rosenberg), 15, 25, 113

Diversity, 8, 12, 20, 26, 67, 71, 86, 211

Domesticity, 3–14, 34–68, 89–110, 134–59, 163–88; and domestics, 50–51, 66; ideology, 23, 44, 89–110, 134–59, 163–84; and literature, 3, 14, 34–68, 89–110, 134–59, 163–89; novels, 4, 34–68, 89–110, 164–84

Douglas, Ann, 1, 38, 89, 90, 94, 98, 106, 128, 166–69

Douglass, Frederick, 26, 39, 46, 59, 111–35, 144, 148–51, 155, 157; and Anna Murray (wife), 122; and Helen Pitts (wife), 59, 122

—Works: *Life and Times of Frederick Douglass*, 116, 123, 130, 132–33; *My Bondage and My Freedom*, 39, 111–33, 144; *Narrative of the Life of Frederick Douglass, The*, 113–35, 149–51, 155

Du Bois, W. E. B., 115

Eagle, American bald, 9–13, 16–18, 31, 64, 181

Economy, 8, 23–68, 83, 92–95, 175–77

Education, 41–52, 59, 114, 117, 134–59

Education of Henry Adams, The (Samuels, ed.), 76, 215–16

Egypt, 58, 129–31; and Pharoah (Rameses the Great), 129–31

Electricity, 7, 8, 72, 75–76, 82–84, 97

Emancipation. *See* Slavery

Emerson, Ralph Waldo, 7, 26–27, 69–86, 90, 112–13, 138, 154, 165, 221–22; "An Address," 83; *American Scholar, The*, 77,
82–83; *Circles*, 69, 83; *Fate*, 69, 72, 83; *Illusions*, 69, 84; *Nature*, 7, 69, 77, 79, 83; *Poet, The*, 7, 83; *Self–Reliance*, 69, 72, 77, 79; and son (Waldo), 222

Emerson in His Journals (Porte), 77, 222

Emotion, 39–68, 84–133, 167, 191–98; agony, 91, 191, 209–10; anger, 119; anguish, 173–74; bereavement/grief/sorrow, 39, 91–96, 134, 170, 191, 198, 205, 222; compassion, 42, 97; despair, 198; disgust/hatred/revulsion, 61, 147, 200–201, 206, 223; empathy, 97–98, 178; fear, 39, 113, 198; fury, 99, 119; guilt, 191; *hérissé*, 82–83; indignation, 39, 91, 135; joy, 75, 84; love, 49–68, 90, 125–33, 176–77, 189–90; passion, 108, 119–20; piety, 42; pity, 97; rage, 97–100, 105; restraint, 42; scorn, 174; shame, 145–59, 200; solace, 92; sympathy, 37–38, 44–45, 113, 217; terror, 122–24, 191–94

Endurance of Frankenstein (Levine and Knoepflmacher), 19

Engendering Democracy (Phillips), 12

England. *See* Great Britain

English/British, 167, 171, 184–85

Enlightenment. *See* Philosophy

Entrepreneurial, 24, 48

Entropy, 172–74, 188

Epistemology of the Closet (Sedgwick), 7, 185

Equal Rights Convention (1869), 148

Escape, 100, 118, 134–59, 170, 201. *See also* Slavery

Essentially Speaking (Fuss), 223

Ethnicity, 66, 105, 212; and ethnocentrism, 68; and ethnology, 129–31

Europe/Europeans, 32, 74, 76, 81, 91, 154, 189–210, 214

Eve (biblical), 6, 52, 96, 110, 164

Evil, 11, 17, 44, 105, 110, 171, 185, 187, 197, 199

Exoticism, 165–84

Fable for Critics, A (Lowell), 73

Family, 31–68, 91–110, 112–59, 164–224

Fantasy, 12–13, 16, 19, 41, 48, 84, 192–201. *See also* Psychoanalysis

Father, 31–40, 64–74, 79, 94, 97, 107, 109, 117–33, 144–59, 163–210, 222; as fictional character, 5, 64–68, 107, 184–210; as figure, 69, 71, 74, 109, 118, 127, 144–59, 163–210; Founding Fathers, 94; as in God the, 79, 97, 181, 185–88; grandfather, 31, 40, 65

Father–Daughter Incest (Herman), 204
Feidelson, Charles, 190, 194, 197, 199–200
Femininity. *See* Gender
Feminism, 2, 8, 23, 25, 34, 98–105, 122,
    148–50, 191–211, 222–24; antebellum,
    11, 25, 148–50; and theory, 2, 25, 98,
    122, 191–211, 222–24
Feminism and Psychoanalysis (Feldstein
    and Roof), 222
Feminism and Suffrage (DuBois), 114, 125
Feminization, 1–10, 15, 72, 112, 118–33,
    168–74, 209–10
Feminization of American Culture, The
    (Douglas), 1, 38, 89, 90, 98, 106, 128,
    166–69
Fiedler, Leslie, 1, 3, 190–96, 216
Fiend, 58, 108, 124, 173–74, 191, 205. *See
    also* Demon
Flag (United States), 64, 211–13
Food, 32, 126–27, 133, 173–74
France, 67–68, 76, 212–13; French, as
    nationality, 67, 80, 82; and the French
    West Indies, 68; revolution, 67, 213
Franchot, Jenny, 112, 120, 122, 129–32
Frankenstein (monster), 17–19, 70
Frankenstein (Shelley), 18
Frederick Douglass (McFeely), 59, 122, 124,
    127, 130
Frederick Douglass (Sundquist), 112, 116–
    17, 126, 136
Frederick Douglass' Civil War (Blight), 112,
    127, 131
Frederick Douglass on Women's Rights
    (Foner), 125, 149
Freedom. *See* Liberty
French Revolution. *See* France
Freud, Sigmund. *See* Psychoanalysis
From Behind the Veil (Stepto), 112, 117,
    135
Fuller, Sarah Margaret, 26, 69–86, 97,
    155; and brother (Robert), 84–85; and
    father (Timothy), 71–74; and husband
    (Count Ossoli), 85; as Margaret Ossoli,
    85–86; and son, 85
—Nonfiction: "American Literature," 69,
    72; *Papers on Literature and Art*, 71, 155;
    Woman in the Nineteenth-Century, 71,
    75–86

Games, 44, 107; gambling, 107
Garrison, William Lloyd, 46, 59, 90, 93,
    111, 113, 116–18, 127
Gender, 5, 8, 10, 18, 22–25, 35–69, 71–86,
    94–159, 163–224; femininity, 1–10, 15,
    24, 42, 67, 72, 83, 90, 100, 112–16, 118–

59, 163–85, 190–210; masculinity, 6, 16,
    72, 105, 110, 113–18, 126, 130–33, 136–
    59, 163–88, 201–10
Gender and the Politics of History (Scott),
    25
*Gender, Fantasy and Realism in American
    Literature* (Habegger), 200
Gender Trouble (Butler), 156
Genealogy, 110, 123, 131–33, 144–59, 176–
    78, 216
Genetics, 84, 132, 176, 216, 221–24
Genius, 69–72, 130–32, 189–90, 203
Genocide. *See* Crime
Germany/German, 63, 73, 80, 154, 213
Ghost, 86, 98, 144, 190–202, 206, 209–10
Gilbert, Sandra, 86, 156
God, 79, 94, 97, 136, 141, 144, 181, 185,
    214. *See also* Jesus Christ; Religion
Golden Age of Black Nationalism (Moses),
    112
Gomorrah. *See* Sodom and Gomorrah
Gorgon. *See* Medusa
Gothicism, 98–99, 111, 165, 172–74, 189–
    215
Grandfather. *See* Father
Grandmother. *See* Mother
Great Britain, 7, 11, 52–53, 69, 94
Greece, 12–13, 20, 22, 67, 74, 84, 109–10;
    as language, 74; and mythology, 12–13,
    20, 22, 84, 109–10; as nationality, 67
Greeley, Horace, 74, 84
Grimké: Angelina ("Devilina"), 1, 215;
    Charlotte Forten, 46, 73; family, 1, 46,
    59, 215; Sarah, 59
Grimké Sisters from South Carolina, The
    (Lerner), 1, 59, 215
Gubar, Susan, 86, 117, 156, 202
Gunning, Sandra, 39, 41, 58, 61, 110, 121

Hamlet (Shakespeare), 10
Harlot. *See* Prostitution
Harper American Literature, The
    (McQuade), 69
Harris, Susan, 9, 128
Hawthorne, Nathaniel, 2–13, 16–18, 20,
    22–23, 25, 70, 72, 74, 76, 85, 151; and
    son (Julian), 85; and wife (Sophia), 85
—Fiction: *Blithedale Romance, The*, 11, 70;
    Marble Faun, The, 11; "Rappaccini's
    Daughter," 11; *Scarlet Letter, The*, 2, 9–
    10, 17, 19, 20–23, 74, 76; *Wonder Book,
    The*, 12–13
—Nonfiction: *American Notebooks, The*, 71;
    "Chiefly about War Matters," 16, 151
Heart Is Like Heaven, The (Baer), 49

Henry, Patrick, 136–42, 148
Henry James (Veeder), 199–200, 215
Herman Melville (Howard), 188
Hertz, Neil, 16, 67
Heterosexuality. *See* Sexuality/Sexualities
Hidden Louisa May Alcott, The (Stern), 195
History of Sexuality (Foucault), 45
Hoffert, Sylvia D., 24, 92–93, 100–1, 106, 145, 185
Holmes, Oliver Wendell, 7
Homans, Margaret, 14–15, 94, 173–74, 192–97
Homosexuality. *See* Sexuality/Sexualities
Homosocial, 185–88, 201–10
Hysteria. *See* Psychoanalysis

Iconography, 1–14, 40, 51, 63–86, 94–159, 163–224; maternal, 1–8, 13–14, 25, 51, 69–86, 94–159, 190–224; national, 9, 11–14, 64, 67, 111–59, 204, 211–24
Ideology, 1–12, 14–25, 31–71, 92–159, 163–88, 211–24; antebellum, 8, 14, 31–68, 94–133, 212; domestic, 23, 26, 34–40, 44, 94–110, 134–88; feminist, 2, 8, 23, 25; liberal, 13, 17, 213–17; multiculturalism, 20, 63; Victorian, 9–20, 66, 94–96
Ideology and American Literature (Bercovitch and Jehlen), 20
Illegitimacy, 5, 46–55, 96, 134–59, 169, 175–78, 190–210; children and, 5, 55, 96, 169, 175–78, 190–210; political, 46, 48
Imaging American Woman (Banta), 11, 111, 204, 212, 215
Immaculate Deception (Arms), 24
Impotence, 123, 178–79
Incest. *See* Psychoanalysis
Incidents in the Life of a Slave Girl (Jacobs), 34–35, 44, 91, 99, 112, 114, 117, 134–59
Indian, 5, 55, 80–81, 165; half–breed, 56; mythology, 80–81; quarter–breed, 56; as "race," 55, 80–81, 165; West Indian, 68. *See also* Native American
Industry, 15, 45–60, 72–92, 116; cotton, 60; publishing, 15, 45, 72, 116, 153–54; textile, 15; urban, 92
Infanticide. *See* Crime
Infant mortality. *See* Death
Inner Civil War, The (Frederickson), 73
Inside/Out (Fuss), 223
Irigaray, Luce, 156, 222
Irish, 151, 153–54
Italy/Italian, 80–85, 191–93

Jacobs, Harriet Ann (Linda Brent), 26, 34–35, 44, 91, 95, 99, 112, 114, 117, 134–59, 165, 215; and grandmother (Aunt Martha/Molly Horniblow), 142–59; *Incidents in the Life of a Slave Girl* (Jacobs), 34–35, 44, 91, 99, 112, 114, 117, 134–59; and son (Benjamin), 151–54; and uncle (Uncle Benjamin/Joseph), 135–43, 157
James, Henry, 9, 20–21, 26–27, 72, 85–86, 189–215
—Fiction: "Altar of the Dead, The," 190; *American, The*, 204; "Author of Beltraffio, The," 210; "Beast in the Jungle, The," 206; *Daisy Miller*, 190; "Jolly Corner, The," 190; "Last of the Valerii, The," 209; "Madonna of the Future, The," 189, 210; *Portrait of a Lady, The*, 189–215; *Turn of the Screw, The*, 190
—Nonfiction: *Hawthorne* (Men of Letters), 9, 20–21, 26; *William Wetmore Story and His Friends*, 86
Jesus Christ, 79, 83, 90–91, 96–97, 105, 108, 185–88
Jeune née, La (Cixous and Clément), 156
Jim Crow, 24, 176–77, 212
Journals of Charlotte Forten Grimké, The (Stevenson), 46, 73
Journey Back, The (Baker), 112, 135
Judaism. *See* Religion

Kahane, Claire, 101, 191–96, 199
Karcher, Carolyn, 5–6, 34, 36, 44, 55, 63–64, 66, 68, 143
Kelley, Mary, 3, 15, 34, 43, 60, 90
Key to Uncle Tom's Cabin (Stowe), 89, 90–91, 112, 125, 135
Knowledge, 52–79, 117–18, 127–59, 194–210; carnal, 52, 117–18; self, 79, 119–59, 194–210
Kristeva, Julia, 7, 121, 174, 197, 218, 222
Kristeva Reader, The (Moi), 197, 218

Labor, 15–47, 60–66, 92, 114, 124, 151–54, 175–77; as in capitalism, 15, 23–24, 42–47, 66, 92, 175–77; slave, 15, 47, 60, 114, 124
Lacan, Jacques. *See* Psychoanalysis
Lady. *See* Woman
Lay of the Land, The (Kolodny), 11, 165
Leverenz, David, 11, 18, 21, 96–98, 102, 105–6, 108–9, 113, 134
Liberty, 3–4, 10–14, 31–37, 46–48, 56, 64–68, 91, 95, 111–59, 211–24; cap, 64, 67;

Liberty (*cont.*)
as figure, 11, 68, 91, 95, 111, 141–42,
159, 213–15, 223; as political ideology,
3–4, 13, 91–95, 111–59, 211–24; Statue
of, 9, 11, 13–14, 31, 68, 213, 223
Life and Letters of Harriet Beecher Stowe
(Fields), 90
Life and Times of Frederick Douglass, 116,
123, 130, 132–33
Life of Harriet Beecher Stowe, The (Stowe),
90
Limits of Sisterhood, The (Boydston,
Kelley, Margolis), 34, 90
Lincoln, Abraham (President), 3–4, 17,
57–58, 94–95; *Emancipation
Proclamation, The*, 217; *Gettysburg
Address, The*, 58, 95; *Perpetuation of our
Political Institutions, The*, 3; *Speeches*, 57
Literacy, 20, 127–59
Literature, 1–8, 17–18, 22–23, 70–86, 116–
33, 139–42, 163–88, 190–224; American,
1, 6, 18, 69–86, 116–33, 163–64, 208–24;
as a cultural form, 1–3, 6–8, 17, 70–72,
86, 208–24; literary, 69–86, 116–18, 127–
33, 139–42, 159, 164, 193, 208–10, 216–
24
Love and Death in the American Novel
(Fiedler), 1, 3, 190–201, 216
Lowell, James Russell, 73–74
Lydia Maria Child (Osborne), 31
Lying-in (Wertz and Wertz), 92

Machine in the Garden, The (Marx), 73
Madness, 46–48, 99–102, 133, 164–69, 181,
206; Bedlamite, 46, 48, 164; paranoia,
206; as prophecy, 181; schizophrenia,
99
Madwoman in the Attic (Gilbert and
Gubar), 86, 156
Manhood and the American Renaissance
(Leverenz), 11, 96–98, 105, 108–9, 113
Margaret Fuller (Miller), 74
Margaret Fuller (Watson), 74, 85
Marriage, 53–55, 65–68, 82–84, 100–10,
122, 169–74, 189–210, 220–21
Martyrdom, 17, 98–105, 110, 125, 150,
185–88
Marx/Marxism/Marxist analysis, 22–23,
139–42, 152–53, 175–78, 204
Mary Shelley (Mellor), 19
Masculinity. *See* Gender
Maternity, 1–19, 23–27, 41–86, 89–184,
189–224; as American, 14, 17, 41, 71–
86, 106, 111, 211–24; and child-rearing,
15, 41–52, 92–94, 175; as concept, 7, 19,

23, 54, 69–86, 99–224; in iconography,
1–14, 25–27, 68, 70–86, 89–224; as
instinct, 13, 112, 118, 209–10, 215–16;
and reproduction, 2, 9, 12, 14–16, 19,
24, 52–68, 75–81, 99–159, 165–74, 176–
78, 198, 208–10, 216–24; as sanctified/
divine/Christian, 1–8, 14, 25–26, 54,
75–86, 89–110, 163, 208; sentimental, 1–
2, 25–26, 76–86, 89–224; and surrogacy,
68, 218–21; as truth, 69–70
Mayflower, The, 16–18
Medusa, 12–13, 16, 67, 98, 172–74
Melancholia, 130–33, 190, 198, 200
Melodrama, 40, 139–42
Melville, Herman, 3, 25, 27, 163–89;
"Benito Cereno," 165; *Billy Budd*, 184–
88, 190; *Confidence Man, The*, 188;
Mardi, 165; *Moby Dick*, 2, 3, 163–84;
Oomo, 165; "Paradise of Bachelors and
the Tartarus of Maids, The" 25; *Pierre*,
164–85, 193; *Typee*, 165–67
Memory, 4, 5, 15, 41, 77–80, 84–86, 115,
128–59, 190–210
Mermaid and the Minotaur, The
(Dinnerstein), 101, 165
Metamorphosis, 150, 157, 177–78
Metaphysics, 7, 26, 69, 72, 86
Mimesis, 122, 185
Mind Children (Moravec), 221
Mind of Frederick Douglass, The (Martin),
112, 125, 127
Miscegenation, 17, 18, 58, 64–68, 73, 108–
11
Moby Dick (Melville), 2–3, 164–84
Monster, 10, 12, 16–20, 58, 70, 165–66,
171, 174; monstrosity, 22, 26, 44, 48, 59,
70, 163–85
Moral Choices (Walker), 44, 47, 95, 113,
123–24, 127, 134, 137
Morality, 1, 3, 31–68, 89–110, 135–59,
187–88, 200, 212, 218
Mother, 1–15, 31–38, 41–52, 60, 68–86,
89–159, 165–224; as alien/monster/
demon, 8, 10, 12, 16, 98, 105, 111–12,
118, 126, 208–10; Britain, 69; and child,
5, 12–13, 15, 24, 41, 44, 50–51, 56, 68–
70, 78–86, 90, 95–105, 107, 111–59, 165–
78, 217, 221–24; and daughter, 50–51,
68, 99–105, 134–59, 190–201, 207–11; as
fictional character, 5, 8, 53, 65–68, 95–
105, 167–78, 190–210; grandmother, 31–
32, 40, 68, 142–59, 220; as icon, 1–4,
13–14, 16–18, 41–52, 60, 68–69, 75–86,
89–94, 182, 208–10, 221–24; as
Madonna (*See also* Virgin Mary), 2, 17,

75–86, 94–96, 101–2, 105, 107–10, 208;
as mammy, 124; mothering/
motherhood, 14, 26, 41–52, 68, 70–86,
89–159, 165–224; as nature, 69–72, 83–
84, 111, 165–67; nursing, 69–71, 111,
165; power of, 1, 3, 26, 41–52, 71, 75–
86, 89–110, 124–59, 190–224; slave–
mother, 24, 68, 98–110, 115, 119–59,
176–78, 217; and son, 78–86, 90, 105,
119–33, 142–59, 166–78, 220–21; and
stepmother, 3, 190–211; as truth, 69–71,
75; and womb, 16, 18, 84, 119, 156,
216, 219–20
(M)Other Tongue, The (Garner, Kahane,
Sprengnether), 101
Mulatta/o, 5–6, 34, 56–57, 65–68, 95–96,
120, 134–59, 177–79, 187
Murchek, John, 61
Murder. See Crime
My Bondage and My Freedom (Douglass),
39, 111–33, 144
Mythology, 12–16, 20, 22, 77, 80–81, 84,
136–42, 147

Nationalisms and Sexualities (Parker,
Russo, Sommer, Yaeger), 52
Nationality/Nationalism, 6–7, 14, 16, 18,
34, 41–52, 60–86, 111–59, 182–88, 204,
211–24
Native American, 5, 53–56, 80–81. See
also Indian
Nature, 48, 69–75, 83–84, 111, 163, 167–
68, 214
Neither Black nor White (Berzon), 34,
120
Nelson, Dana D., 34, 36–38, 44, 64–66,
136
New England, 32, 63, 70, 73–74, 148
New Essays on "The American" (Banta),
204
New Essays on "Uncle Tom's Cabin"
(Sundquist), 89, 90, 97, 109, 163, 176
New Orleans (Lousiana), 63, 148
New Testament, 96, 187
New Woman. See Woman
New-York (Herald) Tribune, 71–74, 118, 155
Nigger, 151–54, 212
Nobility. See Aristocracy
North, the, 17, 24, 44–45, 49, 135, 141–42,
159
Nostalgia, 41, 72, 78, 128, 222

Octoroon, 56, 63
Office of the Scarlet Letter, The
(Bercovitch), 16–19

Of Plymouth Plantation (Bradford), 32
Old Testament, the 97, 185
On Call (Jordan), 151
Operation Rescue, 217–18
Orientalism, 43–44, 67

Paternity/Paternalism, 27, 35, 96, 110,
113, 121–33, 144, 147–59, 165–88, 201–
10
Patriarchy, 23–24, 27, 35–36, 43–49, 52–
53, 96–97, 100–159, 165–88, 201–10
Patriotism, 106, 155–59
"Peculiar Institution," the. See Slavery
Performance, 176–79, 217–18
Phenomenology, 69, 77, 83
Phillips, Wendell, 47, 113
Philosophy, 7–16, 26, 69–86, 163–64;
Enlightenment, 16, 137, 150, 214;
transcendentalism, 7, 26, 69–86, 137
Poe, Edgar Allan, 70
Politics, 8–18, 22–25, 31–68, 70, 89–159,
211–24; and abolition, 22–25, 32–68,
70, 93–159, 217; agrarianism, 47, 92;
civil rights, 60, 176, 217–24;
democracy, 8, 13, 16–17, 26, 48, 60, 72,
93, 97, 184–88, 211–24; liberty/
freedom in, 3–4, 14, 37, 46, 48, 55, 56,
60–68, 95–96, 111–59, 188, 211–24; in
literature, 9, 14, 31–68, 89–188; of
literature, 1, 3, 11, 17, 20, 23, 37, 69–
86, 116–18, 163–88, 208–24; and
religion, 3, 16, 89–110, 171–88;
republicanism, 43, 46–68, 93, 95, 97,
217; suffrage, 24, 26, 60, 114, 125, 148,
183; of the United States, 1–3, 11–12,
14, 16–17, 22–25, 34–36, 40, 46, 64–68,
93–159, 163–224; Women's Rights
Movement, 22–23, 125, 148–50
Politics and Poetics of Transgression, The
(Stallybrass and White), 61
Popular culture. See Culture
Porter, Carolyn, 152, 204
Powers of Horror (Kristeva), 7, 121, 197
Pregnancy, 15, 52, 77, 84, 101, 166, 170,
207, 217–24. See also Maternity
Prejudice. See Race: racism
Prichard's Natural History of Man
(Walker), 128–31
Pricing the Priceless Child (Zelizer), 24,
57
Prison, 189–90, 194, 204
Prison-House of Language, The (Jameson),
194
Private Matters (Hoffert), 24, 92, 100–1,
106, 145

Private Woman, Public Stage (Kelley), 3, 15, 43, 60
Pro-slavery movement, 23, 44, 48, 59, 73, 99, 215
Prostitution, 44, 50–51, 55, 68; bordello, 44, 68; brothel, 47; prostitute/harlot/whore (as figure), 17, 51, 96, 98, 100, 214
Protestantism. *See* Religion
Provisions (Fetterley), 6–7
Psychoanalysis, 12–14, 40–49, 53, 61–70, 84–110, 119–33, 166–224; *anima*, 191; castration, 172–74; consciousness, 172–74, 191–210; desire, 14, 48–49, 53, 61, 100–10, 119–33, 136–224; eros/erotic, 48, 100–1, 137, 156–58, 166, 168, 172–74, 191–96, 205; fantasy/phantasmatic, 12–13, 16, 19, 41, 48, 84, 124, 141, 152, 172–74, 190–210, 217–24; Freud, Sigmund, 22, 119, 172–74, 190–210; hysteria, 67, 99, 113, 147; *imago*, 198; incest, 65, 80, 109–10, 119, 168, 171–74, 191, 203–20; *jouissance*, 70; Lacan, Jacques, 70, 174, 192–201; libido, 47, 197; "Name of the Father," 144, 168, 172–74, 184; Object, 66, 181, 222; objectification, 66; Oedipus complex, 191–96; Other, 66; paranoia, 206; phallic, 40, 114, 172–74; phallogocentrism, 40, 108–10; pre–Oedipal, 192–96, 198; primal scene, 172, 201; primal taboo, 191; psychodynamics, 191–96, 198, 217–24; vagina dentata, 172
Pudd'nhead Wilson (Twain), 17–18, 61
Puritans, 17, 52–53

Quadroons, 34, 56, 68, 176–78
Quakers. *See* Religion
Quayle, J. Danforth, 13, 211, 217

Race, 4–6, 11, 14, 17–18, 22, 25, 34–68, 72–73, 89–159, 175–84, 211–24; racism, 17, 24, 34–68, 99, 117–18, 137, 140, 147–59, 175–84
Ralph Waldo Emerson (McAleer), 74
Rape, 45, 66, 95, 109, 119, 177–78
Recognition of Herman Melville, The (Parker), 164
Reconstruction, the, 27, 46, 59, 109, 184
Reconstructing Womanhood (Carby), 14, 18, 42, 111–12, 114–15, 118, 121, 124, 132, 139, 142–43, 145–48
Religion, 3–19, 24–68, 75–78, 80–81, 89–188; Calvinism, 92, 175–77;

Christianity, 3, 7, 14, 16, 17, 19, 60, 80–81, 89–188; Jewish/Judaic, 67, 123; Protestant, 204, 214; Quaker, 90, 96
Reproduction. *See* Maternity
Reproduction of Mothering, The (Chodorow), 192
Reproductive technology. *See* Technology
Revolution and The Word (Davidson), 49
Rhetoric, 8, 13, 17, 21, 25, 37, 44, 46, 48, 57, 66, 93, 99, 111–59, 175–77
Romance, 21–22, 37, 137, 166
Romance of the Republic, A (Child), 6, 34, 37–38, 63–68
Rome/Roman (Italy), 67, 199
Ryan, Mary P., 15, 19, 24, 43–46, 92, 100, 211

Sánchez-Eppler, Karen, 35–37, 62, 114
Savior, the. *See* Jesus Christ
Sedgwick, Eve Kosofsky, 7, 41, 185, 193, 206
Seduction fiction, 49, 139
Seeing and Being (Porter), 152
Self-Discovery and Authority in Afro-American Narrative (Smith), 112–15, 135, 143, 156, 158
Semiotics, 62, 153–59, 174
Sensational Designs (Tompkins), 2, 4, 9, 96, 107, 128, 164
Sentimentalism/Sentimentality, 1–7, 34–68, 76–86, 89–188, 190, 215–24; conventions of, 34, 76, 116–18, 134–88, 190; as critical term, 7, 26, 62, 116–18, 134–59, 215–24; novels, 5, 34, 37–38, 89–113, 165–84; practice of 1, 4, 25, 35–36, 62–68, 76–86, 89–133, 134–88, 190
Sexuality/Sexualities, 14, 24, 46–58, 69, 76, 82–83, 98–159, 165–224; conduct, 47, 82–83, 98, 164–84, 203; exploitation, 34, 43, 45, 98–110, 134–59, 177, 203, 206–10; heterosexist, 37, 138–59, 166–74, 200, 222; heterosexuality, 14, 24, 37, 56, 108, 138–59, 166–74, 190–210, 222; homosexuality/gay/lesbian, 40–48, 60, 167, 178, 185, 206–10, 222–23; sexual acts, 51, 76, 83, 101, 119, 154, 203
Sexual Personae (Paglia), 21, 223
Shakespeare/Shakespearean, 100, 177
Short Fiction of Sarah Orne Jewett and Mary Wilkins Freeman (Solomon), 107
Sin, 52, 90, 94, 96, 110
Sins of the Fathers, The (Crews), 94
Sister Outsider (Lorde), 156
Slave Culture (Stuckey), 123

Slavery, 5, 15–17, 22–26, 34–68, 76, 81, 90–159, 176–84, 217; and emancipation, 32, 36, 48, 55, 68, 81, 177, 217; fugitives, 56, 98–159, 176–77; as legal fiction, 139–59; mother, 24, 68, 98–110, 115, 119–59, 176–77; "peculiar institution" / "patriarchal institution," 17, 142, 159, 175–77, 217; personified as female, 45, 119–23; slavocracy, 24, 47–48, 57, 109, 128, 133, 136–59, 175–77, 184, 217; whipping, 114–15, 118–33, 174–77

Slavery in the Literary Imagination (McDowell and Rampersad), 34, 44, 108

Smith, James M'Cune, 127, 129

Smith, Valerie, 112–13, 115, 135, 143, 156, 158

Sociology for the South (Fitzhugh), 44

Sodom and Gomorrah, 46, 48, 58

Songs, 31–32, 40, 64, 166, 171, 174, 176–77

Souls of Black Folks, The (Du Bois), 115

South, the, 16–17, 24, 44–45, 135, 159

Southern Commercial Convention, 47, 49

Spillers, Hortense, 34, 41, 57, 108–10, 114–15, 144, 157

Stepto, Robert B., 112–13, 117, 135

Stowe, Harriet Beecher, 6, 26, 76, 89–110, 112, 125, 135, 151, 163–68, 174–84, 212, 215

—Fiction: Uncle Tom's Cabin, 6, 76, 89–110, 125, 135, 147, 163–64, 166, 174–84

—Nonfiction: Key to Uncle Tom's Cabin, 89, 90–91, 112, 125, 135

Sublime Object of Ideology, The (Žižek), 19

Suffrage. See Politics

Suicide. See Crime

Sundquist, Eric J., 89, 90, 97, 109–10, 112–13, 117, 126, 134, 136, 163–64, 175–76, 179

Surrogacy. See Maternity

Technoculture (Penley and Ross), 12

Technology, 42, 72–75, 89–93; artificial intelligence/robots, 221–22; daguerreotypes, 93; dynamo, 76; photography, 89, 223; railway, 72; reproductive, 219–24; steamboat, 178; telegraph, 72; x–ray, 75

Thanksgiving (holiday), 31–32, 40

Thomas, George (illustrator), 101, 102–3 (illus.), 179–80 (illus.)

Thoreau, Henry David, 4, 15, 44–45, 59, 69, 73

Three Lives (Stein), 212

Tompkins, Jane, 2, 4, 6–9, 96, 98, 107, 128, 164, 223

To Tell a Free Story (Andrews), 112, 116, 125, 140–43

"Traffic in Women, The" (Rubin), 204

Tragic Mulatta, 5, 6, 34, 65, 98–105, 147. See also Mulatta/o

Treatise on Domestic Economy (Beecher), 175–77

Truth, Sojourner, 24, 59, 95

Tyler, John (President), 58, 96

Uncle Tom's Cabin (Stowe), 6, 76, 89–110, 125, 135, 147, 163–65, 174–84

"Uncle Tom's Cabin" and the Mid-Nineteenth-Century United States, (Reynolds), 90

Union, the, 17, 58, 63, 94

Unmarked (Phelan), 217

Urban Survival (Sidel), 221

Vice, 49–51, 166, 171

Victimization, 122–24, 128, 132–59

Violence, 17, 100, 115, 132–59, 170, 175–77, 190–210, 216

Virginia Convention, the, 136

Virgin Mary, 72, 75–77, 84, 91, 94, 96, 105, 187

Virtue(s), 42, 97, 138, 166, 171

Vixen, 10, 16–18

Walker, Peter F., 44, 95, 113, 123–24, 127, 129, 134, 137

Walters, Ronald G., 44, 137, 156

War, 16–26, 36, 58–60, 65, 73, 106, 132–59; Civil, 16, 23, 26, 36, 58–60, 65, 73, 106, 132, 136; Gulf, 12, 106, 137, 223–24; Vietnam, 106

Where I'm Bound (Smith), 123

Whipping. See Slavery

White/whiteness, 4–6, 11–14, 24, 34–68, 79, 90, 111–59, 212–24

Whitehead–Gould, Mary Beth, 219, 221

Whore. See Prostitution

Wilson, Harriet, 39, 138

Within the Plantation Household (Fox–Genovese), 124

Witnessing Slavery (Foster), 44

Woman, 2–14, 23–61, 75–86, 90, 98–159, 164–224; fallen, 98–105, 134–59; as "free" workers, 15, 23–24, 92, 175; as lady, 5–14, 68, 101–11, 124, 140, 164–84, 190–210, 213, 215; new, 214–16; as

Woman (*cont.*)
  slaves, 24, 98–159, 175–218 strange, 98;
  as trope, 2, 10, 14, 41–52, 60–61, 75–86,
  90, 98–111, 134–59, 164–224; in True
  Womanhood, 14, 34, 42–43, 75, 139;
  wife, 53, 61, 85–86, 189–210; witch, 98,
  102
Woman and the Myth, The (Chevigny), 74
Womanhood in America (Ryan), 15, 19, 24,
  42–46, 92, 100, 211
Woman, Native, Other (Minh-Ha), 8
Women and Children Last (Sidel), 221
Women & Sisters, 11, 16, 18, 25, 34, 43–44,
  56, 58, 64, 89, 91, 95, 111–12, 123, 137,
  142

Women, Race, and Class (Davis), 114, 125
Women's Rights Movement. *See* Politics
Word in Black and White, The (Nelson), 34,
  37–38, 44, 66, 136
World's Greatest Hit (Birdoff), 110, 212
Wright, Henry C. (abolitionist), 44, 54, 59
Writing, 15, 85–86, 116–18, 125, 134–59
Writing and Sexual Difference (Abel), 117
Writings of Henry David Thoreau (Torrey),
  45

Yarborough, Richard, 96, 98–99, 109, 136
Yellin, Jean Fagan, 11–18, 23–25, 34–35,
  43–44, 56–58, 64, 89, 91–95, 111–12,
  117, 123, 134–59, 137

Reading Women Writing

A SERIES EDITED BY

Shari Benstock and Celeste Schenck

Tainted Souls and Painted Faces: The Rhetoric of Fallenness in Victorian Culture
by Amanda Anderson
Greatness Engendered: George Eliot and Virginia Woolf
by Alison Booth
Talking Back: Toward a Latin American Feminist Literary Criticism
by Debra A. Castillo
Articulate Silences: Hisaye Yamamoto, Maxine Hong Kingston, Joy Kogawa
by King-Kok Cheung
H.D.'s Freudian Poetics: Psychoanalysis in Translation
by Dianne Chisholm
From Mastery to Analysis: Theories of Gender in Psychoanalytic Feminism
by Patricia Elliot
Feminist Theory, Women's Writing
by Laurie A. Finke
Colette and the Fantom Subject of Autobiography
by Jerry Aline Flieger
Autobiographics: A Feminist Theory of Women's Self-Representation
by Leigh Gilmore
*Cartesian Women: Versions and Subversions of Rational
Discourse in the Old Regime*
by Erica Harth
Borderwork: Feminist Engagements with Comparative Literature
edited by Margaret R. Higonnet
*Narrative Transvestism: Rhetoric and Gender in the
Eighteenth-Century English Novel*
by Madeleine Kahn
The Unspeakable Mother: Forbidden Discourse in Jean Rhys and H.D.
by Deborah Kelly Kloepfer
*Recasting Autobiography: Women's Counterfictions in Contemporary
German Literature and Film*
by Barbara Kosta
Women and Romance: The Consolations of Gender in the English Novel
by Laurie Langbauer
Penelope Voyages: Women and Travel in the British Literary Tradition
by Karen R. Lawrence
Autobiographical Voices: Race, Gender, Self-Portraiture
by Françoise Lionnet

Woman and Modernity: The (Life)Styles of Lou Andreas-Salomé
by Biddy Martin
In the Name of Love: Women, Masochism, and the Gothic
by Michelle A. Massé
*Outside the Pale: Cultural Exclusion, Gender Difference, and
the Victorian Woman Writer*
by Elsie B. Michie
Reading Gertrude Stein: Body, Text, Gnosis
by Lisa Ruddick
Conceived by Liberty: Maternal Figures and Nineteenth-Century American Literature
by Stephanie A. Smith
Feminist Conversations: Fuller, Emerson, and the Play of Reading
by Christina Zwarg